MW01174544

China, Sex and Prostitution

How should issues of sexuality and power in China be interpreted? Are China scholars really able to translate linguistically and culturally the 'truth' of China? And to what extent do fieldwork and interviews locate a study in the 'real life' of a country and its people?

China, Sex and Prostitution is an important contribution to the work of critical inquiry in the fields of China studies, feminist studies, and social theory. It engages with debates on the nature and utility of attempts to apply mainstream theories in politico-cultural contexts other than those in which they were originally formulated by examining recent literature on sexuality, power, and prostitution. Starting off with a general critique of China studies scholarship since the Cold War period, the text moves on to a more focused examination of recent writings on sexuality in China. It then outlines the broad parameters of feminist prostitution debates concerning the most appropriate governmental response to prostitution. By analysing the Chinese policing of prostitution as a practice of governmentality, it highlights the unproductive nature of feminist debates concerning the optimal transnational response to prostitution, and hints at the insights a reconfigured form of China studies could bring to these and other critical debates within the new humanities. Specifically, the very diversity of prostitution businesses and practices that exist in present-day China suggests that it is not possible to characterize 'sex work' as a unified target of governmental intervention either in China or more generally.

Elaine Jeffreys' arguments are constructed on the basis of detailed analysis of a wide range of primary texts, including documents, press reports, police reports, and policy and legal pronouncements, and secondary literature in both English and Chinese. The work engages with some key debates in the fields of cultural and gender studies and will be welcomed by scholars in these areas as well as by China specialists, sociologists, and anthropologists.

Elaine Jeffreys lectures in China Studies at the University of Technology, Sydney, Australia.

RoutledgeCurzon Studies on China in Transition
Series Editor: David S.G. Goodman

1 **The Democratisation of China**
Baogang He

2 **Beyond Beijing**
Dali Yang

3 **China's Enterprise Reform**
Changing state/society relations after Mao
You Ji

4 **Industrial Change in China**
Economic restructuring and conflicting interests
Kate Hannan

5 **The Entrepreneurial State in China**
Real estate and commerce departments in reform era Tianjin
Jane Duckett

6 **Tourism and Modernity in China**
Tim Oakes

7 **Cities in Post-Mao China**
Recipes for economic development in the reform era
Jae Ho Chung

8 **China's Spatial Economic Development**
Regional transformation in the Lower Yangzi Delta
Andrew M. Marton

9 **Regional Development in China**
States, globalization and inequality
Yehua Dennis Wei

10 **Grassroots Charisma**
Four local leaders in China
Stephan Feuchtwang and Wang Mingming

11 **The Chinese Legal System**
Globalization and local legal culture
Pitman B. Potter

12 **Markets and Clientalism**
The transformation of property rights in rural China
Chi-Jou Jay Chen

13 **Negotiating Ethnicity in China**
Citizenship as a response to the state
Chih-yu Shih

14 **Manager Empowerment in China**
Political implications of rural industrialisation in the reform era
Ray Yep

15 **Cultural Nationalism in Contemporary China**
The search for national identity under reform
Yingjie Guo

16 **Elite Dualism and Leadership Selection in China**
Xiaowei Zang

17 **Chinese Intellectuals Between State and Market**
Edward Gu and Merle Goldman

18 **China, Sex and Prostitution**
Elaine Jeffreys

19 **The Development of China's Stock Market, 1984–2002**
Equity politics and market institutions
Stephen Green

20 **China's Rational Entrepreneurs**
The development of the new private business sector
Barbara Krug

21 **China's Scientific Elite**
Cong Cao

China, Sex and Prostitution

Elaine Jeffreys

LONDON AND NEW YORK

First published 2004
by RoutledgeCurzon
11 New Fetter Lane, London EC4P 4EE

Simultaneously published in the USA and Canada
by RoutledgeCurzon
29 West 35th Street, New York, NY 10001

RoutledgeCurzon is an imprint of the Taylor & Francis Group

Typeset in Sabon by Wearset Ltd, Boldon, Tyne and Wear
Printed and bound in Great Britain by MPG Books Ltd, Bodmin

British Library Cataloguing in Publication Data
A catalogue record for this book is available from the British Library

Library of Congress Cataloging in Publication Data
Jeffreys, Elaine, 1960–
China, sex and prostitution / Elaine Jeffreys.
p. cm. – (RoutledgeCurzon studies on China in transition ; 18)
Includes bibliographical references and index.
1. Prostitution–China. 2. Sex customs–China. 3. China–Social conditions. I. Title. II. Series.
HQ250.A5J43 2004
306.74'0951–dc22

2003016606

ISBN 0–415–31863–7

Contents

Acknowledgements

I would like to thank my parents, Tom and Jean Jeffreys, and my friends, Ivan Roberts, Xiong Daoqiong, and David Stokes, for helping me to complete this text either by encouraging me to 'get it done' or for insisting that I go out and play traditional Irish music for a change. I would also like to thank all those members of academic institutions – especially Gloria Davies, David Goodman, and Sheila Jeffreys – who offered me diverse forms of assistance. Last but not least, thanks are due to Michael Dutton for introducing me to the academic study of China over a decade ago, and for remaining the major inspiration behind my continued interest in theorizing 'China' to this day.

The author and publishers would like to thank the following for granting permission to reproduce material in this work:

Elaine Jeffreys, 'Feminist prostitution debates: are there any sex workers in China?', in Anne McLaren (ed.), *Chinese Women: Living and Working*, pp. 165–211 (RoutledgeCurzon, 2003) by kind permission of RoutledgeCurzon, London, www.routledge.com.

Every effort has been made to contact copyright holders for their permission to reprint material in this book. The publishers would be grateful to hear from any copyright holder who is not here acknowledged and will undertake to rectify any errors or omissions in future editions of this book.

Abbreviations

ACWF	All-China Women's Federation
CCP	Chinese Communist Party
CEDAW	Convention on the Elimination of All Forms of Discrimination Against Women
COYOTE	Call Off Your Old Tired Ethics
ECP	English Collective of Prostitutes
HIV	human immunodeficiency virus
ICPR	International Committee for Prostitutes' Rights
ILO	International Labour Organization
NGO	nongovernmental organization
PRC	People's Republic of China
STDs	sexually transmissible diseases
UN	United Nations
VD	venereal diseases
WHISPER	Women Hurt in Systems of Prostitution Engaged in Revolt
WHO	World Health Organization

Introduction

Telling tales

In search of authentic native voices

Michel de Certeau (1984: 115) has argued that every story is a travel story and the one I am about to relate is no exception. In August 1993, as the recipient of a scholarship from the Australian Government, I went to live and study in the People's Republic of China (PRC) for a period of two years. My expressed intention in doing so was to improve my standard Chinese language skills and, subsequently, to collect research materials for a proposed doctoral dissertation on the differential construction of 'Maoist' and 'Dengist' political leaders in Western vis-à-vis Chinese biographical discourses. Forearmed with the inevitable cautionary tales provided by more seasoned practitioners of China studies (the moral of which being 'China will change you!'), I anticipated that the broad parameters of this project would alter. Little did I suspect, however, that it would turn into the present work, namely, a text concerned with the question of how to interpret issues of sexuality and power in relation to the PRC, with a subsequent focus on the policing of prostitution. How did such a change come about?

In many respects, my decision to abandon the subject of political biography owed much to the coincidental establishment of a personal friendship. Shortly after my arrival in the PRC, I met a Chinese woman whom I will refer to anonymously as X. She was 19 years old at the time and had come to Beijing from the rural hinterland three years previously to look for work. After obtaining and then leaving a series of menial positions in various work-units and private business enterprises, X eventually started 'working' as a 'hostess' (*sanpei xiaojie*),[1] in what was then a relatively new and flourishing place of entertainment in Beijing, namely, a karaoke/dance venue (*gewuting*).[2]

Initially, X liked her newfound 'employment' for three reasons. First, since she was paid on the basis of tips provided by the male patrons she accompanied in her capacity as a 'hostess', rather than by the management of a given venue, she was not subject to the usual demands of an employer. This meant that she was able to determine the hours and conditions of her 'work' to a relatively large degree. Second, she received more disposable income than she had in previous forms of employment for fewer hours of work.[3] Third, she appreciated the opportunity to meet new people, and enjoy herself at no personal expense, in surroundings that normally would have been prohibited to her by virtue of cost.[4]

Seven or eight months later, however, X was depressed and had started to express contempt for both herself and her 'work'. As she explained it, her dissatisfaction stemmed from a number of interrelated factors. To begin with, women who received financial recompense in the form of tips for the services they provided as 'hostesses' were finding it increasingly difficult to generate something akin to their initial levels of income. Many of the patrons of the venues she frequented appeared to want new – as in different – 'hostesses', and 'hostesses' who would behave in a more explicitly sexual manner. Concomitantly, many of the once 'friendly' managers of such venues appeared unwilling to direct patrons towards 'hostesses' who were known to provide companionship only, a consideration which had seriously affected X's capacity to negotiate a basic income.[5] As a result, X and several of her friends had started 'working' at a number of karaoke/dance venues per week, going to whichever venue was most busy on a given night in order to maximize their reduced income-earning opportunities. Adding to these financial worries, X felt her reputation had been smeared, hence her already low social standing as a rural migrant had been further compromised, by virtue of her presumed association with commercial sexual activities. In consequence, she was no longer convinced that being a 'hostess' constituted a viable occupational choice. But, after embarking on a brief and failed business venture, she doubted that any better options were available to her.

X's indecision over her future was compounded when she discovered that leisure and entertainment venues had become an object of governmental intervention via the implementation of a series of campaigns to fight illegality and pornography. At first, X was not overly troubled by this development because the local police adopted a 'softly softly' approach towards investigating the various commercial enterprises that came under their jurisdiction. For example, the police requested owners and managers of venues in the particular district that X frequented to attend a meeting. At this meeting, they were notified that, as of a future specified date, anyone found operating or managing a karaoke/dance venue without an appropriate licence and clearance from the Chinese public security agencies would be subject to legal sanctions. In addition, they were informed of the relevant regulations regarding the employment of service personnel, and reminded that Chinese law proscribes prostitution, and that the Beijing Cultural Bureau had banned *sanpei* activities (Fan Benji 1994: 83). In short, they were told to make sure that their business operations conformed (or, at least, appeared to conform) to the relevant regulations, or face the consequences of failing to do so at some future date.

This information was relayed to X by the manager of a karaoke/dance venue she frequented. She was informed that the local police intended to visit the venue sometime during the coming week to confirm that business was being conducted in accordance with the law. Consequently, those responsible for managing the activities that occurred within the venue had decided not to liaise between any 'hostesses' and patrons for the next couple of days. This not only meant that X was unlikely to receive a reasonable 'income', it also meant that her presence in the venue would look suspicious unless she was in the company of patrons who could be convincingly presented to the investigating officials as 'friends'.[6] Not surprisingly, X decided to stay at home until the police had finished their investigations.

Although X initially viewed this incident as a minor inconvenience, one that lost her a week's potential income, a year later she had decided that her days as a 'hostess' were numbered. Policy directives aimed at controlling increased rates of commercial sexual activities – activities that are viewed as intimately related to the rapidly expanding nature of the leisure and entertainment market – had resulted in the implementation of stricter policing practices. Briefly, specialized task forces were formed to investigate such venues and they adopted a wide range of tactics. These tactics included: conducting surprise raids on specified entertainment venues; using plain clothes police officers to investigate the activities within such venues; and ensuring that the respective owners, managers, workers, and patrons, of a given venue were subjected to a process of rigorous questioning. Concomitantly, regulations were put in place that outlined a system of penalties for failing to report knowledge of illicit sexual activities in any given workplace, and special plainclothes units were formed to investigate the activities of the investigating task forces themselves. Official announcements also indicated that 'hostessing' activities would become subject to increased scrutiny as a 'known front' for prostitution. In view of these developments, X decided 'hostessing' was not just an increasingly unpleasant 'job', it also constituted a potentially dangerous means of earning a living, since she risked being detained by public security agencies.

As X and I met on a daily basis, and subsequently shared accommodation for almost a year, discussing and attempting to make sense of the forces that were shaping her life was a routine occurrence. My initial interest in debates concerning the nature of *sanpei* activities, and, by extension, the nature of China's prostitution controls, was thus whetted by a desire to comprehend more fully the complexity of X's position. Having travelled to the PRC in order to conduct research, however, this interest almost inevitably became fused to more pragmatic considerations. After all, the new and controversial nature of Chinese debates on *sanpei* and prostitution, combined with the relative paucity of English language materials on such issues, meant that I had inadvertently stumbled on a far more topical and institutionally marketable focus for research than political biography.[7]

In fact, given the recent concern among China scholars to document the 'lives' of Chinese subalterns, and the general interest in theorizing issues of sexuality, power, and difference, that currently permeates the academy as a whole, one could say that I had found an ideal native informant and an ideal topic for research. Or, to use popular academic parlance, one could aver that I was ideally situated to engage in the institutionally sanctioned task of 're-presenting reality, bringing forth the voices of the subaltern, [and] giving space to the perceptions of those whose realities have gone unheard in previous writings of history' (Howell 1999: 38).

Authenticity as academic capital

While it is not conventional practice to mention considerations of personal friendship and institutional marketability in the same breath, I have done so with a particular purpose in mind. Put simply, it constitutes an attempt to be truthful about the practical conditions surrounding the production of this book. I use the term 'truthful' in the sense that reference to my relationship with X may help to explain why I abandoned the subject of political biography, but it does not adequately explain how I, or anyone else for that matter, can suggest that the subject of prostitution comprises an 'ideal' object of intellectual endeavour. It is simply a gesture – calculated to evoke a response from others and to convey an apparently friendly intention – towards the kinds of protocols that inform the Western academic field of China studies, including its prominent subdivision of women's/gender studies. In other words, it constitutes a decidedly rhetorical attempt to situate myself within a particular economy of tertiary knowledge reception/production, one that I want to open to critique.

Therefore, my opening gambit – a travel story which hinges on the coincidental establishment of a personal friendship – entails a certain duplicity at the level of textual strategy. To begin with, the deployment of personalized detail or autobiographical reflection is clearly a conventional component not only of ethnography, but also of many works produced within the field of China studies (e.g., Evans 1997: vii). Such reflections invariably feature in the opening sections of such texts (as they have in mine), and, no matter how briefly related, they play a far from trivial role. They function to anchor the text – what has been said and what has yet to be said – in the intense and authority-giving experience of fieldwork (Pratt 1986: 31–2). This remains the case irrespective of whether the term 'fieldwork' is understood with regard to specific anthropological, sociological, and feminist protocols, or more as an indication that one has completed a rite of passage deemed necessary to confirm one's standing as a China scholar. In the latter case, it confirms that one has seen and experienced 'China' for oneself, and been able to share (at least to some extent) in the daily life of 'the Chinese people', through one's demonstrated ability to communicate in the modern, standard Chinese language.

Recourse to personal narrative or autobiographical reflection is thus a popular textual strategy because it operates as a legitimating device. The provision of personalized detail, however explicitly or surreptitiously mentioned, inserts the voice of the speaking and experiencing subject into the text. In doing so, it helps to establish a particular relationship between the subjects and objects of the ethnographic text – the ethnographer, the native, and the reader (Pratt 1986: 30). And in terms of works produced within Anglophone China studies,[8] it helps to establish a particular relationship between the researcher (the Western China scholar), the objects of research ('the Chinese nation' and 'the Chinese people'), and the reader. It says: 'Trust me; I know what I am talking about because I've been there and I speak the language.'

Viewed in this context, my opening gambit comprises more than a means to introduce the general concerns of this text: it also connotes an institutionally sanctioned attempt to claim the intellectual capital that conventionally accrues to practitioners of China studies by virtue of their linguistic expertise. In Chapter 1, I question the nature and uses of that capital. In particular, I interrogate a founding assumption of China studies, namely, that China scholars are best able to capture the 'truth' or 'reality' of 'China' because they possess the capacity to translate both linguistically *and* culturally. Suffice it to say here, however, that I am obliged to lay claim to that very same capital in order for this text to be viewed as belonging or of relevance to the field. In this respect, my opening gambit is necessarily duplicitous. I am obliged to highlight the specific order of discourse that shapes the parameters for what is considered to be acceptable China studies scholarship, before I can justify the different organizing concerns of this work.

This does not mean that the professional legitimacy accorded to ethnographies, and many texts produced within the field of China studies, stems from recourse to language-as-experience or the provision of personalized detail alone. On the contrary, for a work of intellectual labour to gain professional capital, the voice of the speaking and experiencing subject has to be more or less expunged from the text and replaced with the seemingly objective voice of academic authority. For without suitable reference to the specific order of discourse that governs the shape of a given knowledge field – such as the elaboration of an acknowledged theoretical position and methodological approach, the deployment of familiar tropes, appropriate reference to certain key authors and texts, and the judicious use of institutionally valued source materials – the use of personalized description would probably be dismissed as mere anecdote. In this respect, as my opening gambit serves to suggest, the practice of providing copious endnotes works to ameliorate the quasi-evidentiary status of anecdote, and hence to alleviate the contradiction between the personal engagement called for in fieldwork and the self-effacement called for in formal academic description, by suggesting that the subjective voice is an objective voice, nevertheless.

In consequence, although academic conventions require the voice of the speaking and experiencing subject to be more or less erased from the text – so that the completed work can be adjudged as based on objective, professional criterion – it continues to exist as a 'silent' adjunct to the problematic at issue (Pratt 1986: 32–3). In fact, even when personalized description is provided as a preliminary indication that the text ultimately will be anchored in that institutionally sanctioned, albeit not unquestioned, theoretical artifice called fieldwork, it inevitably serves another function. It surreptitiously grounds the text in that most problematic yet equally intractable of spaces known as 'the real'. This referential grounding further authenticates the text by suggesting that the author has not only internalized and therefore embodies the attributes of the native subject, but has also dealt appropriately with the subjective, sensuous experience of fieldwork, by making such 'attributes' subject to a process of academic rationalization.

Viewed from this perspective, my opening gambit constitutes more than an attempt to claim the intellectual capital that conventionally accrues to practitioners of China studies: it also mimics the realist approach to knowledge that characterizes the field. As mentioned earlier, the narrative of my relationship with X does not explain how, or in what ways, the subjects of *sanpei* and prostitution constitute 'ideal' objects of intellectual endeavour. It simply locates the voice of 'the authentic native' and 'the objective Western scholar' in the same temporal order, and hence anchors the text in the seemingly indisputable (as in prediscursive) world of actuality. In this way, a work of academic labour is not required to reflect on its own textual operations, and their ensuing truth effects, to be positively judged as telling 'the real story'. Rather, as my own preamble would suggest, so long as an account is proffered in a properly empirical and lucid manner – in this instance, through the apparently value-neutral modes of inquiry that are accorded authority within the field of China studies – it will be ascribed intellectual merit.

This is not to say that the classical conception of a mimetic relationship between 'knowledge' and 'reality', or the assumption that the relationship between signification and meaning is essentially transparent, has gone unchallenged within the fields of ethnography and China studies. Ethnographers and China scholars alike have raised questions pertaining to the politics of translation and the nature of classificatory practices (e.g., Clifford 1992; Cohen 1984). What I do want to suggest, however, is that the radical impetus of this style of critique – a mode of criticism that should properly lead to the questioning of dominant modes of representation – has been more or less stymied within the field of China studies.

The radical impetus of theoretical reflections on the nature of representational and translational practices has been curtailed within China studies due to the field's continued affective privileging of linguistic vis-à-vis other forms of professional expertise. Put simply, the very centrality of language study in China studies – encompassing a form of training, or a method of language acquisition, that turns on the presumption that it is possible to render a 'true' translation – has effectively guaranteed the empiricist bias of the field by producing an unconscious justification for a 'realist' approach to knowledge (Dutton 2000a: 4). The field's continued reliance on largely unproblematized models of linguistic 'communication' is demonstrated by the predominance of empirically based studies, as opposed to more theoretically informed works, in the major journals that demarcate the acceptable parameters of the field, such as the *China Quarterly*, the *China Journal*, and *Modern China*. It also goes some way to explain why China scholars frequently mobilize 'theory' as yet another means to realize the assumed (as in desired) transparency of translation that has historically characterized the field.

In short, recent theoretical reflections on the nature of representational practices have had a limited impact on China studies because they are seldom used as a means to interrogate the ontological foundations of the field. Instead, theory has proved to be most acceptable when its deployment gestures towards the now institutionally sanctioned goal of interdisciplinarity, while simultaneously operating as a means to rejuvenate and embellish extant approaches. This approach cleverly mimics theoretical discourse, while doing nothing to address the field's long-standing captivity within the ideological framework of studying-the-other, most succinctly captured in the expression 'China-watching'.

Another native voice: the alternative translator

The preceding discussion has travelled from a 'story' based on personal friendship towards a critique of the kinds of protocols that inform the Western academic field of China studies. The necessity of making a detour through the disciplinary space of China studies seems so evident once it is stated – 'who would dream of describing a journey without having an idea of the landscape in which it was made?' (Bourdieu 1987: 1–7) – that it is difficult to understand why this task is not immediately recognized as the field's first order of academic business. On the whole, however, China scholars have proved remarkably unwilling to engage with the intellectual limitations of knowledge production in the field of area-cum-language studies. In consequence, China studies remains an intellectual enterprise secured along a relatively 'untroubled dividing line between the "object" and "subject" of study'. 'The Chinese nation' and 'the Chinese people' are still essentially 'pre-given' objects to be explored and investigated, while the subjects weighing the pros and cons of these objects (and subsequently speaking for them), are Western China scholars occupying their traditional role as nation-translators (Davies 1998: 178).

Somewhat ironically, the Sinologist's historical claim to professional capital, namely, to 'know' China in a direct and virtually incorruptible fashion, has been augmented in recent years by recourse to the discourse of theory, in particular, the insights afforded by what may be loosely described as poststructuralism, postcolonialism, and feminisms of difference. Critical positions of this kind have done much to foster a cognitive disposition towards intellectual veracity, in the sense of promoting a general willingness to acknowledge and engage with the limitations of knowledge production, especially 'those that dictate one's sense of what it is to "know" as the product of a specific knowledge system' (ibid.: 172). In practice, however, many such accounts are marred by the corollary tendency to adopt a particular ethico-political stance, one that undermines the critical accent of their interventions by leading them back into the referential domain of translation (Dutton 2000a: 4).

The postcolonial emphasis on deconstructing dominant modes of representation, for instance, has all too often been seduced and replaced by nativist propositions, as in claims to have recovered an indigenous voice of resistance. Like neo-Marxist renditions of 'history from below', there is a marked tendency within certain strands of postcolonial/feminist scholarship to champion the non-West, and perceived expressions of female agency, under the sign of a universal ethics of resistance (ibid.: 5). Such accounts ritualistically commence by denying that 'the "Truth" is out there', yet they simultaneously rely upon some assumed proximity to the authentic (native/female) voice in order to demonstrate the superiority of their (theoretically informed) approach. In this way, the use of a 'postrepresentationalist vocabulary' often hides an essentialist agenda (Spivak 1995: 27).

The ethical commitment to a politics of resistance can thus paradoxically function to preclude a critical investigation of the politics of knowledge acquisition by absolving 'the committed' of any need to further interrogate their own modes of reading and writing. Blinded by a desire to expose instances of resistance to the homogenizing effects of dominant discourses, the critical Western (China) scholar easily slips into the role of 'alternative translator' for so-called subaltern voices (Dutton 2000a: 5). In the process, the theoretical unavailability of this task (most succinctly captured in Spivak's contention: 'The subaltern cannot speak') is elided (Spivak 1995: 28); and, instead of using theory to develop a more interrogative praxis within the disciplinary space of China studies, the critical China scholar resorts to the more familiar tactic of using theory as an applied technology for revealing the transgressive nature of 'non-official Chinese voices', and thereby offering new 'truths' against the ongoing 'falsehoods' of the Chinese Communist Party (CCP). Analyses of this kind thus tend to reinforce extant ways of seeing, even as they receive institutional acclaim for providing a new and alternative source of knowledge.

Avoiding this slip into conventional forms of China studies scholarship requires a different order of criticality. Rather than applying theory as yet another, if more sophisticated and fashionable, means to achieve the impossible dream of translating 'the real China', theory might be more gainfully deployed as a tactic to read China studies 'against the grain'. Deconstructive modes of analysis, for instance, increasingly are used by Anglophone China scholars to provide reconfigured commentaries on Chinese texts, events, and situations (Apter and Saich 1994; Hershatter *et al.* 1996). Yet this particular mode of reading has seldom been used as a means to reflect on the historically conditioned nature of our own forms of thinking, and hence to acknowledge the provisional nature of the 'truths' we choose to produce and circulate about China. Instead, the veracity of critical pronouncements on 'things Chinese' tends to be rendered as given, subject to the usual mandatory fillips in the direction of theoretico-political correctness.

To elaborate upon this contention, and subsequently to situate the concerns of this book, I propose to tell another story. This narrative marks a significant departure from my opening preamble since it cannot claim legitimacy on the basis of access to a native Chinese informant, nor can it be authenticated by its implicit conformity to the value-neutral modes of inquiry that characterize the field. Instead, I draw on the methods of the new humanities to offer a close and partial reading of one specific text. In doing so, I venture into the newly reconfigured interdisciplinary terrain of China studies by interrogating a different native voice, namely, that of a prominent China scholar, Gail Hershatter. The value of subjecting this particular voice to scrutiny is heuristic. It illustrates how theory has been 'tamed' to meet the requirements of China studies. In addition, it highlights some of the problematic ways in which the subject of contemporary Chinese prostitution, and hence the relationship between issues of sexuality and power in the PRC, has been rendered as an object of metropolitan intellectual inquiry.

Telling popular institutional tales

In 'Chinese sex workers in the reform period', Gail Hershatter (1996a: 199–224) notes that the re-emergence of prostitution in 1980s' and 1990s' urban China, after nearly three decades of apparent absence, raises a number of pertinent questions for analysis. Among the most important of these, she implies, are not strictly the standard sociological questions: namely, who prostitutes and who patronizes prostitutes?; what factors predispose women to enter prostitution?; and, where do prostitution activities take place and to whose financial benefit? Rather, it is equally, if not more, analytically productive to ask: what meanings have been attributed to the category of prostitution by sellers, buyers, government regulators, and social critics in contemporary China?; how have these understandings affected the daily lives of those classified as prostitutes?; and, what do these understandings reveal about Chinese conceptions of modernity, and the kinds of sex and gender relations that characterize that modernity?

By raising the latter mode of questions, Hershatter usefully suggests that prostitution does not constitute a 'given' or 'known' phenomenon about which it is possible to make general truth statements regarding the nature of its existence and organization. Instead, she points out that the meanings attributed to the category of prostitution are historically and culturally contingent. Moreover, they are constructed in relation to heterogeneous spheres of interest, not solely the interests of governmental regulators alone. In keeping with this interrogative mode of analysis, she further contends that 'official' discourses on prostitution, incorporating patterns of legal regulation and enforcement as formulated by governmental authorities, do not simply describe a pre-existing phenomenon known as prostitution, they also constitute that phenomenon, and having created it, immediately move to alter it (Hershatter 1996a: 201).

This style of criticism owes much to poststructuralist-feminist analyses of prostitution as a discursive domain, including its now common, if contested, construction as a sex-related legal issue. Briefly, such analyses have transformed traditional accounts of prostitution by pursuing three interrelated propositions. First, prostitution does not constitute a transparent category of analysis; even the referent, 'the flesh-and-blood female body engaged in some form of sexual interaction in exchange for some kind of payment, has no inherent meaning and is signified differently in different discourses' (Bell 1994: 1–2). Second, it is unproductive to view prostitution as a set of practices whose politically relevant features exist prior to or independent of its current legal and moral status. Third, it is equally unproductive to assume that the nature and organization of such practices can be 'read off' the nature of existing prostitution controls. This is because the socio-cultural production of prostitution occurs via mechanisms that are exclusive neither to the law nor to prostitution alone: for example, the Western 'cultural denigration of chastity (especially among men), the attribution of various disorders to "not getting any", and the equation of a "healthy" sex life with general well-being, all serve to encourage prostitution' even as laws prohibit it (Zatz 1997: 304).

Theoretical reflections of this kind are avowedly political in that they aim to show how prostitution has been constructed within various discursive domains, and hence to reconfigure the subject of prostitution as an object of governmental intervention. Once invoked within the field of China studies, however, such reflections tend to become little more than a means to demonstrate that Chinese prostitution *too* can be read and represented using the discourse of theory. Hershatter, for instance, offers an interesting sketch of 'life' in the Chinese sex trades, an account that is buttressed by her own eye-witness observations or ethnographic fieldwork. She also details how Chinese commentators have chosen to construct 'the problem of prostitution' and thereby influenced the nature of its regulation. But the radical impetus of this style of critique, one that purports to explain the particularity of Chinese discourses on prostitution, is ultimately stymied by her implicit endorsement of the Western concept of sex work – simplistically rendered as preferable to the term 'prostitution' in that it draws attention to the labour involved in transactions involving sexual services, and is therefore morally less prejudicial – as a measure by which the failings of the Chinese response to prostitution can be highlighted and assessed.

Despite explicit claims to the contrary, Hershatter's main contention is that Chinese understandings of prostitution are flawed because reform-era prostitution has rarely been formulated as work, or, more precisely, as a phenomenon shaped in part by labour market conditions.[9] To illustrate this contention, Hershatter divides Chinese commentators on prostitution into two arbitrary yet supposedly discrete groupings. The first group are described as 'state commentators' (presumably the CCP and the Ministry of Public Security), and the second group are described as professional or 'non-state commentators', including researchers for the All-China Women's Federation (ACWF), sociologists, legal scholars, journalists, and 'creators of reportage literature' (Hershatter 1996a: 214, 199–201).

By dividing Chinese commentators into what amounts to the voice of 'the state' versus that of 'the non-state', Hershatter is able to acknowledge the diversity of Chinese discourses on prostitution yet simultaneously insist that they are inadequate, as in one-dimensional. According to Hershatter (ibid.: 210), China's 'state authorities' are committed to an outmoded and disintegrating analytical framework, one that simultaneously defines female prostitutes as 'victims' of human traffickers and 'victimizers' of the social and moral order. Consequently, they cannot accept that prostitution is shaped by inequitable labour market conditions and may constitute a viable occupational choice for many women. The problem here, or so Hershatter (ibid.: 221) concludes, is that until 'state authorities' in China recognize prostitution as work, or else devise policies that will make other types of labour for women more available and attractive, the PRC will continue to pursue an ineffective and discriminatory policy of prohibition.

In contrast to the alleged rigidity of 'the Chinese state', Hershatter (ibid.: 204–5, 221) maintains that 'non-state commentators' have proved more willing to acknowledge the specificity of prostitution in the reform era. This willingness, she suggests, stems from the fact that they are not wedded to the same disintegrating framework, one inherited from the 'bad old days of [China's] semicolonial weakness . . . and the good old days of the 1950s when the [Maoist] state successfully closed [China's] brothels'. Unlike 'state authorities', therefore, 'non-state commentators' are inclined 'to attribute more agency to individual prostitutes, to concern themselves more with the question of motivation, and to take seriously the economic lure of prostitution for many women' (ibid.: 214–15). Like China's 'state authorities', however, Hershatter concludes that 'non-state commentators' also view the sale of sexual services and work as mutually exclusive, since they tend to describe instances of 'voluntary' prostitution in terms of personal deviancy.[10] That is to say, they refer to prostitution as a choice made by women who dislike work but who want to get rich quick, rather than as a legitimate strategy designed to achieve specific economic and psychological ends (ibid.: 216–18).

While correctly noting that prostitution has not been constructed as an acceptable form of female employment in the PRC, Hershatter's corollary contention that Chinese commentators have refused to acknowledge the relationship between prostitution and labour market conditions is flatly contradicted by the evidence which she subsequently mobilizes to support this claim. To substantiate this contention, Hershatter compares a report, written by a Hong Kong journalist in November 1988, on the growing problem of unemployment in Hainan Province's capital of Haikou, with a statement made four months later by the Party secretary of Hainan on allegedly the same subject. The journalist, she notes, indicated that the massive influx of people to the newly created Special Economic Zone had created a serious (un)employment problem, and simultaneously contributed to the growth of a visible and lucrative 'sex industry', with women who offered sexual services earning up to twenty times more than they could by working in conventional forms of employment elsewhere in China (ibid.: 218–19). Yet when the Party secretary took up the same topic, she continues, he chose to classify prostitution, along with gambling, as an 'ugly social phenomenon' brought about by a massive influx in population, inadequate policing controls, and an increase in the number of people pursuing decadent lifestyles. He did not, she concludes, acknowledge that unemployment might be a factor inducing women in particular to work as prostitutes, nor did he acknowledge that prostitution was a particularly lucrative line of work for women. Instead, his 'proposed solution matched the problem as he had defined it', namely, to crack down on serious criminal activities, to exercise firmness with regard to the eradication of an ugly phenomenon, and to implement tougher controls on the migration of people into the province (ibid.: 218–19).

As far as Hershatter is concerned, the Party secretary's refusal to acknowledge that prostitution is shaped by changing labour market conditions is replicated in the growing literature on the rising transient population in China's major cities. As she points out, '[t]ransients move about China, principally *to find better-paying work* [my italics, since this comment implies that transients do not necessarily leave their place of origin due to lack of employment] and they frequently send remittances home' (ibid.: 220). 'Women make up roughly a third of all transients and transients as a group tend to be young' (ibid.: 219). Prostitutes comprise a not insignificant part of the female transient population, with many young women from the rural hinterland working as lower-class prostitutes in China's cities and many higher-class prostitutes being women who have migrated from one metropolis to another. Despite the clear connection between prostitution and changing labour market conditions, however,

Hershatter (1996a: 220) avers that 'Chinese writings on transients make virtually no mention of prostitution or its relative desirability as a work option for female transients'.

These conclusions are both theoretically and empirically spurious: rather than demonstrating the refusal of Chinese commentators to analyse prostitution in terms of labour, they highlight Hershatter's refusal to engage with Chinese discourses on their own terms. To begin with, pressure on job security, especially in relation to female employment, has undoubtedly been building in the PRC ever since managers were given the power to dismiss workers in 1988. However, given that middle-aged women have been most adversely affected by such policies (Rosenthal 1998), and female prostitutes in China are predominantly single women under 25 years of age, Hershatter's causal explanation for the existence of reform-era prostitution may be just as one-sided as the approach she attributes to 'the Chinese state'.

In addition, although *Chinese writings on transients* may make little mention of prostitution and its relative desirability as a work option for female transients, *Chinese writings on prostitution* routinely cite the economic lure of prostitution, in conjunction with the unchecked migration of people from rural areas to urban centres, and from one metropolis to another, as a major reason for the continued growth and rapid spread of prostitution in China today (Beijing dongcheng gongan fenju 1993: 14–17; Niu Yangzi 1993: 32–4; Ouyang Tao 1994: 15–18). In fact, even the Party secretary, whom Hershatter so strenuously condemns, clearly points to the relationship between prostitution and the floating population, and hence to an acknowledged connection between prostitution and altered market conditions. The only discrepancy between Hershatter's and the Party secretary's understanding of the situation is that the latter's description of prostitution as an 'ugly social phenomenon' obviously conflicts with Hershatter's implicit endorsement of sex work as both a viable occupational choice and a positive expression of female agency.

Hershatter's tendency to construct the absence of public discussion on sex work in China as a lack – and hence as a sign of the PRC's failure to conform with some universalized (Western) idea of development and modernity – is highlighted by the way she raises and deals with the following question. To use her own words: 'Why do China's state authorities and social scientists by and large find a labor market framework uncongenial?' While noting that '[g]ood historical method cautions against hypothesizing about something that does not happen', she promptly proceeds to ignore her own sound advice in order to affirm that she can tell us about something that does (Hershatter 1996a: 220). In the process of confirming her ability to translate 'the Chinese nation', Hershatter not only reinstates the notion of sex work as a measure by which the failings of the Chinese response to prostitution can be assessed, she also proffers an ahistorical and contradictory form of analysis.

In keeping with the predictive ethos of China studies, for instance, Hershatter (ibid.: 223) contends that 'non-state commentators' may eventually come to see prostitution, 'if not as a form of work, then at least as an income-generating activity that looks more attractive than other available options'. At the moment, however, China's 'new social scientists' are more inclined to look at prostitution through the lens of crime, or else as a sign of women's unequal status and resultant victimization, due to a particular combination of factors. These factors include: the relative newness of crime as a category of analysis in China; the fascination of China's new social scientists with Western social science theory; a general lack of interest in the category of labour as 'an old and shopworn topic', which was 'exhaustively (even numbingly) discussed throughout the prereform period'; and the active retreat of scholars who pay attention to 'women's issues' from a Maoist analytical framework which took 'employment as the sole criterion of women's liberation' (ibid.: 220).

While China's new social scientists may be somewhat crime-obsessed and bored with Maoism, it bears stating that none of the above-mentioned frameworks preclude an analysis of prostitution in terms of labour market conditions. On the contrary, both Western and Chinese accounts of prostitution as crime and female deviancy, or as a sign of women's subordinate status and resultant victimization, are invariably constructed with reference to the limited economic and social opportunities that are made available to women vis-à-vis men (Acton 1857; Benjamin and Masters 1965; Ding Juan 1996; Wang Jinling *et al.* 1998). Likewise, although mainland Chinese scholars who pay attention to 'women's issues' have challenged various Maoist precepts, they have far from abandoned Maoism as a vehicle for realizing social change. In fact, the vaunted achievements of the Maoist era – including the eradication of prostitution and the full participation of women in productive labour – have been used as political leverage to ensure that the current leadership reaffirms its historical commitment to women's emancipation, by guaranteeing female employment and eliminating prostitution (Wang Zheng 1997: 126–52). What these interpretative frameworks do not allow, and this is the issue that truly troubles Hershatter, is the understanding of prostitution as an autonomous expression of female sexuality, and hence as a positive sign of female agency.

Hershatter's commitment to the broader feminist project of detailing the agency involved in women's experiences thus leads her to equate a labour market analysis with understandings of prostitution as sex work. This theoretical slippage results in considerable textual confusion. Post-structuralist-feminist proponents of sex work, for instance, have documented the various deleterious ways in which Western psychological and criminological discourses literally created the female prostitute subject as a marginalized socio-sexual identity (Bell 1994: 40–72). Yet Hershatter virtually condones the tendency of China's new social scientists to psychologize and pathologize the female prostitute subject, flowing from their relatively recent access to the kinds of analytical frameworks that make up Western social science. Hershatter's paradoxical privileging of 'non-state commentaries' on prostitution does not flow from any intrinsic respect for the now bedevilled social sciences, but rather from her adherence to a popular China studies convention. Like many China scholars, she assumes that the work of China's new social scientists has to be more 'progressive' than anything constructed in the 'stifling' and 'has-been' language of Chinese Marxism.

In contrast to her 'gentle' treatment of China's new social scientists, Hershatter roundly berates China's 'state authorities' for responding to the problems currently surrounding female employment by attempting to return women to stable work and family situations. As she puts it, 'state authorities' have adopted this strategy in the hope of realizing the desired goal of modernization, while resisting the 'disruptions engendered by bourgeois liberalization' (read Western influences, incorporating changing sexual mores and patterns of consumption). The problem here, she continues, is that Party and government leaders have constructed modernity as 'simultaneously displacing women (who are both victimized and set loose) and requiring that they be resituated (both protected and contained) with the help of strong state authority' (Hershatter 1996a: 220). In this formulation, 'prostitution appears as an interruption of stable work and family, rather than as a form of work that may, in fact, be helping to support many Chinese families'. Hence the real issue at stake, or so Hershatter (ibid.: 220) concludes, is 'the very control of what modernity looks like and means, as well as what "women" are and should be'.

What Hershatter means by this rhetorically impressive but surprisingly empty contention is that prostitution controls in the PRC are reflective of nothing more than the patriarchal/paternalistic nature of 'the Chinese state'. I use the term 'empty' for three reasons. First, she has clearly abandoned the suggestion that prostitution practices, and also the mode of their regulation, are constructed in relation to a heterogeneous set of discourses and interests. It is now a phenomenon with definite, as in potentially liberatory, characteristics that is negatively acted upon by 'the (monolithic) Chinese state' for the sole purpose of controlling independent expressions of female agency and sexuality.

Second, Hershatter's contention that China's prostitution controls are revealing of Chinese conceptions of modernity, as well as the kinds of sex and gender relations that should characterize that modernity, makes very little sense unless one is familiar with feminist rewritings of the history of prostitution in nineteenth-century Britain and North America. Briefly, late nineteenth-century and early twentieth-century campaigns against prostitution as vice, including those launched by first-wave feminists, have been accused of effecting a rigid form of social control by imposing bourgeois or middle-class moral values on all levels of society. In the process, or so it is claimed, these campaigns denied female (working-class) prostitutes any agency or autonomy by attempting to return and confine them to the home (Walkowitz 1980). Hershatter replicates the broad parameters of this interpretive framework by suggesting that the CCP is attempting to control all women, through the imposition of some out-dated form of socialist, as opposed to bourgeois, morality.

Finally, it is precisely Hershatter's unquestioning transportation of these debates to the analysis of contemporary China that renders her conclusions so untenable. Far from explaining how prostitution has been constructed as an object of discourse in the PRC, she interprets the nature of Chinese prostitution, and the manner of its regulation, through a grid supplied by recourse to a particular strand of revisionist feminist history. In the process, Hershatter makes exactly the same mistake as her mentors (i.e., late twentieth-century feminist historians of prostitution in nineteenth-century Britain and North America). She allows her opinions regarding the primacy of sexual pleasure in contemporary feminist theory, and the problematic nature of sexual repression, to overshadow the actual subject matter of her inquiry.

The 'wrong-headed', if well-intentioned, nature of this approach is highlighted by the fact that Hershatter herself is not exactly enamoured of the prostitution as sex work formulation. In marked contrast to the pro-work thrust of 'Chinese Sex Workers in the Reform Period', Hershatter (1996a: 203) concludes the text by stating that she is not saying that prostitution is '"really" labour' and 'all Chinese commentators are operating under the cloud of false consciousness'. Rather than interpreting Chinese discourses on prostitution in an 'imperialistic' fashion, she finds it preferable to look at the formulations by which people choose to understand prostitution, as well as the ones they foreclose. Moreover, if she could make her 'own personal favourite formulation of prostitution', it would pay as much attention to questions of sexuality (both male and female), marriage markets, trafficking in women, disease, and Chinese constructions of modernity, as it would to labour.

If Hershatter recognizes the neocolonialist and homogenizing implications of saying that prostitution *is* work, then why does she fail to confirm that Chinese commentators have addressed the issue of prostitution in most (if not all) of her favourite terms? Even more curiously, given this gesture towards the characteristic anti-essentialism of postcolonial theory, why does Hershatter conclude by suggesting that prostitution *looks* like work and therefore needs to be reconfigured as labour after all? The answer to this about-face lies in Hershatter's unexamined commitment to a particular brand of identity politics and her concomitant failure to question the informing assumptions of China studies, particularly the field's continued reliance on empiricist modes of information retrieval.

In both respects, Hershatter's conclusion exemplifies how theory has been 'tamed' to meet the requirements of China studies. To extrapolate,

Hershatter concludes 'Chinese sex workers in the reform period' by making three inter-related observations. First, Hershatter (ibid.: 223) notes that the women (read prostitutes) whom she observed in a Shanghai hotel approached customers with the kind of concentration and seriousness that she, for one (and presumably all of us), would associate with work.[11] Second, Hershatter points out that if the work of the prominent Chinese sexologist, Pan Suiming, is anything to go by, then the occupation of prostitution 'involves much of the drudgery, even alienation, often associated with work'. To substantiate this claim, she cites the following passage from Pan's work:

> Individual interviews with prostitutes found that the majority of them describe their experience as 'tiresome', 'indifferent', 'no alternative', 'have to tolerate' . . . There is [a] popular joke today: 'The prostitute says to her customer, move your head, I am watching TV.'
>
> (ibid.: 223)

Finally, Hershatter (ibid.: 224) concludes the text by stating that Pan Suiming comes closer to a labour market analysis than any other Chinese scholar, once again via an authorized joke:

> A family of three were talking about prostitution. The husband said, 'One act of a prostitute in xx city is worth three years of my salary!' The wife immediately responded, 'Then, never visit a prostitute.' The daughter unexpectedly said, 'I should do this work' [sic].[12]

This conclusion rings with the voice of authority, even though it is completely lame theoretically. At the level of textual strategy, Hershatter's conclusion is persuasive because it affirms popular understandings of the nature of prostitution. By this I mean we all *know* that women prostitute for money and due to the absence of better alternatives. Moreover, our (common-sense) perception of how things 'really are' has just been confirmed by the eye-witness observations of a prominent China scholar and the work of one of the PRC's most famous new social scientists, based on his own personal interviews with Chinese 'prostitutes'. In consequence, the fact that words such as 'drudgery' and 'alienation', and phrases such as 'no alternative' and 'have to tolerate', are quite in keeping with radical feminist constructions of prostitution as sexual exploitation (Barry 1995), and completely antithetical to the movement for prostitutes' rights' celebratory reconfiguration of the prostitute subject as a self-employed businesswoman who uses the market as a means to realize sexual and financial autonomy (Bell 1994; Nagle 1997), is rendered a 'non-issue'.

Viewed at the level of theory, however, this belated elision of the 'pro-sex' side of the prostitutes' rights platform is decidedly disturbing, not least, because Hershatter has consistently valorized the agency entailed in prostitution and, conversely, decried the adherence of China's 'state authorities' to the so-called victim model. In fact, this *volte-face* undermines the rather neat division that both underpins and ascribes authority to her account. This is the implied opposition between a 'wrong' approach to prostitution – the one adopted by China's 'state authorities' – and some 'better' approach to prostitution – the one endorsed by Hershatter, by China's new social scientists (albeit, in the near future), and by 'us' (as a presumably sympathetic China studies/women's studies readership).

Hershatter literally gets away with this about turn due to the timely provision of personalized detail. Anecdotal evidence – presented as a combination of eye-witness observations, interviews with prostitutes, and vernacular jokes – functions to verify Hershatter's account by shifting the perceived point of 'true knowledge' away from textual representations of prostitution towards 'real-life experience' itself. In this way, it does not matter whether the account provided is 'true' or not. Rather, as noted with regard to my own preamble, what matters is the mode of presentation; and, in this case, it is the point of repetition. Following her review of Chinese (textual) discourses, Hershatter's concluding stratagem effectively meshes the voice of 'the objective (Western and Chinese) scholar', 'the Chinese prostitute', and 'the Chinese people'. In doing so, it intimates that Hershatter is telling the 'real story' because she has given voice to the voiceless. She purportedly has entered the voice of those who have been excluded by 'official state categories' into 'history', namely, the most elusive, as in both gendered and proscribed, voice of the subaltern, Chinese prostitute subject.

The fact that this 'voice' is merely a truth-effect derived from the use of specific representational practices is likewise rendered a 'non-issue' because it is counterintuitive to the empiricist protocols of China studies and the humanistic idealism of the alternative translator. Hershatter's concluding stratagem thus exemplifies how the very commitment to revealing oppositional discourses can paradoxically function not only to elide the issues surrounding the translation problematic, but also to cocoon the field from the possibility that there may be other ways of 'doing China studies'. Embracing other ways of 'doing China studies' does not require the complete abandonment of this ethico-political stance. Rather, as Rey Chow (1998: xxii) suggests, it entails following the alluring traces of such idealism via the deployment of

> a reading practice that is always tactical, that seeks to uncover the theoretical part of even the most specific 'cultural' study, on the one hand, and the implicit cultural presumptuousness, aggressivity and violence in even the most pristinely 'theoretical' pronouncement, on the other.

For in the absence of such a practice (and despite the collective desire and assorted claims of China scholars to be 'writing from somewhere else'), we will continue to speak for subjects that can only be spoken for, and spoken of, by way of a transition narrative that will always ultimately privilege 'the modern', namely, the sovereign theoretical space of 'Europe'.[13]

Reading 'China' differently

Bearing the preceding comments in mind, it should come as no surprise that this is not a straightforward China studies text, that is, an account of prostitution in present-day China based on my friendship with X, and buttressed by references to generalized feminist insights, and the work of China's non-state commentators. Since both the Anglophone and Sinophone fields of China studies are inevitably framed in terms of the problematics posed by a transition narrative that always defines 'the modern' in relation to the hyperreal space of Europe, I do not propose to replicate extant approaches by striving for a truer translation or re-presentation of contemporary Chinese 'lives'. In recognizing that we cannot step 'outside' of this hyperreal space (despite our assorted claims to professional capital as historians, ethnographers, critical and feminist theorists, and so on), I have a different project in mind.

To provisionalize my opening travel metaphor, I intend to take theory or 'Europe' for a 'walk'. Rather than purporting to speak for subjects that can only be spoken for and spoken of via a transition narrative that privileges the masterful language of the Anglophone humanities, I want to employ a different order of criticality from 'within'. This deconstructive strategy entails bringing the impossible dream of providing a 'perfect translation', and the controversial identity politics that have shaped our readings of China, into question. Showing how the truth-statements generated within the institutional praxis of the China field are constituted, and then tactically redeploying them to challenge the ways in which the PRC is conventionally read, is a necessary precursor to providing other ways of 'doing and seeing'. In short, interrogating our assumptions – not just 'theirs' – is a crucial task if the field of China studies is to have a critical input into the formation and development of theory and retain its integrity as a pedagogic practice.

Challenging the traditional dichotomy between 'Euramericans' as theory makers and 'China/the Chinese' as objects of theorization means questioning 'the directional tyranny that names as East the place we go to study', and asking: 'Where is it that we really start from, where is the place that enunciates this itinerary?' (Harootunian 1999: 128). Accordingly, Chapter 1 assesses recent claims to the effect that the Western academic field of China studies, at least in its theory-minded manifestations, now constitutes an integral component of the metropolitan university precinct. While agreeing that recourse to the discourse of theory offers one of the most effective means of promoting China studies as a research-based programme in the current academic marketplace, I demonstrate that the recent deployment of theory within Anglophone China studies has taken a decidedly anti-theoretical turn. Most notably, even though 'the impact of theory' has opened new avenues of research in China studies, especially with regard to popular and institutionally sanctioned subjects like gender, sexuality, and power, theory has often been applied in a manner that reinforces, rather than challenges, the conventional parameters of the field.

Chapter 2 contextualizes these remarks by examining the various hierarchical divisions that currently condition the field of China studies as a subset of the new humanities and human sciences. Specifically, it illustrates the ways in which the institutional packaging of theory as more generalized ways of reading and writing has encouraged the perception that 'doing theory' is somehow an automatic sign of intellectual superiority. It also shows how this tactic has, conversely, led non-practitioners of theory – including those who utilize the kinds of discourses that circulate within the PRC – to be viewed as generating a form of knowledge that relegates them to a lower-class stratum within the academy. With reference to recent Anglophone China studies scholarship on the nexus between sexuality and power in the PRC, I suggest that this negative and asymmetric staging of theory has left us unable to account for the kinds of changes that are occurring in China today.

Chapter 3 begins to re-situate accounts of the nexus between sexuality and power in the PRC by focusing on the example of prostitution as an internationally contested sex-related legal issue. Prostitution is now identified as a transnational issue requiring global solutions in relation to its regulation and legislation, but the question of what constitutes a properly feminist response remains a matter of dispute. Ongoing conflicts within Western feminist circles over the meanings of sex and sexuality for women, combined with the United Nations' acknowledgement of women's rights as human rights, have produced two divergent conceptions of prostitution as a legitimate target of governmental intervention. The chapter therefore explains how feminist prostitution debates have come to be characterized by the fierce opposition between those who insist that prostitution constitutes a violation of women's human rights and those who maintain that prohibitory and abolitionist laws constitute a violation of individual and civil rights. This examination of feminist prostitution debates is a first step towards indicating how the Chinese response to prostitution might be read as a theoretical point of departure for rethinking, rather than re-rehearsing, existing debates within the new humanities.

The subject of prostitution in the PRC offers a vehicle for interrogating the utility of travelling theories, chiefly because the emergence of prostitution as a renewed object of metropolitan concern has coincided with the emergence of prostitution as new object of discourse in China. This convergence affords Anglophone China scholars an opportunity to engage in topical mainstream debates, both by virtue of their ability to show how the subject of prostitution has been constructed as an object of discourse in the

PRC, and their ability to interrogate the explanatory capacity of metropolitan prostitution debates with regard to the study of China. Accordingly, Chapter 4 outlines the various domestic and international issues that have informed the renewed problematization of prostitution as an object of intellectual and governmental concern in present-day China. By highlighting the different genealogical underpinnings of Western and Chinese prostitution debates, it demonstrates that the PRC's response to prostitution has been presented – and hence translated – for consumption by an Anglophone readership in a manner that reifies the idealized space of 'Euramerica'.

Anglophone scholarship on issues of sexuality and prostitution in the PRC largely turns on the 'problem of the state', and hence problems of legitimacy, the notion of ideology, and the question of who possesses power and who does not. This approach has resulted in a generalized critique of the Chinese government for adhering to a supposedly ideological (read moralistic and out-dated) understanding of prostitution and thereby failing to recognize that prostitution is better understood as a legitimate form of work. Unfortunately, exponents of this approach claim all the kudos that accrues to those who speak with moral indignity against the Chinese government and on behalf of the 'downtrodden subaltern', without the accompanying ethical burden of investigating whether the strategy that they want adopted will work in different cultural contexts in a way that is unambiguously better than the strategy that they want replaced. Thus, despite its seeming 'political correctness', the statist bias of this approach renders it both empirically and politically limited.

In consequence, Chapters 5 and 6 outline an alternative reading of the PRC's response to prostitution with reference to the Foucauldian concept of governmentality (Foucault 1979: 5–19). Recourse to the concept of governmentality allows us to observe the manifold ways in which subjects such as sellers and buyers of sex have been transformed into objects of governmental concern and intervention, rather than encouraging us to see the exercise of power in China as necessarily top-down, static, and rigidly ideological. In doing so, it demonstrates that the PRC's response to prostitution can be translated in a manner that both acknowledges the difference of that response, yet also allows that difference to be actively admitted within a transnational dialogue. Certainly, the diverse forms of selling and buying sex that have been identified by governmental authorities in China would suggest that prostitution in China cannot be treated as a homogeneous category that, in order to be effectively addressed, needs to be redefined as work. Likewise, the fact that campaigns to curb the activities of 'hostesses' within commercial places of entertainment have wound up problematizing the conduct of corrupt government officials would suggest that the effects of implementing prostitution controls are far from predetermined.

As the conclusion to this text in Chapter 7 suggests, a critical appraisal of the Chinese case not only brings into sharp relief the unproductive nature of metropolitan debates concerning the optimal transnational response to prostitution, but also hints at the insights a reconfigured form of China studies could bring to these and other critical debates within the new humanities. An analysis of Chinese policing as a practice of governmentality demonstrates that the problems surrounding the PRC's response to prostitution are neither reducible to the nature of the 'Chinese Party police state', nor amenable to resolution via the imposition of some idealized, transnational, feminist response. Indeed, the very diversity of prostitution businesses and practices that exist in present-day China shows that it is not possible to characterize 'sex work' as a unified target of governmental intervention either in China or more generally. Recourse to the Foucauldian concept of governmentality thus underscores the analytical redundancy of mobilizing theory in an applied fashion to prove that our 'ideological identity papers are in order', and subsequently to intimate that our capacity to speak on behalf of the 'truly downtrodden' knows no political or cultural borders.

1 Changing China

Changing China studies

The impact of theory

Given the traditional isolation of China studies from mainstream debates, one of the most striking aspects of contemporary sinological studies[1] is the growing tendency for China scholars to interpret 'China' through the lens of Western critical theory. By 'theory', I am not talking about 'high theory' or theory with a capital 'T', such as the overarching philosophical-political metanarratives of Marxism, Liberalism, and Feminism. Instead, I am referring to what has become more generally known as poststructuralism and deconstruction. I realize that these terms are somewhat problematic since, as Michèle Barrett (1992: 201) explains, they unify 'a diverse and often contradictory group of ideas on the specious basis of what preceded them in a chronology of Parisian thought'. But the fact remains that they are both understood, and commonly circulated, as a kind of shorthand for ways of reading that have transformed the nature of intellectual endeavours over the past three or more decades. Suffice it to say, therefore, that I am not using these terms in an exact sense, but rather as a means to discuss the impact of theory on Anglophone China studies.

As Rey Chow (1998: xiii) notes, 'the one unmistakable accomplishment of "theory" understood in this restricted sense is what one might call the fundamental problematization of referentiality'. Here, Chow is referring to the general poststructuralist-deconstructive tendency to destabilize positivistic and universalizing conceptions of 'the real', irrespective of whether 'the real' is defined as 'language', 'the author', 'the individual', 'Woman', 'the Nation', 'the State', and so forth. The interrogative impetus of this style of critique has had an enormous impact on the academy in general. Most notably, it has eroded the seemingly natural barriers that once existed between the disciplines. It also continues to resonate throughout the new humanities via inquiries into the ways in which discourses on power, sexuality, race, and subjectivity, are both constituted and mutually constitutive of each other.

The effective reorganization of the humanities and human sciences into academic subdivisions that are either 'inside' or 'outside' of theory has inevitably questioned the nature of China studies, not least by suggesting that the field will end up occupying an even more isolated outpost on the institutional map, unless it starts to engage in the production of new theories and practices (Davies 1992: 67–86). As a result, although scholars who utilize poststructuralism–deconstruction for the analysis of China remain a minority within the field as a whole, texts that take China as their object of study, and deploy the insights made available by recourse to the discourse of theory, have begun to fill an identifiable niche in the publishing market. Texts that deal with issues of power, gender, sexuality, and race in China, for instance, are definitely on the increase. For China scholars who engage with theory, then, this is a moment of opportunity, a moment when the study of China has the perceived capacity to contribute to mainstream theoretical debates by highlighting their heretofore largely Euramerican contextual bias (see Apter and Saich 1994; Dikötter 1995; Evans 1997; Gilmartin *et al.* 1994; Hershatter *et al.* 1996; Zito and Barlow 1994).

But the relationship between theory and China studies is far from straightforward. The question of what theory can do for the study of China and, conversely, what the study of China can contribute to mainstream debates, is complicated by what Gloria Davies (1998: 179) describes as the 'ill-disciplined' nature of China studies as a field of 'knowing', and the 'symptomatic lack of an adequate grounding for much of what is practiced' in theoretically informed studies throughout the various knowledge fields. Here, Davies is referring to both the unwillingness of most China scholars to examine the intellectual limitations of knowledge production in the field of 'area-cum-language studies', and the effective 'taming of theory' via its institutional packaging as more generalized ways of reading, writing, and 'seeing'. As Davies (1998: 176) and other critical theorists have noted, in the absence of attention to historico-cultural specificity, the adoption of theory in different knowledge fields can amount to little more than the deployment of an 'easily learnt and fashionable skill' (Chow 1998: xviii; Parker and Gagnon 1995: 5).

The continued disjunction between the perceived utility of theory and the actual nature of its employment in different knowledge fields can be illustrated by focusing briefly on three texts produced within the Anglophone field of China studies: *Engendering China: Women, Culture and the State*, edited by Christina Gilmartin, Gail Hershatter, Lisa Rofel and Tyrene White (1994); *Remapping China: Fissures in Historical Terrain*, edited by Gail Hershatter, Emily Honig, Jonathan Lipman and Randall Stross (1996); and *Body, Subject and Power in China*, edited by Angela Zito and Tani Barlow (1994). These texts facilitate an examination of the relationship between China studies and theory and thus the newly reconfigured disciplinary space of the field for several reasons. To begin with, all are edited collections, rather than the product of a single authorial voice, and they aim to introduce a theorized version of China studies to a general readership. Accordingly, the introductory chapter of each text offers a broad outline of the perceived utility of theory for the study of China and, conversely, a brief account of how the study of China itself may function to reconfigure the concerns of the new humanities. In addition, all of these texts engage with the insights afforded by recourse to postcolonial and feminist positions, as well as Foucauldian conceptions of discourse, power and sexuality.

Having said this, it should be clear that the institutional marketability of analyses of gender, sexuality, and power in China both derives from and trades on the structuring concerns of the new humanities. Despite important differences, therefore, *Engendering China*, *Remapping China*, and *Body, Subject and Power in China*, are marked by a common set of concerns. All of these texts aim to explore the possibilities afforded by recourse to new frameworks of analysis, to problematize familiar reference points with regard to the study of China, and to show what the empirical study of China may reveal about the limitations of various forms of Western theorization. In this respect, they appear to have adopted the basic principle of poststructuralism–deconstruction, namely, to engage in the fundamental problematization of referentiality, and thereby question the certainty of the knowledge bases of both China studies and 'the disciplines', via the theoretical exploration of difference (Chow 1998: xiii).

As a result, all three texts adopt a deconstructive-constructive mode of criticism. According to the editors of *Remapping China*, the aim of the text is threefold: first, to interrogate notions of nation, state, and peoplehood, and hence to historicize gendered bodies; second, to remap the familiar geographical, regional, and ethnic boundaries that have been used to denote the entity known as China; and, third, to reconfigure the familiar signposts that have conventionally charted the course of the Chinese revolution (Hershatter *et al.* 1996: 1–9). Similarly, the editors of *Engendering China* contend that the aim of the text is to complicate unitary conceptions of Chinese women. As Gilmartin *et al.* (1994: 1–24) argue, this objective will be achieved by pursuing a three-pronged methodological strategy: first, by examining the multiple subject positions that Chinese women may occupy due to the differential effects of class, ethnicity, age, and regional background; second, by highlighting instances of women's agency; and, third, by addressing issues of representation, and thereby showing the centrality of gender to questions of state formation and policy-making.

Partaking of the same critical impetus, albeit in a somewhat different vein, the editors of *Body, Subject and Power in China* suggest that neo-Marxist, feminist and Foucauldian insights have made once dominant conceptions of China as a single, essential unity, inherently unstable (Zito and Barlow 1994: 1–19). In doing so, Zito and Barlow evidently reject the definition of China studies as an area of applied knowledge – a field where suitably cultivated experts are seen to access the 'truth' of China via their linguistic expertise and recognition of China's cultural uniqueness – for retaining a problematic epistemological relation between the 'real' and 'thought', or what Chow (1998: xiii) describes as 'a persistent reflectionism in representation'. Instead, they maintain that a judicious combination of Marxisms, feminisms, and Foucauldian insights redirects scholarly attention towards questions of agency, the importance of classificatory practices and strategies, and towards a focus on subject positions instead of 'individuals' or holistic conceptions of 'the Chinese' (Zito and Barlow 1994: 9–10).

Thus the incursion of theory with a small 't', or, as the editors of *Remapping China* put it, the use of 'analytical frameworks formulated first in the context of intellectual and political traditions of the United States and Western Europe', appears to be transforming the study of China (Hershatter *et al.* 1996: 5). Quite apart from opening new avenues for research, as my brief review of the proposed subject matter of the above-mentioned texts would suggest, the growing tendency for China scholars to utilize the insights made available by recourse to the discourse of theory marks an important shift away from the traditional position of isolation occupied by China studies in relation to mainstream debates. Not surprisingly, the perceived potential for a more interdisciplinary form of China studies is a subsidiary, but no less important, theme of each text.

For example, in *Body, Subject and Power in China*, Zito and Barlow (1994: 15) note that the utilization of theory for the analysis of China entails a double move. It not only allows them to rethink fundamental questions of power, subjectivity and corporeality in Chinese contexts, but also through the concomitant obligation to consider the specific historical genealogies that accrue to such concepts in the PRC, it enables them to challenge the universalizing, and ideologizing, function of much Western social science. Likewise, the editors of *Engendering China* contend that their attention to difference – a vital problematic in recent theorizations of gender via postcoloniality, minority discourse and psycho-analytic theory – enables them to explore the broader question of what 'China will become and represent, both to those who live in China and to those who look on from other places' (Gilmartin *et al.* 1994: 4). Having made this claim, Gilmartin *et al.* further contend that they have not simply adopted feminist insights and superimposed them onto the Chinese case. Instead, they insist that their attention to cultural specificity with regard to subjects such as 'sexuality, prostitution, work, political participation and bodies', should function to challenge the universalizing tendency of much feminist theorizing in the West (ibid.: 7). Finally, and in a more celebratory tone, the editors of *Remapping China* suggest that social and political changes in the PRC, combined with 'the impact of theory', have broken down the conventional lines of demarcation that formerly prevented one group of scholars from speaking to another. In consequence, China scholars are no longer preoccupied with speaking solely to each other; they have moved out of the ghetto and into the 'cross-disciplinary polyglot metropolis' (Hershatter *et al.* 1996: 3).

Given the general resistance to theory that still permeates the field, it is tempting to endorse these claims. However, before celebrating the belated coming-of-age of area-cum-language studies (as indicated by the ability of China scholars to engage with mainstream debates), we need to ask two questions. How has this perceived change come about? And what are the implications of this perceived change for an understanding of China studies as a truly interdisciplinary endeavour, rather than some fashionably reconfigured branch of Asian studies?

In raising these questions, I do not wish to align myself with China scholars who oppose the use of theory on the grounds that it is Eurocentric, and subsequently revert to the traditional defence of the field on the grounds that China is unique or culturally exceptional (Ryckmans 1984: 18–20). But we should question the automatic privileging of post-structuralism–deconstruction on the grounds that it is theoretically superior, especially when such claims may be premised on a simple insistence, rather than demonstration, that it is non-essentialist and hence more revealing of heterogeneity. Put differently, we need to question the all-too-easy valorization of theory, especially when claims to theoretical superiority may mask the elision of a related critical imperative, namely, the task of ensuring that the very terms and conditions under which a given project is undertaken are subjected to ongoing and stringent analysis. This task is necessitated by a recognition that failure to examine the informing assumptions of a given knowledge field tends to result in reformulated categories and concepts being treated as little more than 'tools' to be borrowed and used. One vocabulary is simply replaced by another and the original problematic venture – whether it is 'History' (characterized by a belief in the notion that it is possible to faithfully document lived reality) or 'Sinology' (characterized by a belief that language constitutes the key to 'true' knowledge of China) – continues unchallenged.

Problematizing China studies

It is precisely Zito and Barlow's acknowledgement of the dual imperative of theory that makes *Body, Subject and Power in China* such an exemplary text. Their understanding of the Janus-faced nature of 'doing theory' is signalled from the outset. They begin the text by highlighting the need to disrupt accepted regimes of scholarly 'truth', in particular, the kinds of commonsensical assumptions that function to occlude a recognition of difference. Stemming from this commitment, the text is structured around the difficult methodological task of acknowledging, on the one hand, how Western regimes of scholarly 'truth' are structured, while, on the other, never forgetting that the text aims to explain the common sense of others. Hence, in a move that is often dismissed by those who object to the incursion of theory (the impatient 'why can't they just get on with it and say what they have to say about China!'), Zito and Barlow (1994: 3) point out that it is impossible to explain how Chinese subjects understand and experience their lives without first examining our own common sense, that is, without excavating the kinds of assumptions that have historically organized the field of China studies.

To appropriate Zito and Barlow's words, therefore: 'What are some of the assumptions that have structured China studies in a post-World War II United States [namely, in the postcolonial setting]?' As they note, the influence of the Cold War upon the field of China studies cannot be overstated (ibid.: 3). This is because, following the end of the Second World War, the United States inherited what Chow (1998: 5) describes as 'Western Europe's former role as military-aggressor-and-cultural-imperialist-cum-saviour around the world'. The rapid growth of area studies in the USA during the 1950s, and, to a somewhat lesser extent, in Britain and Australia, was thus intimately related to the universities' perceived function as a support for foreign policy. In effect, the special task of the area specialist was to report on 'other civilizations', 'other regimes', and 'other ways of life'; and, in the case of the China expert, it was to report on the 'otherness' of 'Red China'. Consequently, 'the specific version for China studies of what has come to be called the self/other problem was communist world versus free world' (ibid.: 3).

Until the arrival of theory, the self/other problematic within the field of China studies was expressed in two main ways. During the 1950s and early 1960s, the Chinese polity was viewed primarily, albeit not always, through the grid of what is now known as the 'totalitarian model'. Simplistically speaking, this model focused on the ideology, structures, key personalities and activities of the so-called 'Party police state', and assumed that the Chinese Communist Party was able to exert a monolithic control over all aspects of Chinese society. The result was a highly persuasive portrayal of the PRC as an authoritarian state populated by an army of dehumanized 'blue ants' (Guillain 1957; Paloczi-Horvath 1962). To caricaturize this position, communist China was portrayed as utterly different from Western society, as something equivalent to our worst collective nightmare.

During the late 1960s and early 1970s, however, this rendition of 'Red China' as yet another bastion of communist-style totalitarianism began to be questioned. And, in striking contrast, the People's Republic was held up in various Western discourses as an exemplary society and a model for actual or existing socialism. In fact, it was often claimed that the Chinese revolution (unlike the Russian revolution) had to a large extent established the preconditions for a truly egalitarian society, incorporating the emancipation of Chinese women. In such accounts, the PRC was still portrayed as fundamentally different, but it was no longer depicted as the antithesis of all that was 'good' and 'healthy' about Western-style liberal democracy.

Instead, in the words of Zito and Barlow (1994: 3), 'China held out hope for a utopian egalitarian alternative to a corrupt bourgeois American society'. It was like our own best, if as yet unrealized, self.

While the initial tendency to denounce 'communist China' stemmed from the perceived threat posed by rapid changes taking place in formerly colonial and/or third-world countries, the tendency to idealize 'Mao's China' stemmed, in no small part, from political and social developments within the West itself. Put simply, growing opposition to North American imperialism in the form of the Vietnam War challenged the Cold War division of the world into those who were with the USA in the fight for freedom and democracy, and those who were with the former USSR in the fight to establish international socialism. Given that Sino-Soviet relations had effectively collapsed by the start of the 1960s, this encouraged more positive readings of Chinese society and politics. Social and intellectual changes ensuing from a conjunction of other historical forces also predisposed scholars to view the PRC as an alternative model. Among the most important of these were: the emergence of second-wave feminism; the sexual revolution; student demonstrations against established authority; struggles for gay rights; and the black power movement. A further important development was the 'crisis within the socialist camp', and the subsequent proliferation of neo-Marxism(s), flowing from Khruschev's denunciation of Stalin in 1956. This action not only ended the former Stalinist monopoly over extant interpretations of Marxism; it also resulted in an exposure of the many atrocities that had occurred in the Soviet Union, especially the horror of the Gulag.

Political and social changes in the USA and Western Europe – changes from which the organizing concerns of the new humanities can be traced – thus encouraged arguments to the effect that China was essentially a socialist democracy. A basic contention here was that the PRC did not operate on hierarchical and tyrannical lines as did the USSR; rather, it operated on the basis of participatory and egalitarian politics, as evidenced by the mass participation of the Chinese people in the implementation of policy (Blecher 1986; Selden 1971). Moreover, and in contrast to the situation of many women in the West, it was argued that Chinese women had been largely liberated from their economic and social dependence on men due to their active engagement in the labour force (Broyelle 1977; Milton 1973: 180).

Nowadays, it is standard practice for China scholars to criticize the type of binary oppositions that were fostered in a field defined by an '"area studies" sensibility, born of the Cold War and nourished by marginality to the Euramerican intellectual agenda of the universities' (Hershatter *et al.* 1996: 1). It is also routine practice for China scholars to point out that both the 'totalitarian school' and the 'pro-Maoist school' were trapped within the confines of the same discursive formation. For rather than seriously challenging the conceptual parameters of the field, those who launched the initial counter-offensive against established paradigms simply inverted the claims of former authorities, often by recourse to information disseminated by the CCP itself. In this way, totalitarian China became the land of participatory democracy, the Party that oppressed the masses became the Party that acted in the interests of the masses, and the country that had oppressed its women for centuries under the system of Confucian patriarchy became the country that had begun to liberate its women via the establishment of socialism, and so on.

It is also standard practice for China scholars today to aver that we are no longer constrained by the essentializing binary framework of 'East/West', 'us' and 'them'. According to the editors of *Remapping China*, 'the field of modern Chinese history has changed, sometimes imperceptibly, and sometimes dramatically, over the past two decades' (Hershatter *et al.* 1996: 1). As they argue, the former obsession of eminent China historians with naturalized conceptions of China's cultural uniqueness, and the question of how traditional China reacted to its 'encounter with the West', has been complicated by changes both in China and abroad (ibid.: 2). This shift commenced with the kinds of socio-political changes noted above, changes that encouraged scholars to view 'Mao's China' as an alternative developmental model. In more recent years, however, 'China's reorientation away from socialism' (read the introduction of market-based economic reforms), the popular movement of 1989, and the collapse of almost all socialist regimes, have dampened the enthusiasm with which China scholars sought to 'fashion utopias distant in time and place' (ibid.: 2). Consequently, we are allegedly no longer trapped within a framework that led us to alternate between excessively denigrating and overly idealizing 'them'.

As far as the editors of *Remapping China* are concerned, therefore, political changes combined with the altered nature of first-world academic labour have transformed the field of China studies. As they argue, increased access to the PRC and regular interchange with mainland Chinese scholars (flowing from the introduction of the Open Door policy) have broadened the scope of the field. In addition, the proliferation of new areas of inquiry in the discipline of history as a whole – following from the inclusion of the formerly excluded (usually by virtue of race, class, gender, sexuality, etc.) – has destroyed the customary boundaries that left China specialists talking only to other China specialists. Hence China studies (at least in its historical manifestations) is now well and truly a part of the metropolitan university precinct (Hershatter *et al.* 1996: 1–3).

The editors of *Engendering China* are similarly keen to situate feminist sinological studies within the disciplinary space of the new humanities and an increasingly globalized academy. The production of knowledge about China, they aver, now takes place in a multivocal environment, 'one that involves a proliferation of research agendas, an expansion of conversations, and an enhanced attention to the diversity of Chinese women's experiences' (Gilmartin *et al.* 1994: 8). During the 1970s, the growing momentum of second-wave feminism in the USA and Western Europe first challenged the masculinist and state-orientated focus of research agendas in the areas of Chinese history and politics. Feminist concerns to explicate the condition of 'Woman', combined with the expressed commitment of socialist revolutions to the liberation of women, led to a proliferation of research on 'Chinese women' (Broyelle 1977; Croll 1978; Davin 1976; Kristeva 1977; Stacey 1975, 1976; Wolf and Witke 1975; Young 1973, 1976). By the early 1980s, however, disillusionment with CCP policies towards women, and what Jinghua Teng (1996: 127) describes as a general decline in 'the fashion for leftism', 'meant that fewer nonsinologists chose to write about women in China'. As a result, 'China' once again became marginal to mainstream feminist concerns, even though the study of Chinese women continued to develop as an important subdivision of China studies.

In fact, according to the editors of *Engendering China*, the relationship between feminism and sinology is currently more sophisticated than ever due to three considerations. First, developments within feminism itself, most notably the shift away from a focus on 'Woman' (understood as a unitary category of analysis) towards a focus on the differences that exist between and among women, have resulted in a new emphasis on diversity and agency. Second, the CCP's move 'away from socialism', combined with the 'death of Marxism', has meant that old stories about communist China have faded, and sinologists are now faced with the challenge of 'identifying, interpreting, and reshaping the multiple narratives that circulate about China' (Gilmartin *et al.* 1994: 9). Third, new conditions of research in the PRC, combined with the emergence of gender as an arena of contestation in China itself, have enabled feminist sinologists to challenge the traditional 'dichotomy between Europeans and Americans as theory makers and Chinese women as objects of theory'. At this moment in time, therefore, feminist sinologists are ideally situated to offer a more vital cross-cultural perspective to women's/gender studies 'at home' (ibid.: 6–7).

Although the above-mentioned claims highlight a strong desire to forge a new disciplinary identity for China studies, they are problematic insofar as they imply that the phenomenon of orientalism has somehow disappeared (at least, for those of 'us' who possess the critical awareness and critical tools to deal with it). In this respect, the claim that China studies has moved out of the ghetto and into the institutional mainstream may rest on little more than the transparent ability of a growing number of China scholars to command the 'newspeak' of theory, and thereby present themselves as alternative translators. To elaborate upon this contention, however, it is necessary to consider the background against which these celebratory claims have been both formulated and accepted. Specifically, we need to examine the long-standing conflict as to whether sinological or disciplinary methods constitute the best means for revealing the 'truth' of China, and the ways in which this debate has been played out in an era when poststructuralist-deconstructive reading practices have colonized many realms of discourse in the new humanities and human sciences.

The uses and potential misuses of theory

Since the early 1960s, practitioners of China studies have been criticized by their disciplinary counterparts for producing work that may be caricaturized as untheoretical and overly empiricist ('Symposium on Chinese Studies and the Disciplines' 1964: 505–38). Accusations of this kind originally stemmed from the area-based focus of China studies – hence the related tendency for China scholars to privilege 'language' and 'culture' – which was viewed as particularistic and inferior to the more disciplinary-minded concerns of the Western social sciences. More recently, and undoubtedly due to the erosion of former disciplinary boundaries, this kind of criticism has been increasingly levelled at the field of China studies by China scholars themselves (and I include myself in this category).

In-house criticisms of the current 'state of the field' stem from the evident need to challenge the general resistance to theory that permeates the field. I say 'need' in the sense that this resistance flows from the traditional Sinological belief that China studies should be exempt from engaging with the latest paradigms and critical positions that inform the larger discourse of the Humanities 'by virtue of the "otherness" of its object of study' (Davies 1992: 78). This traditional defence of the field is anachronistic given the rise of postcolonial and cultural studies. These two fields are defined by their characteristic concern with the affirmation of otherness and the negation of Western meta-discourses. Moreover, both fields would be inconceivable without 'the radical reformulations of language and discourse, of the relation between high and low culture, and of the relation between representation and politics, which were enabled by poststructuralist theory' (Chow 1998: 4). In-house calls to 'theorize' the field thus constitute a necessary recognition that adhering to old ways of 'doing China studies' may well render the field obsolete (other than as a provider of language-teaching programmes), especially in a political climate where the market increasingly determines what forms of teaching and research activities receive funding and support.

Despite the transparent institutional success of poststructuralist-deconstructive reading practices, however, it remains the case that any China scholar who engages with theory runs the risk of being criticized by other China scholars for producing work that may be crudely caricaturized as elitist, obfuscatory, and not really about China at all (i.e., lacking an adequate empirical basis).[2] Such arguments are largely rhetorical and lack substance for a simple reason. They tend to constitute a blanket dismissal of theory in that they fail to engage with the issues raised by the deployment of theory itself. Certainly, arguments concerning the 'empirical weakness' of theoretically informed sinological studies routinely elide the fact that different textual practices produce the need for different 'empirical' approaches, ones whose 'truth claims' cannot be dismissed as invalid simply because they are not constructed in terms of the conventional discursive protocols that inform the field of China studies.

Given the continued disjuncture between China studies and the organizing concerns of the new humanities, the arguments put forward by the editors of *Engendering China*, *Remapping China*, and *Body, Subject and Power in China*, are pertinent because they appear to be advocating a different way of 'doing China studies', one that promises to overcome the kinds of divisions that have conventionally separated practitioners of theory from practitioners of China studies in various hierarchical ways. The suggestion that we now have access to a form of theory that enables us to highlight cultural specificity, for instance, basically constitutes a claim to have met two formerly contradictory requirements, namely, to be both a 'China expert' *and* to possess disciplinary expertise. In other words, it constitutes a claim to possess valued intellectual capital, to have acquired or cultivated a set of habits that should ensure recognition and acknowledgement by academics on both sides of the language/disciplinary divide.

The arguments put forward by the respective editors of *Remapping China*, *Engendering China*, and *Body, Subject and Power in China*, are doubly pertinent because they appear to be advocating the intellectual mainstreaming of China studies, as opposed to the addition of more Asian content to the university curricula. This latter conception of mainstreaming amounts to a demand that the disciplines recognize their Eurocentricism and introduce more Chinese literature, Chinese history, and Chinese politics, etc., into the curriculum. In this respect, it is a demand for more of the same, only with the addition of more 'China'. Not surprisingly, proponents of this delimited conception of mainstreaming tend to explain the institutional marginality of China studies in terms of the lack of receptivity displayed by the dominant disciplines towards Asian-centred applied knowledges. Although there is some truth to this claim, their criticism of disciplinary and theoretical hegemony is simply that the disciplines have occupied a position of superiority for long enough, and that it is time for Asianists to enjoy the same institutional privileges (Chan, A. 1994: 21; Schwartz 1964: 537–8).

Intellectual mainstreaming, however, is not about reproducing the forms of privilege and intellectual capital that have traditionally accrued to the disciplines via their relocation to the field of Asian studies. Rather, it entails problematizing the certainty of the knowledge bases of both the disciplines and China studies via the theoretical exploration of difference. In this regard, as the editors of *Engendering China*, *Remapping China*, and *Body, Subject and Power in China* variously suggest, the judicious use of poststructuralism–deconstruction, Foucauldian insights, and postcolonial-feminist positions, may well result in a more interdisciplinary form of China studies. This is because all of these terms ultimately refer to a reflexive critical practice, one that aims to interrogate the legitimating structures inherent in the production of knowledge itself.

Nonetheless, if the above-mentioned texts gesture usefully towards a new disciplinary identity for China studies, there is a certain impatience about the ways in which the editors of *Remapping China* and *Engendering China*, in particular, demarcate the new disciplinary space of the field. I, for one, question their assumption that since Marxist socialism has collapsed in the USSR, and the PRC has seemingly moved away from socialism, old frameworks of analysis have either faded or vanished, and the space is literally 'there' to create new ones (at least, for those of us who have the necessary political awareness and theoretical 'know-how' to do so). Certainly, the work of many feminist and postcolonial scholars would point towards the opposite conclusion.

As many feminist scholars have noted, the 1990s' emphasis on identity politics and sexual preference has often resulted in a paradoxical endorsement of the phallocentric logos of Western liberal humanism (Valenze 1996: 189). This is because struggles for equality on the basis of identity and sexual rights are more or less obliged to leave liberal conceptions of 'the self' intact, a move that sits rather uneasily with the expressed aim of certain strands of feminist theory, and lesbian and gay activism, namely, to undermine hetero-patriarchal discourses. In a not dissimilar fashion, postcolonial scholars have consistently noted that Western scholarship in the 1990s has proved unable to capture the 'uniqueness of race, its historical flexibility and immediacy in everyday experience and social conflict' (John 1996: 98). This latter recognition informs Dipesh Chakrabarty's clarion call for postcolonial scholars to provincialize the hyperreal space of 'Europe', a project that entails a radical critique (not a facile rejection) of liberalism and its associated teleological narratives of citizenship and modernity, as well as an acknowledgement that we are all 'doing European history' even though we may be utilizing non-Western archives (Chakrabarty 1992: 1–26).

Chakrabarty's contention that we are all 'doing Europe', even as we claim and are seen to be writing about other places, suggests that arguments concerning the transformed nature of contemporary China studies may be premised on a sleight of hand. After all, the call to provincialize Europe, and thereby acknowledge the deep-seated Eurocentricism of knowledge produced at the institutional site of the university, offers no comfort to those who wish to reify the native subaltern subject or promote a project of cultural relativism. For while advocating the programmatic adoption of a project that aims to displace 'Europe' from the centre of other histories, Chakrabarty simultaneously notes the impossibility of this very project. As he explains, it is not possible to provincialize Europe within the disciplinary space of the university because the 'globality of academia is not independent of the globality that the European modern has created' (ibid.: 23). Hence, rather than endorsing the popular ethico-political project of retrieving authentic or resistant voices – a project that turns on the teleological suspension of the theoretical by intimating that the subaltern ultimately *can* speak – Chakrabarty argues for a political practice that is always deconstructive and employs a strategy similar to Spivak when she writes of the impossible 'no', namely, a strategy 'wherein one critiques the very structures one inhabits intimately' (Dutton 2000a: 27).

Chakrabarty's critique of nativist strands of postcolonial scholarship undermines the celebratory contention that China studies (at least in its theory-minded manifestations) has been transformed by questioning the expressed goal of the alternative translator, to reveal an 'inside-resistant' perspective that is 'outside' of Europe. As Dutton (ibid.: 27–30) suggests, however, Chakrabarty's call to provincialize Europe could paradoxically offer succour to the alternative translator because it re-emphasizes the desire for an 'outside' viewpoint even as it insists on the impossibility of realizing that desire. By this Dutton means that calls to provincialize Europe could function to affirm existing ways of 'doing China studies' by appearing to offer another strategy towards, rather than away from, the long-standing goal of achieving a 'true' translation or, more recently, the positivist goal of achieving a truly 'China-centred' translation. Dutton therefore suggests that the project of provincializing Europe might be better understood as the process of provisionalizing Europe, not simply by highlighting the Eurocentric bias of Western forms of theorization, but also by reading our own translations, or the knowledge we choose to produce about China, against the grain.

Chakrabarty's and Dutton's calls to provincialize and provisionalize Europe undermine the contention that the field of China studies has undergone a radical transformation by redirecting scholarly attention towards the translation problematic. For while claims to possess intellectual capital on the basis of a dual privilege – by virtue of having access to the latest theoretical insights and the cultural entity known as China – are undoubtedly an effective means of promoting the continued viability of China studies as a research-based programme in the current academic marketplace, these claims clearly trade on, and therefore reinforce, the traditional claim of the Sinologist to be a nation-translator (that is, an objective and authoritative spokesperson for things 'Chinese'). In this respect, despite the evident desire of theory-minded China scholars to distance themselves from the now denigrated positivism of Sinology, they may be unwittingly reproducing extant conditions that apply to the production of knowledge about China.

For instance, contrary to the implication of much China studies scholarship, the Western academic field of China studies has been shaped by a history that long predates the Cold War. Foreign policy imperatives tied to broader academic requirements indubitably exerted an enormous influence on the field of knowledge production/reception that we now call China studies. But the area studies 'sensibility' of the field is not the child of Cold War politics alone. The field's characteristic preoccupation with the gathering and documentation of empirical data (a preoccupation fuelled by the Sinological belief that language constitutes the key to 'true' knowledge) is the product of a much older parentage, namely, the wedding of philology and Oriental studies.

As Dutton (2000a: 6–16) explains, philology or the 'scientific' study of the historical and comparative basis of language(s) commenced in the form of a romantic quest to find the language of God, an assumed original, universal language which existed prior to the 'confusion of tongues' imposed on humankind at Babel and therefore constituted a perceived means of recovering original knowledge and the wholeness of humankind. This theologically informed quest led scholars to investigate various arcane languages, resulting in a focus on the ancient and mysterious texts of the East in the belief that they held the key to plotting history's unfolding path, and hence to understanding the (Western) present. The European 'discovery' of Sanskrit in 1785, a language that was demonstrably older than Hebrew and thereby intimated that the textual past could not be confined solely to the biblical tradition, not only served to intensify this focus on the Orient – especially on India and China – it effectively buried the classical philologist's universalistic dream of discovering a general grammar in a quagmire of detail, thus encouraging the more empirically focused direction of comparative philology, and, in turn, Oriental studies (see also Dutton 2002: 495–538).

Although the 'discovery' of Sanskrit, or, more precisely, the articulation of its link with European languages, had the effect of pushing history back in time and geographically towards the East, it did not destroy the element of romance in classical philology. Instead, it sparked a new romantic curiosity in 'the East', one that was both disguised and legitimated by way of reference to 'science' (Dutton 2000a: 17–18). Under the influence of classical philology, for instance, early translators were not overly concerned whether their translations transmitted the linguistic and semantic meanings of the original text or not. The object of translation was basically to enrich the language of the translator. With the rise of comparative philology, however, this approach changed. Translation studies embraced the new concern to explicate different language structures and grammars in terms of the language of science, yet simultaneously reinscribed the romanticism of classical philology, by demanding of itself the impossible, namely, the word-for-word replication of the original text or a 'perfect translation'. In this way, perfecting the science of translation, rather than discovering the language of God, became the key to 'revelation', even as scholars began to provide detailed empirical knowledges of Oriental languages and Oriental peoples to suit the requirements of imperialist rule. It was precisely this potent mix of 'romanticism' and 'science', fuelled by the utilitarian imperatives of imperialism, which led to the emergence of Oriental studies, and ultimately was to find new expression with the development of Asian-based area studies.

Put simply, the fields of philology, Oriental studies, and Sinology, share certain genealogical affinities at the level of method, even though they have radically different organizational bases and objects of concern. All of these fields are concerned with the question of how best to translate, the problem of how to render the original in a different linguistic form without destroying the singularity of the original. To realize this goal, all of these fields have placed a core emphasis on language training and the acquisition of particular translation skills, epitomized by the practice of rote learning, or the subjectifying act of immersing oneself in 'other' languages, texts, and contexts, so as to internalize the perceived means for acquiring a genuine understanding of another social and cultural formation. Thus both the underlying aim of achieving a 'true translation' and the methodology used to realize that goal are virtually identical (Dutton 2000a: 3).

As Dutton (ibid.: 18–22) suggests, however, the initial focus of comparative philologists on textual translation, or the word-for-word duplication of the original, gradually became fused with the notion of social translation, namely, the translation of different places and different peoples. This slippage from textual to social translation flowed from a combination of historical factors, including: a recognition of the impossibility of the philologist's quest; the development of linguistics; the eighteenth- and nineteenth-century rise of positivist science; and the 'informational' requirements of imperialist rule. Hence despite the late eighteenth-century and early nineteenth-century shift towards 'specialization' and 'scientism', practitioners of Oriental studies were not viewed solely as linguists or translators. Rather, their hard-earned acquisition of a specific set of language/translation skills was accorded both the privilege of a 'science' *and* the privilege that had formerly accrued to the philologist's theologically informed quest for 'the Word'. Practitioners of Oriental studies thus came to be viewed, and, indeed, to view themselves, as erudite scholars who could provide unproblematic empirical details on the nature of 'other peoples, other cultures and other nations', because they embodied the combined skills of a philologist, a linguist, an anthropologist and a translator. In effect, they were nascent multidisciplinary social scientists.

The Oriental scholar's claim to be a multidisciplinary translator of 'other worlds', a claim underpinned by the philological-theological rendition of language as the key to all knowledge, clearly informs the traditional Sinological defence of China studies from disciplinary attack. Writing in 1984, for example, Pierre Ryckmans dismisses Edward Said's critique of Western representations of non-Western cultures as irrelevant to the field of China studies. Ryckmans rejects Said's attack on the methodology of area studies – particularly the implication that Sinologists lack the means to grasp the difference of China because the field is geographically rather than intellectually defined – by arguing that the field is *linguistically* defined.

According to Ryckmans (1984: 20), China studies is 'one global multidisciplinary humanistic undertaking, solely based upon a specific language pre-requisite'. Elaborating upon the privilege that accrues to this solitary requirement, Ryckmans notes that 'mastering the Chinese literary language' requires such a difficult and demanding training that it can 'seldom be combined with the acquisition and cultivation of another discipline'. But, he concludes, this situation is actually advantageous because 'Chinese civilization has an essentially *holistic* character which condemns all narrowly specialized approaches to grope in the dark and miss their target', as demonstrated by 'the spectacular blunders of *nearly all* the Contemporary China Specialists' in the 1970s (read the pro-Maoist school). Unlike China scholars who engage with disciplinary concerns, therefore, Ryckmans (ibid.: 18–20) intimates that 'good Sinologists' cannot be seduced by theoretical abstractions, nor can they be accused of Eurocentricism, because the study of China offers the most 'powerful antidote' to the temptations of Western ethnocentrism and disciplinary excess.

As this classic defence of the field illustrates, the China scholar's traditional claim to intellectual capital rests on more than the ability to translate, as in reproduce, texts. Instead, the method of language acquisition itself is seen to enable a 'good Sinologist' (i.e., one who has not been seduced by Western disciplinary concerns) to 'know' China in a most direct and virtually incorruptible fashion. In this respect, language study has clearly operated as more than a rite of passage within China studies. The methods learnt to master the 'Chinese literary language' have also fed back into the general scholarly programme of the field by producing an unconscious justification for a 'realist' approach to knowledge (Dutton 2000a: 4).

In consequence, while Ryckmans' response to Said's *Orientalism* exemplifies the conservative knee-jerk reaction to theory that permeates much of the field, his refusal to engage with the translation problematic is far from exceptional, even among China scholars who affiliate themselves with disciplinary rather than Sinological concerns. Certainly it bears noting that the first detailed response to Said offered within China studies, namely, Paul Cohen's (1984) *Discovering History in China: American Historical Writing on the Recent Chinese Past* basically uses the concept of Orientalism to promote an unreconstructed form of empiricism, one that enjoins China scholars to work harder at translating the 'reality' of China (Dutton 2000a: 5). Likewise, one of the few responses to postcolonial scholarship generated within the 'acceptable' theoretical outskirts of the field, 'The subaltern talks back: reflections on subaltern theory and

Chinese history' by Gail Hershatter (1993), effectively dismisses Spivak's contention that 'the subaltern cannot speak' to argue in favour of a rearticulated commitment to the very translation project that Spivak irrevocably problematizes, i.e., the ethico-political project of retrieving authentic, and resistant, native voices. Despite varied attempts to distance China studies from the linguistically based positivism of Sinology, therefore, it seems the field's claim to be a 'scientific' or applied form of interdisciplinary knowledge continues to be informed by the romanticism of philology, or the colonizing and universalizing presumption that everything is translatable.

Given the unconscious complicity of even disciplinary-minded China scholars in retaining the goal of truly translating China, Dutton's warning that Chakrabarty's call to provincialize Europe could be appropriated to affirm extant ways of doing China studies is timely. After all, the suggestion that China studies is now an integral component of the metropolitan university precinct – because China scholars have better access to theory, better access to China (hence language), and can engage in more scholarly exchange with China scholars – may ring true, but it also elides a crucial issue. This celebration of new conditions of access does not address the continued problem of representation, or, more precisely, the politics of translation. It simply displaces such issues by suggesting that 'we' are no longer guilty of representing 'them' (because we are aware of the asymmetrical power relations that are entailed in such a move), and because 'they' are now able to represent themselves (i.e., they can now utilize categories that do not belong exclusively to the official language (read Marxism) of 'the Chinese State'). In short, the impact of theory may be opening up new avenues of research in China studies, but theory is frequently applied to offer yet another way of 'doing China' that fails to interrogate the enunciative modalities of the nation-translator.

Contemporary sinological studies revisited

Proponents of a reconfigured form of China studies are fond of claiming that due to the end of the Cold War, the altered nature of the academic marketplace, and the changed nature of the PRC, the institutional and conceptual parameters of the field have irrevocably changed. While such scholars usually credit an earlier stream of scholarship with exposing the ideological blinkers of the 'totalitarian school', the implication here is that we are no longer operating within the confines of an oppositional discourse. For if the 1970s' tendency to idealize 'Mao's China' stemmed from a desire to challenge the imperialistic interests of the US government, it also stemmed from the fact that China scholars had limited physical access to the PRC until the early 1980s. As a result, scholarly and other impressions of the PRC were largely gleaned from materials (read propaganda) released by the CCP, or from eye-witness accounts by the few visitors who were allowed to live in or enter the PRC, in order to see and hear what was permitted by the CCP. Thus scholars who mounted the first internal challenge to the organizational bases of the field were basically agreeing, as opposed to disagreeing, with what the CCP had to say about 'Mao's China'.

Delineating the disciplinary space of the field in this fashion has proved to be a popular strategy because it appeals to common sense. On the one hand, it avers that due to the implementation of the economic reforms and the Open Door policy, China scholars now have genuine access to the PRC, Chinese language sources, in-country language training, and the Chinese people themselves. On the other hand, it intimates that the altered nature of first-world academic labour has enabled China scholars to transcend the kinds of problems that have dogged the field since its inception. In short, it suggests that China studies scholarship is now premised on rational and empirical as opposed to ideological or idealistic grounds.

Despite its evident popularity, the practice of delineating and thereby legitimizing the current state of the field in this fashion entails a certain sleight of hand. Most notably, it does not challenge the Sinologist's traditional claim to privilege as a nation-translator, nor does it adequately question the kinds of assumptions that have historically organized the field. It simply avers that contemporary China scholars are doing an even better job of what China scholars have always done best, namely, revealing the 'reality' of China. This legitimizing tactic is significant in its failure to consider how the institutional praxis of China studies might militate against the critical imperative of 'doing theory' itself.

It should be clear, for instance, that Western accounts of the PRC as an alternative social formation did not fall into serious disrepute solely due to the incursion of theory, and hence the advent of a more critical and self-reflexive moment within Anglophone China studies. Instead, such accounts were primarily called into question as a result of the CCP's 1981 negation of the Cultural Revolution (*Resolution on CPC History (1949–81)*). The main impetus of this negation was to salvage the Party and justify the implementation of economic reform by repudiating a particular set of 'erroneous' theories and policies that were attributed to the late stages of Maoism (i.e., the 'disasters' of the Great Leap Forward and the Cultural Revolution). This negation has proved to be so effective that attempts to positively assess the continued relevance of Maoist techniques and practices for an understanding of China today are virtually non-existent within both the Anglophone and Sinophone fields of China studies.

Attempts to positively assess the continued relevance of Maoist techniques and practices for an understanding of China today are few and far between for an obvious reason: it is widely accepted that the introduction of a market-based economy in China signals, or at least, *should* signal, a complete break from revolutionary Maoism. Somewhat ironically, this is precisely the political line put forward by the CCP, although unlike most practitioners of Anglophone China studies, the CCP denies that this shift constitutes a move away from socialism. That said, I am not interested in debating here whether the economic reform period constitutes a radical break from 'Maoism' and a move away from socialism or not. Rather, I am concerned to show what effects the presumption of a 'break' has had on recent literature produced within the Anglophone field of China studies. Put simply, if disciplinary-minded and left-wing scholars in the 1970s were inclined to endorse the CCP's idealistic vision of the PRC in order to challenge the hegemony of the totalitarian school and Cold War frameworks of analysis, the overwhelming majority of China scholars today tend to accept the political line put forward by the CCP in order to turn it back on the CCP, that is, to show how and where the CCP and Chinese Marxism have failed.

During the late 1980s and early 1990s, for instance, scholarly proponents of Maoism in the West either recanted or disappeared into the oblivion occasioned by lack of academic interest in, or total disregard for, their formerly popular if still highly marginalized research topic. Instead, following the parameters established by the CCP's negation of the Cultural Revolution, politically conservative China scholars such as Pierre Ryckmans (alias Simon Leys) basically cried: 'See! We were right all along. The PRC *is* a totalitarian state!' (see, for example, Leys 1977, 1981, 1989). Concurrently, left-wing and disciplinary-minded scholars who had once supported the goals of the Chinese revolution, such as Mark Selden (1971, 1995), affirmed that 'Mao's China' was a far more repressive and underdeveloped society than they had originally believed, and that the introduction of the economic reforms and the Open Door policy under Deng Xiaoping was exactly what China needed.

Viewed in conjunction with international condemnation of the PRC, following the brutal suppression of the student-led protest movement in Tiananmen Square in June 1989, the tendency of left- and right-wing China scholars alike to regard 'Chinese politics' in a hostile fashion has enabled Cold War-style readings of China to regain something akin to their former popularity. While such readings are now configured predominantly in the language of human rights, rather than in terms of a political opposition to Marxism or Communism per se, the founding premise of such readings – that the Chinese people want political and social reform, but the CCP does not – has a decidedly familiar ring. As with earlier 'totalitarian' readings of the nature of government in the PRC, they function to preclude the possibility that there might be anything positive or productive about the operation of power in China.

In short, intellectual and socio-political changes may not have radicalized the field of China studies at all. As Zito and Barlow (1994: 3) point out, the diplomatic offensive of the Cold War may have ended, thus removing the overarching binary of communism versus the free world, but the self/other problem for China studies has not entirely disappeared: the 'ideological underpinnings of the Cold War years' have yet to be dismantled. Adding to this contention, it strikes me that the altered nature of first-world academic labour, combined with the so-called 'death of Marxism', may have rendered the task of dismantling Cold War paradigms and questioning the traditional, linguistically based privilege of the Sinologist, even more difficult, and necessary, than before. This is because the effective result of such changes has not only been to foster an active intellectual hostility towards Chinese governmental practices, it has also encouraged and enabled China scholars of all political persuasions to occupy a position of safe, respectable liberalism.

Certainly, practitioners of China studies who choose to resist the incursion of theory on the conventional grounds that it is universalizing and Westerncentric can continue to valorize China's cultural uniqueness, safe in the knowledge that, nowadays, everyone is (or, at least, should be) into recognizing cultural diversity. In this way, the Sinologist's traditional claim to intellectual capital, namely, to have a specialized knowledge of a non-Western culture, by virtue of their linguistic expertise and recognition of China's 'uniqueness', may actually gain in credibility due to the popular veneration of localization as the basis for a liberal pluralism that recognizes all cultures in their multiplicities and diversity.

Conversely, those who celebrate the incursion of theory into the field of China studies often promote a different and more covert form of liberalism. I mentioned earlier, for instance, that many of these scholars lay claim to a position of double superiority by virtue of their privileged access to theory *and* the cultural entity known as China. This claim to dual privilege has not been adequately challenged even though many of these scholars merely apply the insights made available by recourse to the discourse of theory, rather than using them as a means to examine the intellectual  limitations of knowledge production in the field. The result has been a recent spate of publications that claim the status which accrues to the use of theory, while simultaneously endorsing the problematic 'other' of poststructuralism–deconstruction (i.e., the philosophical-political tradition of liberal humanism), in order to expose and condemn the difference (still understood as fundamental 'otherness') of the CCP-led regime (see Apter and Saich 1994; Dikötter 1995; Evans 1997; Hershatter 1997. For critical reviews of these texts see Dutton 1996: 172–6; Jeffreys, E. 1998: 215–18; Jeffreys and Ross 1998: 207–10).

This is a sweeping statement that will not go unchallenged, but it is meant to highlight the peculiar way in which Western accounts of gender, sexuality, and power in the PRC tend to become variations on the already known 'history of Europe'. As noted at the outset of this chapter, the institutional marketability of analyses of gender, sexuality, and power in China both derives from, and trades on, the structuring concerns of the new humanities. In consequence, those who participate in the production of this new textual industry 'can be assured that what they say does generate "new" truths about China', ones that do have very real effects on the way

China and more particularly the Chinese government are perceived on a global scale (Davies 1992: 83). But the fact that these commentators resort, for rhetorical effect, to the modality of the universal (that is, their implicit rejection of Chinese governmental practices leads them to implicitly valorize Western liberal conceptions of democracy, citizenship, modernity, and sexual rights) renders them incapable of providing a self-reflexive critique of the relationship between sexuality and power in China today. Such commentators can only offer 'new truths' against the 'falsehoods' of the Chinese Communist Party without considering how their critique of power might be constrained by their own doctrinal commitments, as the following chapters demonstrate.

2 Changing institutional categories and academic legitimacy

The ins and outs of the poststructuralist academe

One way of provisionalizing the knowledge we now choose to produce and circulate about China is to demonstrate that the emergence of popular objects of intellectual inquiry such as sexuality and gender is intrinsically related to the development of the new humanities. Writing in 1987, Arnold Davidson begins an article entitled 'Sex and the emergence of sexuality' with the following words:

> Some years ago a collection of historical and philosophical essays on sex was advertised under the slogan: Philosophers are interested in sex again. Since that time the history of sexuality has become an almost exceptional topic, occasioning as many books and articles as anyone would ever care to read.
>
> (Davidson 1987: 16)

In '"Gender" for a Marxist dictionary: the sexual politics of a word', Donna Haraway (1991: 136) similarly notes that the term 'gender' only truly entered the academic lexicon in the 1970s. By monitoring the occurrence of keyword entries under gender in US social science research over a 20-year period, Haraway discovered that the number of entries in sociological work increased from none at all between 1966 and 1970 to 724 between 1981 and 1985. And the number of entries in psychological work for the same periods increased from 50 to 1,326.

The current pervasiveness of the term 'gender' attests to the powerful influence of the second-wave feminist movement and the subsequent rise of academic feminism. Likewise, the importance now attached to the study of sexuality can be traced to early feminist concerns with issues of sexual difference (Firestone 1970; Rich 1980: 631–60; Wittig 1981: 47–54), even though contemporary studies on sexuality would be inconceivable in their present shape and form without Michel Foucault's (1978) seminal work on the nexus between sexuality and power. Certainly Foucault's innovative contention that sex is a product of regimes of sexuality, and hence not a ground of the 'real' or a biological base onto which a superstructure of gender and sexuality can be securely added, has brought classic feminist analyses of sex and sexuality into question. At the same time, it has opened the space for feminist theorizations of the body, or attempts to account for the fact that sex and sexuality are marked and lived according to whether it is a male or female body that is being discussed, without reinstating the now problematic early feminist sex/gender distinction (Butler 1990, 1993; Grosz 1994, 1995). Feminism and Foucault thus 'constitute the principal theoretical discourses that have stimulated and shaped the new studies on sexuality, even by the tensions between them' (Stanton 1992: 21; see also Diamond and Quinby 1988; Ramazanoglu 1993).

Yet if critical theorists are now speaking the language of gender and sexuality, it bears noting that they are no longer speaking the language of Marxism. Few scholars today seem prepared to echo Sartre's contention that 'Marxism is the one philosophy of our time which we cannot go beyond' (cited in John 1996: 97).[1] Instead, the collapse of Marxist–socialism in Eastern Europe and the former USSR, combined with the introduction of market-based economic reforms in the PRC, has given many a gleeful commentator the opportunity to proclaim the 'death of communism' and the 'triumph of capitalism'. Concurrently, although the language of Marxism still resonates within Western academic discourse, it has clearly lost much of its former authority. Once dominant debates on the structuring effects of capitalism and the possibilities of socialism are now on the sidelines. The different feminisms and cultural-critical theories of the 1980s and 1990s have undermined most Marxist categories of analysis, and shifted scholarly attention away from a concern with 'high politics', and even away from issues of class and labour, towards a new interest in the subjects of gender, sexuality, and power, and, more recently, to questions of race, the politics of identity, and the politics of difference (Levine 1996: 208–13; Valenze 1996: 181–92).

The embattled status of Marxism and the concomitant rise of 'theory' have had quite pronounced effects on contemporary China studies scholarship, not least on the field's prominent subdivision of women's studies. As discussed in Chapter 1, the recent spate of publications on subjects such as gender, sexuality, and power in China owes much to the growing popularity and institutional prestige of theory, particularly in North America. Participants in this new textual industry thus lay claim to professional capital on three consecutive grounds: first, by displaying a familiarity with the insights made available by recourse to the discourse of theory and subsequently deploying them for the analysis of China; second, by suggesting that recent intellectual and political changes have transformed the traditional parameters of the field; and, finally, by intimating that China studies should be properly located inside – not outside of – the poststructuralist academe. In short, participants in this new textual industry imply that

China studies constitutes a transdisciplinary, not simply an interdisciplinary, enterprise, because its concerns extend beyond those of the Euramerican concerns of most sectors of the new humanities.

As also discussed in Chapter 1, although recent claims concerning the transdisciplinary nature of contemporary sinological studies evince a strong desire to forge a new disciplinary identity for China studies, they are seldom grounded in the institutional praxis of the field. My reference to the rise of theory and the decline of Marxism thus marks an attempt to contextualize the nature of our recent interest in certain categories for the analysis of China, and to suggest that a reconfigured form of China studies might be better achieved by examining, rather than eliding, the kinds of divisions and hierarchies that currently condition the field as a subset of the new humanities and human sciences. As Harry Harootunian (1999: 128) puts it, if practitioners of China studies truly wish to challenge the traditional dichotomy between Euramericans as theory makers and China/the Chinese as objects of theorization, then we need to start questioning 'the directional tyranny that names as East the place we go to study', and ask: 'Where is it that we really start from, where is the place that enunciates this itinerary?'

Certainly, if sexuality emerged as *the* intellectual topic of the late 1980s, an article by Zillah Eisenstein (1990) indicates that the term 'socialism' ceased to name North American feminism at precisely the same time. Eisenstein's contention that the term 'socialism' had ceased to actively name feminism in the USA by the end of the 1980s is remarkable not because it underscores an obvious political 'truth', but rather because it indicates the extent to which feminist theorizing had altered in the course of barely a decade. After all, one of the best-known texts to have foregrounded the relationship between feminism and Marxism is the collection of essays edited by Lydia Sargant in 1981, *Women and Revolution: A Discussion of the Unhappy Marriage of Marxism and Feminism.* Taken as a whole, this text enters into a long-standing debate regarding the levels of generality and specificity that should characterize feminist theory and activism, but it does so without the benefit of the critiques of the sex/gender binary that began to characterize feminist discourse in the 1980s, or the poststructuralist critiques of foundationalism and essentialism that are more common today. Although this text raises issues that are quite compatible with contemporary feminist concerns – such as the question of how to theorize issues of gender, sexuality and race within the broader dynamics of global market capitalism – it nonetheless appears decidedly dated for a simple reason. The text argues for more feminist space, given the entrenched political and intellectual dominance of Marxism (John 1996: 80–2).

Somewhat paradoxically, if the language of Marxism still 'speaks' to contemporary feminism, it does so most clearly through the work of radical feminists, namely, those who most vociferously rejected Marxism–

socialism in the 1970s for being a strictly 'boys only' club. In *Toward a Feminist Theory of the State*, Catharine MacKinnon (1989: 3) effectively exchanges Marx's central concept regarding the alienated nature of labour under capitalism with the alienated nature of female sexuality under capitalism/patriarchy by declaring: 'Sexuality is to feminism what work is to marxism: that which is most one's own, yet most taken away.' In continuing to posit sex/gender and sexuality as the fundamental ground of female oppression, however, radical feminists have opened themselves to the same kinds of criticisms that have ensured the intellectual marginalization of Marxism, namely, accusations of essentialism, lack of theoretical rigour, and adherence to limited understandings of the nature of power and subjectivity (see Bell and Klein 1996). As a result, if the term 'Marxism–socialism' no longer defines feminism today, then neither does the language of radical feminism, at least for those who position themselves on the poststructuralist-deconstructive side of the clash within US feminism over the meanings of sex and sexuality for women, or what has been simplistically labelled 'the sex wars' (see Leng 1997: 77–103).

This reference to the embattled status of radical feminist theorizations is not intended as a précis for a more sustained discussion of their continued significance. Although many of the issues raised by radical feminism warrant further attention, I personally concur with Gayle Rubin's feminist-Foucauldian insistence that gender and sexuality are not the same thing, even though they are historically and structurally imbricated in one another (Rubin 1984: 3–31). Hence feminism as a theory of gender oppression cannot automatically assume that it offers a theory of sexual oppression. Expressed differently, however, Rubin's suggestion that sex and gender *do* have an important place in feminist thinking about social relations, but sexuality and sex/gender are connected in ways that need to be examined, rather than assumed, is apposite precisely because it poses a challenge to *all* generalized feminist accounts, irrespective of their denominative labels as radical, liberal, poststructuralist, etc. Rather than arguing for or against radical feminism, therefore, I merely want to indicate that whereas early second-wave feminists were struggling to articulate a feminist space that would overcome the so-called gender-blindness of Marxism, queer theorists and feminist-Foucauldian scholars today are attempting to construct a theoretico-political space that will overcome the perceived sexuality-blindness of classic gender Feminism, incorporating certain strands of contemporary radical feminism, often erroneously equated with cultural feminism. In short, within the disciplinary space of the new humanities, the language of theory has superseded the language of Marxism and classic gender Feminism.

I thus make reference to the embattled status of Marxism–socialism and radical feminism because it intimates that there are certain *class distinctions* at work within the poststructuralist academe. By class, I do not mean the standard economic marker of social stratification, but rather what

John Frow has described in terms of the acquisition and use of knowledge, and hence the particular processes of socialization and cultivation of habits that give academics (as members of 'the knowledge class') 'certification to live among certain sectors of the professional community' (cited in Chow 1998: xvi). Adding to Frow's conception of intellectuals as 'the knowledge class', Chow points out that the knowledge class itself is fractured along hierarchical lines. And, given the kinds of turf battles that surrounded the formation of the new humanities, these divisions have encouraged the privileging of critical theory as *real* intellectual labour and, conversely, led non-practitioners of theory to be perceived as generating a form of knowledge that relegates them to a lower-class stratum within the academy. Consequently, those who are deemed fluent in the language of theory are accorded more intellectual capital than those who are not. And scholars who utilize Foucauldian and/or poststructuralist approaches can lay claim to more professional legitimacy than those who continue to speak in the now 'out dated' languages of Marxism–socialism and classic gender Feminism.

The hegemonic or 'upper-class' status of theory is routinely credited to its anti-essentialist impetus and hence its undeniable capacity to generate new and often highly productive approaches. In practice, however, this initial apprehension of theory's critical utility has become increasingly complicated. For while a minority of theorists continue to stress the importance of engaging with the limitations of theory itself, the institutional sanctioning of theory has not only facilitated the effective taming of theory's critical agency (via its institutionalized packaging as more generalized ways of reading, writing and 'seeing'), it has also promoted the perception that 'doing theory' is somehow an automatic sign of intellectual rigour and political correctness. To cite Spivak (1986–7: 55), 'the greatest problem with theoretical production has been its sense of being right'.

In this respect, as Mary John (1996: 104) suggests, claims regarding the critical utility of theory are frequently mobilized in a negative rather than a productive fashion. The accusation of essentialism, for instance, often operates less as a precursor to showing why things are not *essentially* so and more as a sanction of dismissal. The extent to which disputes over the perceived utility of theory can amount to little more than an ill-mannered taking of political sides over what constitutes 'real' academic labour-cum-activism is illustrated by the out-of-hand rejection of radical feminist debates by numerous scholars on the grounds that they neither acknowledge nor utilize the insights made available by recourse to poststructuralism–deconstruction (ergo they cannot be saying anything worthwhile). It is also evidenced by the radical feminist rejection of queer theory, and poststructuralist-feminist accounts of sexuality, on the equally facile grounds that they cannot possibly be *feminist* because they draw on the work of gay male theorists like Foucault (see Bell and Klein 1996).

This hierarchization of the different types of intellectual labour that make up the new humanities is further complicated by what Rey Chow (1998: xvi–xvii) describes as the institutionalized racialization of intellectual labour. Here, Chow is referring to the fact that prior to the advent of cultural studies and postcolonial studies, the upper-class status of theory derived from its acknowledged position as the subversive 'other' within the Western logos, until the belated recognition of a different kind of otherness – in the form of non-Western cultures – began to challenge this presumption. The rise of cultural studies implicitly challenged the institutional hegemony of theory, not by questioning critical theory's superiority per se, but rather by intimating that claims regarding the radical nature of 'doing theory' had assumed 'the proprietariness of a firmly established tradition', and hence become the mark of a select group within the knowledge class. As Chow explains:

> In the light of cultural studies, it becomes possible to realize that 'critical theory' is, after all, a process which, despite its claim to radical alterity and heterogeneity, operates by demanding of its adherents a certain conformity with its unspoken rules, rules that have gone without saying until they are revealed for what they are: 'deconstruct the best you can – but continue to center on the West!'
>
> (ibid.: xviii)

Although the rise of cultural studies and postcolonial studies has highlighted the Euramerican bias of many theoretically informed endeavours, the asymmetrical hierarchization of knowledge produced within the institutional site of the university – a hierarchy premised on the distinction between theory and other forms of intellectual labour, as well as the division between 'white' and 'non-white' cultures – continues apace. As Chow and Chakrabarty variously suggest, the subalternity of the non-West, and, by extension, the study of the non-West, is underscored by the fact that non-Western authors and texts are simply not accorded the same kind of 'verbal, physical, theoretical density and complexity' that is endowed upon Western authors and texts (Chow 1998: xxi). Moreover, while relative ignorance of the non-West seldom detracts from the perceived quality of work undertaken by Western scholars, third-world scholars, as well as postcolonial and other scholars of the non-West, cannot afford to ignore the 'Western canon' without taking 'the risk of appearing "old-fashioned" or "out-dated"' (Chakrabarty 1992: 2).

These problems notwithstanding, the institutional success of cultural and postcolonial studies has also complicated the hierarchical division of labour within the new humanities. With reference to the critical imperatives of postcolonial theory, various scholars have noted how the importance currently attached to issues of race and ethnicity, once combined with popular conceptions of identity politics, has facilitated the institutional privileging of the 'non-white' professional academic as an authentic cultural spokesperson. While appearing to redress the hierarchical divisions that exist between 'white and non-white' scholars and cultures, Davies (1998: 174) suggests that this supposedly 'correct' ethico-political privileging of the academic of colour is problematic in practice, because it translates 'into asymmetries that render postcolonial theory pedagogically and critically ineffective'. Most notably, the investment of authority and hence institutional legitimacy in academics of colour as the stratum within the knowledge-class that is most fit to pronounce on the experience of colonialism effectively splits the postcolonial field in two. On the one hand, there is a minority of highly visible academics of colour with carte blanche to pronounce on the postcolonial condition; on the other, there is a majority of 'others' who, for various reasons – including a misplaced sense of guilt over being the 'beneficiaries of Western imperialism' and/or for fear of being challenged by the 'culturally authentic' – feel compelled to write only within the borders staked out by the former (Davies 1998: 174).

Concomitantly, although certain theorists as academics of colour have indicated how these divisions can function to constrain the critical agency of postcolonial theorizations, even self-reflexive observations of this kind tend to be utilized as yet another 'authoritative cultural source' that can be appropriated to revitalize extant approaches (ibid.). As noted in Chapter 1, Chakrabarty's call for postcolonial scholars to provincialize the hyperreal space of Europe, and hence to accord non-Western authors, texts, and histories, the same degree of theoretical complexity that has been historically endowed upon 'the West', could paradoxically offer succour to extant forms of China studies scholarship by appearing to offer another strategy towards, rather than away from, the long-standing Sinological goal of providing a 'true' (nation) translation. Certainly Spivak's insistence that the subaltern cannot speak has already been reinscribed within the disciplinary space of the field to suggest that it is possible to recover the resistant, albeit elusive, voice of the gendered, subaltern subject, and thus to challenge the dominant discourses of 'the Chinese Party state' (see Hershatter 1993: 103–30). In the process, practitioners of China studies who engage in the popular institutional task of retrieving 'resistant voices' are effectively transmogrified into living agents-cum-witnesses for the 'oppressed and voiceless' Chinese people, and thereby absolved of any need to acknowledge the problematic status of the 'new truths' generated by their own attempts to recover 'the history of the oppressed' (Chow 1994: 133; Dutton 2000a: 4).

This all-too-easy appropriation of theory to recuperate extant approaches highlights a very real need to *historicize* the informing categories of the new humanities, or to acknowledge

> the extent to which theory, in the moment of its institutional legitimation and its (troubling) success in public culture as 'postmodern truth',

has lent its name to so many different and contradictory projects in the ever-growing 'global' business of theorizing.

(Davies 1998: 180)

At the same time, the popular conflation of 'doing theory' with intellectual rigour and political correctness suggests that it is no longer sufficient to draw attention to the question of who is speaking and from what critical standpoint. Rather, as Davies (ibid.) suggests, 'if theorizing is to remain true to its critical interventionist brief', then the question of 'who it is who is doing this studying?' needs to be grounded in the more practical question of 'who benefits from doing this studying?' Bearing the preceding observations in mind, it is worthwhile recounting some of the ways in which the institutional legitimation of theory has impacted on the Western academic field of China studies.

The ins and outs of China studies

Given the kinds of hierarchical divisions that currently condition the poststructuralist academe, the emerging upper-class stratum of China scholars within the disciplinary space of the new humanities – but not within the conventional parameters of China studies – are those who are seen to have access to 'theory' and 'language', and can thus lay claim to a position of dual privilege by virtue of the status that accrues to theory as the subversive 'other' within the Western tradition, *and* by virtue of their professional 'otherness' as academic representatives of a non-Western culture.

This dual privilege functions to grant such scholars the status of alternative translators, as in more intellectually engaged and politically correct spokespersons for 'the Chinese people and the Chinese nation'. Concurrently, although practitioners of China studies who resist the impact of theory in the name of cultural exceptionalism continue to occupy a lower-class position within the new humanities per se, they can still lay claim to a broader institutional privilege by virtue of their specialized knowledge of a non-Western canon, tradition and history. Thus the traditional defence of Asian-based area studies, namely, to act as an institutional counter to the deep-seated Eurocentricism of mainstream disciplinary concerns, has achieved renewed currency in recent years due to the complex politics of multicultural inclusion that condition the poststructuralist academe.

The increasingly globalized nature of the metropolitan university precinct has also increased claims regarding the transdisciplinary nature of the China field by intimating that the concerns of Western and mainland Chinese scholars have somehow converged. I say 'somehow' in the sense that celebratory claims concerning the multivocal, cross-cultural environment in which knowledge about China is now produced elide the still formidable difficulties associated with generating productive exchanges across asymmetrically divided 'fields', languages, and forms of cultural production. For example, the contention that feminist sinologists are now in a position to challenge the traditional dichotomy between Europeans and Americans as theory makers and Chinese women as objects of theory (Gilmartin *et al.* 1994: 7), flowing from new conditions of access to the PRC and the emergence of gender and sexuality as objects of contestation in China itself, posits a false equivalence between the organizing concerns and informing categories of Anglophone and Sinophone China studies scholarship. Moreover, it implies that feminist sinologists are now engaged in the analytically productive task of demonstrating what the difference of China can reveal about the limitations of theory, when they are more commonly showing that 'China' too can be read using the discourse of theory, and, in the process, affirming the superiority of their own critical vantage point vis-à-vis classic gender Feminism, orthodox Marxism and the Western social sciences, and ultimately in relation to the kinds of discourses that circulate within the PRC.

One way of highlighting the narrowness of our own critical enterprise is to acknowledge both the asymmetrical nature of knowledge production within the metropolitan university precinct and the continued dissonance between the organizing concerns of Anglophone vis-à-vis Sinophone scholarship. As Davies (2001a: 1–3; 2001b: 17–22) explains, Anglophone China studies accounts of contemporary Chinese intellectuality are usually constructed in terms of the re-emergence of a more open intellectual scene in China, flowing from the kinds of changes that have accompanied the economic reforms and the Open Door policy, rather than in terms of issues pertaining to the emergence of theory and postcolonialism per se. Once overlaid with the popular, and decidedly romantic, Western perception of Chinese intellectuals as protagonists of change, or post-1989 dissidents opposing a repressive regime, this particular way of constructing Chinese intellectuality has crudely distorted both the nature and content of mainland Chinese debates. Most notably, it elides the extent to which so-called non-official discourses have been implicitly sanctioned by 'the Chinese state', and it fails to acknowledge that many of China's so-called new social scientists actually view their efforts as complementing or even consolidating the government-led programme of modernizing China. The inherent bias of our own critical enterprise is further underscored by the fact that if non-official discourses are viewed as consonant with, rather than opposed to, the official discourses of 'the Chinese state', this congruence is invariably explained in negative terms. Namely, it is held up as a sign that the CCP may have lost its former stranglehold on independent thought but it still retains a formidable degree of social control. Thus Anglophone China scholars frequently aver that China's non-state commentators are no longer confined to speaking in the 'tired and has-been' language of Marxism, but they have yet to realize the political and intellectual benefits associated with (post)modernity in the West.

Furthermore, although the asymmetrical nature of knowledge production within the China field has led to various hostile exchanges between mainland-based and overseas-based Chinese intellectuals, this debate has hardly been mentioned within the Anglophone field of China studies, 'let alone in the larger discourse of theory of which postcolonial theory is a branch' (Davies 1998: 180–1). For instance, in 'Jingti renwei de "yangjing-bang xuefeng"' ('Watch out for "purposeful pidgin scholarship"'), Liu Dong (1995: 4–13) accuses overseas-based Chinese scholars of deliberately misreading the complexities of the mainland intellectual scene by adopting inappropriate Western interpretative frameworks in their Chinese publications. And, in 'Chanshi "Zhongguo" de jiaolü' (The anxiety of interpreting 'China'), Zhang Yiwu (1995: 12–35) contends that many Chinese scholars have not only endorsed Western 'authorship' of knowledge about China, but also reinforced the long-standing asymmetrical power relation between 'the intellectually advanced with the blueprint of history in hand' and 'indigenous critics in their difficult circumstances', by presenting Western liberal humanism as a value common to all humanity. In different ways, therefore, Liu and Zhang both suggest that the adoption of Western forms of theorization by certain Chinese scholars has led them to 'misrecognize' the complex 'realities' of political, cultural, and economic progress in 1990s' China, and that the 'form' of present-day China has become a ready-made segment of knowledge production largely determined by the hegemony of Western culture (Davies 2001b: 27–32).

The question of how to interpret 'China' both within and outside the hegemonic space of 'modern Euramerica' also informs recent mainland scholarship on the history and nature of sexuality in China. In *Zhongguo xing xianzhuang* (The State of Sex in China), Pan Suiming (1995) maintains that the history of sexuality in China is not unlike the history of sexuality in Britain and North America in that sex was made the subject of prohibition in all these cultures during the nineteenth century. Apart from this chronological similarity, however, Pan concludes that the forms of asceticism which provided the rationale for enforcing a taboo on sex in 'China' and 'the West' were qualitatively different, being underpinned by Confucian and Protestant values respectively. In consequence, the historical consequences of prohibition were completely opposite. So far as Pan is concerned, sexual repression in 'the West' proved to be a positive precondition for the development of capitalism, whereas sexual repression in Qing dynasty China resulted in social stagnation and decline. This process of stagnation, he continues, was halted by the CCP's rise to power in 1949, but it was only truly rectified after the Cultural Revolution with the implementation of the economic reforms and the Open Door policy, and the governmental sanctioning of popular sex education in order to realize the objectives of the One-child Family policy. According to Pan, these recent changes have generated something akin to a sexual revolution in present-day China.

It bears noting, however, that Pan's implicit valorization of the Western trajectory of historical development does not constitute an endorsement of Western modernity per se. Rather, it flows from his Marxist-informed belief that the traditional prohibition on sex in China was a product of feudal and therefore retrogressive values, whereas prohibition in the West flowed from the needs of capitalism and hence incorporated various progressive aspects. This adherence to teleological Marxist conceptions of historical development also accounts for Pan's suggestion that China will ultimately develop a more advanced (i.e., socialist) science of sex.

In a somewhat different vein, in *Zhongguo nüxing de xing yu ai* (Sex, Love, and Chinese Women), Li Yinhe (1997) maintains that the status of sex in China cannot be measured by way of comparison with 'the West' because it is the distinct product of a specific cultural time and place (trans. Sigley 1998: 25–31). While crediting Freud, Marcuse, and Foucault as being the three most important thinkers on the subject of sexuality, Li concludes that their respective analyses are of limited relevance for understanding the history and nature of sexuality in China. Yet, Li then proceeds to appropriate Foucault's work in order to argue that, contrary to Western constructions of sexuality in the PRC as repressed, 'the Chinese people' are currently in a 'pristine state of uncorrupted preknowledge regarding sex'. Li's argument here is that, unlike their anxiety-ridden counterparts in 'the West', the Chinese people have not been obliged historically to make sex the truth of themselves, hence they are neither defined nor constrained by the obligation to recognize themselves as individual subjects in terms of Western-style guilt-based distinctions between correct or incorrect, normal or abnormal, and licit or criminal, forms of sexual behaviour. For Li, it is this culturally based difference, rather than the existence of governmental constraints, which accounts for the lack of public debate on issues pertaining to sexual rights and identity politics in the PRC today.

While these debates could be opened to criticism as indicative of the historicist and neo-conservative impetus of much contemporary Chinese scholarship (see Chan, S. 1999: 173–83), I want to resist this move for a simple reason. Speaking from my own critical vantage point as a Western-trained academic versed in the discourse of theory, and involved in the study of China, a generalized pronouncement here on how the East–West dyad or the nature of sexuality *should* properly be read would only make 'the Chinese versions' appear naïve or theoretically inept. And it is precisely this implicit relegation of mainland Chinese debates to a lower-class stratum of knowledge production within the metropolitan university precinct – a relegation that is paradoxically confirmed by the privileging of the work of some of China's new social scientists within the Anglophone field of China studies, in order to empirically ground and subsequently confirm the more knowledgeable nature of our own critical pronouncements on China – that I want to bring into question. Rather than using these debates to comment on 'the real China', they might be better read as an attempt to elucidate how various postmodern positions are being staked out within the Anglophone and Sinophone fields of China studies, and hence as a preliminary effort to negotiate the ways in which the presupposed relation between 'China and the West', 'tradition and modernity', functions both to enable and constrain the act of knowledge production in various hierarchical ways (see Davies 2001a: 3–5; 2001b: 29–32; 37–8; also 2000: 1–42).

Put another way, the exploration and critique of theory pursued within the Chinese-speaking world are grounded in an emerging politics of place and cultural representativeness that cannot readily be accommodated within the existing parameters of Anglophone China studies. On the one hand, any attempt to reinscribe these debates as providing a characteristically or uniquely Chinese critical perspective from the traditional purview of China studies would fail to address the field's long-standing captivity within the ideological framework of studying-the-other. On the other hand, the more recent strategy of ascribing intellectual merit to non-official Chinese discourses as resistant or opposed to the official discourses of 'the Chinese state', while simultaneously decrying their lack of congruence with the organizing concerns of metropolitan discourses, simply confirms the asymmetrical relationship between theory (as core, upper-class knowledge) and China studies (as a lower-class subset of exotic case studies within cultural studies, conceived as a subset of theory) within the Anglophone humanities (Davies 2000; 2001a; 2001b). In short, reading strategies of this kind either fail to disrupt the conventional Eurocentric/Sinocentric framing of modern China, or else they elide the discrepancy that exists between the plenitude and effectivity of Chinese discourses when viewed within their own idiom and context, as opposed to their apparent impoverishment once represented in the masterful language of the new humanities.

This continued elision of the translation problematic is anachronistic, given the rise of postcolonial studies and the ongoing debate within Sinophone China studies over how the China–West dyad should be negotiated. Certainly, Zhang Yiwu's criticism of the 1990s' advocacy of 'the humanist spirit' (*renwen jingshen*) in the PRC on the grounds that it not only affirms Western authorship of knowledge about China, but also cannot account for the cultural consequences of rapid commercialization in the PRC, makes supposedly objective Anglophone China studies accounts of the unfulfilled promise of humanism in China sound decidedly lopsided and surprisingly metaphysical. Likewise, the recent concern of mainland Chinese scholars with the politics of place, or questions concerning the different speaking modes adopted by overseas-based and mainland-based Chinese intellectuals, and the different forms of institutional legitimation that accrue to Sinophone scholarship as it circulates in different cultural contexts, make recent (Anglophone) claims concerning the multivocal and heterogeneous nature of contemporary sinological studies sound remarkably hollow and self-justificatory.

It bears noting, for instance, that works produced by overseas-based Chinese scholars – the émigré Chinese intellectual speaking both as and for the other, and supposedly able to speak more freely due to their new location in 'not-China', as well as works produced by mainland-based non-state commentators, supposedly speaking as authentic cultural spokespeople from a muted but still audible position of subversive, internal 'otherness' within the dominant discourses of 'the Chinese Party police state' – are frequently valorized on the basis of nothing more than the assumed oppositional status of such scholars as physical or intellectual exiles from post-1989 China. This valorization stems from a complex interplay of factors, including: the neo-liberal revitalization of Cold War-style readings of the PRC following the brutal suppression of the student protest movement in June 1989; the popularity of an unproductive kind of identity politics which has the corollary institutional effect of privileging the academic of colour as an authentic cultural spokesperson; and the transparent unwillingness of most Anglophone China scholars to challenge the prescriptive assumption that China's economic reforms *should* culminate in a particular type of socio-political reform. The net effect of such considerations, however, is that scholars who raise issues that seemingly challenge the nature of Chinese governmental practices are accorded more intellectual capital than those who do not. And it is precisely this way of hierarchizing knowledge production within the China field – a process that invariably presents the PRC as still vegetating on the edge of world history – that many Chinese intellectuals object to, but also encounter enormous difficulties in confronting, for the simple reason that any attempt to do so runs the risk of being automatically dismissed as neo-conservative or overly nationalistic.

Our inability to accept that crucial discursive shifts may be occurring within the socio-political space of the PRC owes much to the continued dominance of post-1989 neo-liberal readings of the Chinese polity and the decline of Marxism. The inglorious fall of the European socialist states was a belated death certificate that put an end to the long-standing crisis within Western intellectual circles over the continued relevance and political viability of Marxism. In terms of Anglophone China studies, however, the disillusionment of disciplinary-minded and left-wing scholars with Marxism–socialism cannot be separated from the CCP's negation of the Cultural Revolution, and hence the highly embarrassing suggestion that those who first attempted to revolutionize the field, namely, those who were held up in the late 1970s and early 1980s as the most intellectually sophisticated and politically concerned of Asian scholars, had been the ones most literally duped by Marxism–Maoism (read CCP propaganda). Viewed from this 'we've-already-been-burnt-once' perspective, the events of June 1989 have been construed by many Anglophone China scholars as a timely and equally nasty reminder that things are not always how they look in the People's Republic, and therefore as confirmation that the economic reform programme may have changed the 'face' of post-Mao China, but that it has not altered the oppressive nature of the CCP's historical exercise of power.

Our now ingrained hostility towards viewing the Chinese polity *productively* is underscored by the popular understanding that the CCP's negation of the Cultural Revolution has brought the entire course of the Chinese Revolution into question. To cite Alessandro Russo (1998: 183), 'the fact that, after 1976, the Cultural Revolution's political content was totally denied (*chedi fouding*) could not but discredit all the political events that Mao and his followers presented as their own historical forerunners'. Furthermore, attempts to limit this official repudiation to the so-called errors of the late Mao 'have been patently fictitious, a crude compromise aimed at safeguarding state legitimacy rather than offering a tenable historiographic thesis'. Russo thus concludes that the Chinese themselves are in a condition of stolid embarrassment over how to conceive their own past and present, since even the celebrated precursor to the CCP's victory in 1949 – the May Fourth Movement of 1919 – cannot be thought of today as anything other than 'an exhausted, worn-out, foundational myth'.

There can be little doubt that the CCP's negation of the Cultural Revolution combined with the embattled status of Marxism–socialism has engendered a massive re-reading of the PRC's often not-so-revolutionary history on both sides of the East–West divide. But this does not mean that the recent Anglophone China studies' project of revisiting our early and overly idealized accounts of 'Red China', in order to expose the 'violence' that accompanied the very inception of the communist regime, can be equated with mainland Chinese efforts to re-read their own past in order to reconfigure their own present and future. Dismissing key moments in the PRC's revolutionary history as foundational myths wrapped up in the once powerful but now exhausted language of Chinese Marxism may provide psychological compensation as well as an explanation for our former failure to recognize what was 'really' happening in 'communist China', but it has the corollary effect of rendering us unable to account for the kinds of changes that are occurring in the PRC today.

Most notably, our reluctance to view the Chinese polity as anything other than a 'living dinosaur' makes us blind to the positivity of Chinese governmental practices, as well as the effectivity of the language of Chinese Marxism as it continues to permeate and organize the Chinese social formation. Researchers associated with the All-China Women's Federation, for instance, have been engaged in the dual task of deconstructing and reconfiguring 'Maoism' so as to develop programmes designed to maintain and improve the position of Chinese women. This project is unified under the rubric of the 'Marxist Theory of Women' and refers to the entire discourse on women's liberation in revolutionary China, from the May Fourth Movement of 1919, through the Maoist era, and into the present day. In doing so, this project does not refer to a fixed set of principles. Rather, it refers to a strategy designed to garner the support of governmental authorities for a broad platform of gender equality. Thus, in marked contrast to the androgynous or sex-sameness model that was promoted during the Maoist period, this project is also premised on the assertion of fundamental sex-based differences between women and men, differences that are said to have been elided during the Maoist era (Wang Zheng 1997: 126–52).

Although this new concern with naturalized conceptions of femaleness appears to replicate the insights of Western radical and cultural feminism, it owes much to the CCP-led rejection of the politics of the Cultural Revolution and the ensuing neo-Marxist critique of the Maoist regime for alienating the 'true nature' of the Chinese people and the Party itself. As Wang Zheng (ibid.: 136–9) notes, Li Xiaojiang, the prominent Chinese feminologist (a term used to differentiate the concerns of women's activists in mainland China from those of Western feminists), has criticized the Maoist version of women's liberation for failing to transform patriarchal culture and institutions. However, Li's contention that the 'ultra-left' egalitarian policy of the Cultural Revolution distorted women's true nature or unique femaleness, simply replicates Wang Ruoshui's renowned (at least in the PRC) theoretical critique of Maoism for alienating the human nature of the Chinese people, with the claim that such policies alienated the true nature of Chinese women.

Unfortunately, the rhetorical and symbolic strength of the different moral and cultural propositions that inform this project cannot readily be accommodated within the institutional praxis of contemporary China studies because we already know that Marxism-cum-Maoism is out-dated and gender-blind, and that classic gender Feminism is not just sexuality-blind, it has long since passed its political use-by-date. Assessed within the traditional purview of Anglophone China studies, therefore, strategies of this kind are read and (re)presented as 'tired' repetitions of already worn-out foundational myths, or belated articulations of an already superseded critical position, rather than as repetitions with a difference, or strategies that have very real and transformatory effects. In this respect, our ingrained reluctance to ascribe any utility or explanatory capacity to the language of Marxism-cum-Maoism has left us unable to account theoretically for the kinds of changes that are occurring in China today. This problem is particularly pronounced in Western commentaries on sexuality in the PRC.

Sexuality is 'in' and sex is 'back' in China

Although the institutional marketability of recent analyses of sex in China owes much to the organizing concerns of the new humanities, it is augmented by the perception that sex is 'back' in China. To use the words of

Linda Jaivin (1994–5: 3): '[s]exuality has gone from being one of Chinese society's greatest taboos to one of its most ardent obsessions'. In contrast to the Maoist period, books and magazine and newspaper articles now abound on the subject of sex. These texts not only encompass such diverse topics as accounts of ancient sexual practices, guides to contemporary sex education, and various portrayals of prostitution, but also display a wide variety of approaches, ranging from the scholarly to the journalistic and even to the pornographic. Whether on advertisement billboards or on the covers of popular magazines, in articles by sexologists or in the display counters of China's new sex-shops and sex-exhibitions, images of and information about sex are now omnipresent in the PRC (Evans 1995: 357; McMillan 1999: 10–26). Even open displays of sexual interest, such as holding hands or kissing in public, have gained some degree of social acceptability and are no longer treated as indisputable signs of promiscuity (Bulbeck 1994: 95–103).

For popular commentators, the emergence of sex as a prominent feature of public life in the PRC marks a dramatic shift from the perceived sexual puritanism of the Maoist era. According to the *Newsweek* reporter, George Wehrfritz:

> Mao's government regarded the masses' libidos as a major threat to the Communist Party's authority. As soon as he took power in 1949, his troops went to work shutting down the country's brothels. That was just the beginning.
>
> (1996: 8)

In *China Pop: How Soap Operas, Tabloids, and Bestsellers are Transforming a Culture*, the émigré Chinese commentator, Zha Jianying (1995), similarly contends that, under Mao, sex practically vanished from sight in Chinese culture. To use her own words, the Chinese Communist Party promulgated a strictly 'antibody, antiflesh, antisexuality attitude'; and, even though Mao himself was a notorious lecher, the Party 'systematically eradicated all palpable signs of bodily interest and institutions of carnal pleasure' (ibid.: 139). Hence she infers that the antisexuality attitude of the CCP explains why one of the first actions undertaken by the new regime was to shut down all of China's brothels.

In the eyes of popular commentators, therefore, the PRC is now either engaged in its own belated sexual revolution, or else it would be if not for the repressive policies of the CCP-led regime. Accounts of this kind are routinely buttressed by comparing the 'richness' of erotic life in traditional China with the 'sexual prudery' of the Maoist era, and subsequently suggesting that the loosening of social controls (flowing from the economic reforms), has liberated the minds and bodies of the Chinese people, if not necessarily those of the Chinese government. Wehrfritz (1996: 9), for example, contends that the 'prudery of Mao's social policies owed a larger debt to the Victorian notions of the Marxist philosopher Friedrich Engels than to anything Confucius ever said'. Consequently, now that Marx and Engels are buried again at last, 'China's sexual attitudes are quickly reverting to the permissive standards of precommunist life'. Conversely, although the émigré Chinese sexologist, Fang-fu Ruan, shares Wehrfritz's conception of sexuality as natural and inherently liberatory, he is far more pessimistic regarding the Chinese people's ability to enjoy the freedoms associated with sexual liberation in the West, due to the continued existence of the 'totalitarian CCP'. According to the editorial comment that opens Ruan's *Sex in China*, sexuality used to be glorified in traditional China, but today's political climate is 'one of sexual repression' (Green, in Ruan 1991: v).

Journalistic accounts of sex in the PRC appeal to a Western readership because they fall into what Gail Hershatter (1996b: 78) describes as 'the "just like us" category of China reporting'. Now that former constraints have been lifted, or so we are enjoined to believe, 'the Chinese' are starting to behave like 'us'. They now have sex shops, radio call-in shows providing sexual advice, a commercial sex industry, a growing gay and lesbian scene, and so forth; and, somewhat unfortunately, they are also experiencing some of the same problems as 'us', in that crimes such as rape are on the increase, sexually transmissible diseases including HIV/AIDS are spreading rapidly, and prostitution and pornography are now widespread. In the final analysis, however, what makes 'the Chinese Long March toward "modern" sexuality' so newsworthy is not just the 'newness' and 'titillating' nature of its subject matter, but the fact that it appears decidedly quaint by our 'already-had-a-sexual-revolution' standards (Hershatter 1996b: 78). Thus, Wehrfritz (1996: 11) concludes his catchily titled 'Unbuttoning a nation' by informing us that the director of a Shanghai Male Sexual Function Rehabilitation Centre (a clinic which treats problems such as impotence and premature ejaculation) believes his work is serving the country. Wehrfritz cites the director as saying: '[p]utting sex in the proper perspective will build strong families for the next millennium', to which Wehrfritz sardonically quips: '[h]e doesn't appear to be joking'.

Most academic accounts of sex in the PRC also fall into 'the "just like us" category of China reporting' except, to extend Hershatter's metaphor, this particular mode of writing might be more accurately, if inelegantly, termed 'the China that would be "just like us" if it could only get rid of the CCP genre of China reporting'. Ruan's work, for instance, turns on the premise that sex was free from constraint in traditional China, but sex in the PRC is subject to overt political suppression. What this particular mode of scholarship enjoins us to believe is that the retreat of 'the Chinese state' from the economic arena has yet to be replicated in the arguably most personal and 'private' arena of the sexual. Hence, in an emotionally charged chapter of *Building a World Community*, entitled 'Sex repression in contemporary China', Ruan and Bullough (1989: 201) inform us that the greatest repression of sex in the whole of history has not occurred due to religion, but rather due to the CCP – 'a modern secular government that claims to know what is best for its people'. For, they continue, any country which did not have a sex education programme until 1988, where individuals need permission to attempt to conceive, where sex is still tied to procreation, and where people's natural sexual urges are suppressed, leading to increases in crimes like rape, can only be described as 'the ultimate police state'.

Ruan and Bullough's conclusions could be open to criticism on a number of grounds. Feminists would challenge the assumption that rape is the inevitable consequence of attempting to repress the 'natural' male sex drive; and scholars who claim a theoretical debt to the work of Foucault would question their reliance on 'the repressive hypothesis', or the assumption that sexuality constitutes an inevitable target of power because of its natural and inherently liberatory capacity.[2] Yet Ruan and Bullough's conclusions are not only echoed in most popular accounts of sexuality in China, Ruan's *Sex in China* is also cited as an authoritative and unproblematic source in texts produced by some of China studies' recognized theorists. In a special edition of *Chinese Sociology and Anthropology* entitled 'Sex', Linda Jaivin (1994–5) similarly intimates that the desires of the Chinese people are still subject to political repression and that the incidence of rape is related to the fact that prostitution is illegal in the 'fuddy-duddy' PRC. And, despite his professed theoretical debt to Foucault, Frank Dikötter (1995: 183–4) cites Ruan in the epilogue of *Sex, Culture and Modernity in China* to indicate that male homosexuality is treated as a crime in the PRC, one that incurs summary arrests and long prison sentences, or else as a mental illness susceptible to treatment by electric shock theory, and many Chinese lesbians end up in correctional institutions.[3]

Although Dikötter only makes this one reference to Ruan's work, it highlights the problematic status of his supposedly critical pronouncements regarding the state of sexuality in present-day China. So far as Dikötter (1995: 184–6) is concerned, the PRC is still a totalitarian state and the reasons we can adduce this include: (1) the fact that discourses on sex in the PRC, unlike those in twentieth-century Europe, have never been dissociated from procreation, hence the rights of individuals to be their own unique selves (lesbian, gay, an unmarried active heterosexual, and so forth), have not been acknowledged; (2) the coercive nature of China's birth control programme; and (3) because 'the degree of convergence between state and intellectuals in the recent proliferation of debates on sexuality' in China highlights the CCP's continued monolithic control over the production of discourse. Like Ruan's *Sex in China*, therefore, Dikötter's work turns on an unexamined commitment to the repressive hypothesis: he assumes that the act of talking about and engaging in sex is inherently liberatory and therefore diametrically opposed to the interests of power.

Dikötter's adherence to libertarian-totalitarian conceptions of the nexus between sexuality and power is problematic, not least because it turns on the implicit valorization of Western forms of thinking. The cultural presumptuousness of Dikötter's seemingly objective pronouncements is underscored by the way in which he denies contemporary discourses on sexuality in the PRC any explanatory capacity and ultimately installs himself (the theory-minded Western academic) as the most authoritative spokesperson on sex in China. For having damned the CCP and official discourses on sexuality, Dikötter informs us that Chinese intellectuals who talk about sex may occupy a position of privilege due to the oppositional nature of their knowledge vis-à-vis established power, but their claims to 'enlightenment' should not be given too much credence. This is because 'intellectuals in the PRC who crusade for "sexual liberation" often speak the same language when dealing with sexuality as the regime from which they most wish to distance themselves' (Dikötter 1995: 186).

Leaving aside for a moment the problems associated with defining the relationship between sexuality and power in terms of repression, the question Dikötter's conclusion begs is: precisely what language should intellectuals in the PRC who are allegedly engaged in a crusade for sexual liberation be speaking? With regard to extant Anglophone China studies scholarship, the answer is surprisingly simple and accomplished through little more than the work of negation – they should not be speaking the language of Marxism-cum-Maoism. Why? Because armed with the kinds of theoretical insights that inform the new humanities, we know (even if mainland Chinese scholars do not) that discourses of this kind are premised on intellectually inferior (as in essentialist) understandings of the difference between the two sexes. Moreover, we know (even if mainland scholars do not) that the language of Marxism-cum-Maoism is unable to deal with the complexities of sexual politics and identity politics. In consequence, Chinese discourses on sexuality are portrayed as irretrievably gender-blind and sexuality-blind.

Dikötter's tactic of relegating Chinese discourses to a lower level of knowledge production, and simultaneously affirming the superiority of various Western categories of analysis, is replicated by Harriet Evans in *Women and Sexuality in China*, with the effect that she reaches similar conclusions. According to Evans (1997: 15), the recent proliferation of publications and debates on sex-related issues in China has functioned less to encourage 'new voices and opinions' and more to reinforce key aspects of the dominant 'official discourse' on sexuality, a discourse that the CCP set in place during the 1950s to promote the new Marriage Law. This discourse, she continues, privileges the model of monogamous heterosexuality and propagates women's subordination as a natural condition of biological differences between the two sexes. Furthermore, although the ideological parameters of the Maoist era enabled the naturalized gender hierarchy of this dominant discourse to coexist, albeit uneasily, with messages of empowerment to women, this has not proved to be the case in the commercialized reform era. Instead, Evans concludes that the routine conflation of biological sex with gender in China today – a conflation which she contends is not disrupted by efforts to mobilize an essentialist discourse of sexual difference in order to contest Maoist-style masculinist standards of sexual equality – has been used 'to sustain fundamentally hierarchical views about what women and men can and cannot do, in nearly all areas of social and sexual life' (ibid.: 220, 29).

For Evans (ibid.: 218–19), the impoverished nature of Chinese discourses on sexuality is demonstrated by the fact that the dominant 'representation of female sexuality as a naturally responsive complement of the powerful male sex drive, invariably orientated to the needs of procreation, ignores the female subject as an autonomous site of pleasure'. The theoretical question of how mainland Chinese scholars might go about mobilizing an understanding of gender that does not fall back onto some conception of the natural, biologically sexed body, while simultaneously enabling them to explore what it means to be specifically a woman as opposed to a man, is not addressed by Evans, and nor does she explicate what the notion of an autonomous site of female pleasure actually entails. But just as Dikötter does not have to explain what particular language he believes Chinese crusaders for sexual liberation should be speaking, Evans can afford to ignore such questions because the general feminist point is clear: sex is synonymous with marriage in the PRC; and, therefore, unlike 'us', Chinese women can only occupy a very limited range of subject positions. Or, as Hershatter (1996b: 93) similarly opines, female sexuality – in the sense of a display of bodily postures, adornment, and narratives designed to encourage male desire – may be increasingly visible in the PRC, but 'female desire remains a transgressive, almost impossible, subject'.

Although these claims appeal to popular understandings of the nature of sexuality and appropriate feminist concerns, they could be refuted simply by inverting Dikötter's textual strategy and valorizing the opposing claims of other 'Chinese' commentators as the most authoritative and authentic cultural spokespersons on sex in China. In marked contrast to the suggestion that sexuality in the PRC is subject to overt political suppression, for instance, Xu Xiaoqun (1996: 383) contends that 'the Chinese state' has virtually abandoned its Cultural Revolution practice of intervening in the private lives of ordinary people. In fact, apart from sex-related legal issues that attract *international* controversy [my emphasis], such as prostitution, rape, and the kidnapping and selling of women, Xu (ibid.: 388) maintains that issues pertaining to love, marriage, and sexuality, are all open to public discussion, with a clear indication of the changed environment of the reform period being that the Maoist cliché of two partners persisting in a marriage out of a regard for the building of a 'perfect society' has been replaced by a new concern with female sexual and emotional fulfilment, and a recognition that female sexuality should not be bounded by conventional conceptions of the sexually virtuous woman. Moreover, contrary to those who see this more relaxed approach as a natural extension of the PRC's abandonment of Marxism, Xu (ibid.: 401) contends that this new rhetoric of love, and the related increasing tolerance of female-initiated divorce and female extra-marital affairs, is informed by a rereading of Friedrich Engels' *The Origin of the Family, Private Property, and the State* ([1884] 1972) a work that became familiar to most educated Chinese during the Cultural Revolution era.

Xu is not the only commentator to suggest that sex in the PRC is largely free from governmental constraint, that the historical link between sex and procreation in China has been severed, and that the language and practices of Marxism-cum-Maoism can be reconfigured to suit new purposes. Li Yinhe (1997) and Pan Suiming (1993) also reject the understanding that China lags behind the West because sexuality is tied to procreation and the Chinese people are thereby denied their rights as autonomous sexual subjects. For Li Yinhe (1997), the Western discourse of sexual rights is 'meaningless' when located in the Chinese context because it turns on Western liberal conceptions of the individual subject, and therefore presupposes a particular kind of distinction between 'the public and private spheres' that has not historically informed and organized the Chinese socio-political formation. And, in contrast to those who view China's birth control programme in strictly negative terms, Pan Suiming (1993: 3) contends that the CCP, via its implementation of the One-child Family policy, is responsible (albeit perhaps unintentionally) for severing the historical link between sex and procreation in China and thereby promoting the current emphasis on the importance of female sexual pleasure.

This new discourse on female sexual pleasure might be more accurately described as an 'economy of pleasure', since official and academic publications alike *do* tend to discuss female sexuality in relation to harmonious, monogamous marital relations (see the series of translations in Sigley 1998). But the same cannot be said of China's burgeoning genre of journalistic literature *(jishi wenxue)*. As Xu Xiaoqun (1996: 381–3) points out, although this body of literature smacks of tabloid commercialism, it plays an important role in defining contemporary Chinese sexual culture by offering diverse portrayals of the purportedly real-life experiences of sexually independent women, participants in the prostitution transaction, and people involved in gay and lesbian relationships. In fact, contrary to Hershatter's suggestion that female desire remains a virtually impossible subject in the PRC, some of these accounts not only provide positive representations of female adultery, they also suggest that a husband who cannot sexually satisfy his wife should wholeheartedly and unashamedly support her other involvements (see Jaivin 1994–5: 84–92). Popular fiction or not, such accounts present a reversal of traditional notions of male attitudes towards female sexuality that is far from common in Western literature.

Playing the popular academic game of 'tit for tat' is ultimately unproductive, however, because it simply reactivates the unreflexive commentary principle that permeates the field of China studies. In what is broadly called commentary, the hierarchy between primary and secondary text plays two roles which Foucault (1981: 51–77) suggests are in solidarity with each other. On the one hand, the originary and permanent status of the primary text enables the (endless) construction of new discourse in the form of secondary texts. On the other hand, the role of the commentary is always to reiterate what was said in the original, while simultaneously appearing to articulate something other than or 'beyond' the primary text. For Foucault, this sense of 'beyondness' or newness is something of a sham since it masks the dependence of the secondary text on mere recitation, or the repetition of what has already been said in order to expose what was never said, but is paradoxically presented as intrinsic or integral to the original, nevertheless.

Although the commentary principle is a standard component of academic practice, its activation within the new disciplinary space of China studies has two significant effects. First, via the uninterrogated process of translation, it enables practitioners of China studies to reiterate endlessly the work of native Chinese commentators on sex-related issues, while simultaneously pointing to the impoverished nature of such discourses vis-à-vis the masterful language of the Anglophone humanities. In other words, the activation of the commentary-principle-as-translation allows Western China scholars to empirically ground their conclusions in the work of native Chinese commentators. In doing so, they can claim the professional capital that conventionally accrues to practitioners of China studies by virtue of their linguistic expertise, while simultaneously intimating that they have gone beyond the act of mere recitation, and should therefore be granted additional intellectual capital, because their access to the insights made available by the Western social sciences or the discourse of theory enables them to speak the 'truths' that their Chinese sources and informants cannot express in the final analysis.

Second, given the kinds of hierarchical divisions that currently condition the China field as an untheorized subset of the new humanities, the activation of the commentary principle-as-translation effectively functions to ensure that the work of those who benefit from commenting on China cannot be opened to serious interrogation. Certainly, it bears noting that, within the conventional parameters of China studies, the work of scholars who use theory to interrogate the Eurocentric/Sinocentric framing of modern China tends to be defined as 'not-China studies' because it is not deemed to be saying anything new about China per se (i.e., it fails to activate the commentary-principle in the form of an extended recitation of Chinese language sources or information derived from in-house fieldwork). One way of illustrating this point is to note that Rey Chow's work is considered marginal to the field, even though her name features regularly in the metropolitan discourse of theory. This marginality is arguably the result of self-marginalization, or a reflection of Chow's desire to be affiliated with the more fashionable and theory-informed fields of postcolonial and cultural studies. But it bears noting that those whose reputations as theorists are largely confined to the field of China studies have had little, if no, impact on the production of new theories and practices within the broader disciplinary space of the new humanities, for the simple reason that they tend to apply, rather than engage with, mainstream theoretical concerns.

Obfuscation of the kinds of hierarchical divisions that condition China studies as an untheorized subset of the Anglophone humanities means that practitioners of China studies can use theory to expose the problematic forms of rationality that underpin mainland Chinese discourses on gender and sexuality, without having to undertake the related critical task of examining the problematic forms of rationality that underpin their own conclusions. Given the acknowledged theoretical debt of scholars such as Dikötter, Evans, and Hershatter, to the work of Foucault, for instance, it strikes me as decidedly odd that their respective analyses are premised on an implicit commitment either to liberal conceptions of sexuality, or else to libertarian-totalitarian conceptions of 'the state' as the form against which civil society – understood in oppositional terms as embodying values such as the freedom and autonomy of the individual – is pitted. In fact, even though these scholars claim the professional capital that accrues to the use of theory, and thereby intimate that their work is more sophisticated than that of popular commentators, most Western accounts of sexuality in the PRC turn on a juridical conception of power, with the corollary effect that the CCP are routinely presented as repressive, sexual puritans.

Repression, as the work of Foucault (1978: 17–49) makes clear, is a concept used above all in relation to sexuality. In defining the relationship between sexuality and power in terms of repression, however, one adopts a purely juridical conception of power. Power becomes associated with a law that says no or something that operates with the force of a prohibition. For Foucault, this negative and skeletal conception of power is analytically unsatisfactory, despite its widespread popularity, for the simple reason that if the only function of power were to repress, it would not be tolerated. Instead, Foucault contends that what makes power hold good, what makes it accepted, is its technical and positive nature, the ways in which it induces pleasures, creates knowledge, and produces discourse. The *positivity* as opposed to *negativity* of power has proved difficult to grasp, however, because conventional analyses of power are invariably framed in terms of the legitimate reach of 'the state', and hence in terms of law and repression. While never denying the existence of governmental constraints, the originality of Foucault's work lies in showing how the modern discourse of repressed sexuality emerged from a particular conjunction of historical forces, including the re-articulation of seventeenth-century confessional practices within the disciplinary apparatuses associated with the eighteenth-century state, and the rise in the nineteenth century of such new knowledge forms or 'sciences' as medicine, pedagogy, psychiatry and law (Foucault 1978: 135–59). In doing so, Foucault (ibid.: 119–22) demonstrates that analyses of the relationship between sexuality and power must necessarily extend beyond traditional liberal concerns regarding the limits of 'the State': first, because 'the state', for all the omnipotence of its apparatuses, cannot occupy the whole field of actual power relations; and, second, because 'the state can only operate on the basis of other, already existing power relations'.

Unfortunately, Foucault's insistence on the positivity of power has gained little critical purchase within the boundaries of what is considered to be acceptable China studies scholarship. This remains the case even though a number of scholars have drawn on the Foucauldian concept of governmentality to reconfigure extant understandings of the operation of power in the PRC, and, in turn, to show how empirical observations about China can be used as a theoretical point of departure to challenge the growing body of Western scholarship on the subject of liberal-style governmentality (Bray 1999; Dutton 1992; Sigley 1996b). Instead, scholars such as Dikötter, Evans, and Hershatter, tend to endorse Foucault's rereading of the popular history of sexuality, while simultaneously ignoring his insistence on the positivity and effectivity of the diverse techniques and practices that make up all governmental programmes of intervention.

Hershatter (1996b: 42–93) and Evans (1997), for instance, offer a potentially constructive challenge to the journalistic contention that China is currently undergoing a sexual revolution, and hence becoming 'just like us', by highlighting the dependence of such analyses on an assumed opposition between the repressive puritanism of the Maoist era and the seeming liberalization of today. In doing so, they explicitly or implicitly draw on Foucault's suggestion that the history of sexuality cannot be adequately explained in terms of a period of repression, followed by the development of more liberal and permissive attitudes to sex, since, in the West at least, the very mechanisms that prompt us to see and speak of sex as the truth of ourselves are inseparable from the historic exercise of power, and thus the veritable explosion of discourses on sex and sexuality that occurred in the eighteenth and nineteenth centuries (despite the common construction of this era as a period when sex became subject to severe repression). Once applied to the analysis of the PRC, however, Foucault's contention that talking about sexuality may be neither inherently liberating, nor diametrically opposed to the interests of power, turns into an insistence that the recent proliferation of sex-related discourses in China has not entailed any transformatory effects, a move which surreptitiously reinstates the repressive hypothesis. Consequently, Western commentators can continue to portray the CCP as a patriarchal and sexuality-blind 'monolithic controller' of discourse with predictable, deleterious effects for Chinese women and men.

Even more bizarrely, Frank Dikötter (1995: 185) uses a Foucauldian-style methodology to demonstrate that Western and Chinese discourses on sex and sexuality have different genealogies, only to reach the negative conclusion that, in contrast to discourses on sexuality in twentieth-century Europe, sex has not been dissociated from procreation in China. This conclusion would be laughable – given that the One-child Family policy exhorts couples to engage in sex for non-procreative purposes – except that we are already primed to accept that it is not possible to 'live' one's sexuality as an expression of one's unique personal identity in puritanical-totalitarian China. Indeed, it is precisely due to the continued dominance of the popular understanding that sexuality is a natural and pre-given attribute of the universal, individual subject, that Dikötter can claim to be revealing the different genealogical underpinnings of Chinese discourses on sexuality, yet conclude by berating the CCP and mainland Chinese intellectuals for failing to acknowledge the inalienable rights of the autonomous sexual subject, a subject that Foucault (1978) and Li Yinhe (1997) variously suggest may be a specifically Western invention.

Despite their alleged concern to highlight the specificity of the Chinese case, therefore, all of the above-mentioned scholars assume that it *is* possible to predict the outcome of the particular nexus between Chinese modernity, the economy, and sexuality, in similar terms to the West, because of their unexamined commitment to Western conceptions of the individual as an autonomous sexual subject. For even as they reject teleological and Westerncentric forms of historical analysis, they *want* economic development to result in the formation of a 'new' kind of Chinese individual, one that does not necessarily have sexuality placed at its core, but one that can claim all the rights that accrue to the Western sexual-political subject nonetheless: that is, the 'right' to sexual self-determination, to be homosexual, to be promiscuous, to look at pornography, and work in the sex industry, and so forth, without being made subject to undue interference by 'the Chinese state'. As a result, any Foucauldian hint of optimism regarding the impossibility of reducing the relationship between power and sexuality to one of pure repression is omitted from their work. Cold War-style readings of the CCP are readmitted through the back door and the old sinological game of prophecy and prediction continues to be pursued, albeit in a modified form.

In sum, the unexamined adherence of most Western commentators on sex-related issues in the PRC to a juridical conception of power leaves them unable to account for the diversity of forces that are entailed in making governmental programmes of intervention operable, or for the ways in which points of congruence are established between the aspirations of Chinese government authorities and the activities of other individuals or groups. Tied to a reductive understanding of power as an institutional and prohibitory phenomenon, CCP-led attempts to govern diverse aspects of the Chinese population are read as outmoded forms of patriarchal-socialist repression, and the concern of Chinese intellectuals to establish how such interventions can be implemented most effectively is viewed as indicative of their historic and ongoing subjection to 'the Party police state'. To demonstrate how such analyses misconstrue the nexus between sexuality and power in the PRC, however, requires a more specific focus than the all-encompassing subject of sexuality. In this regard, I can think of no better example than a contentious sex-related issue like prostitution.

3 Feminist prostitution debates and responses

Prostitution and the new humanities

Prostitution is now identified as a transnational issue requiring global solutions in relation to its regulation and legislation. As such, it is not possible even to begin to elucidate metropolitan debates regarding prostitution in the PRC without understanding, in the first instance, the contested status and complex evolution of discourses on prostitution more generally. After all, the extent to which feminists are divided over the issue of prostitution is substantial, and this discord is due in no small part to recent developments in the new humanities.

Put simply, feminist theorists and activists disagree about the nature and effects of prostitution and, consequently, about its appropriate moral and legal status. Some view prostitution as the ultimate in the reduction of women to objects that can be bought and sold, and in terms of a sexual slavery which lies at the root of both marriage and prostitution, forming the foundation of women's oppression (Barry 1995; Jeffreys, S. 1997). Others see prostitution as an unconventional if sometimes demeaning form of work that nonetheless women have the right to choose (Thorbek and Pattanaik 2002). Yet others portray the female prostitute subject as a transgressive sexual-political minority, one whose challenge to the opposition between erotic/affective activity and economic life could have potentially liberatory effects for all women (Delacoste and Alexander 1987; Nagle 1997).

These competing accounts of prostitution cannot be reconciled by moving out of the 'ivory tower' and listening to the 'subaltern voice' of the female prostitute subject. Advocacy groups for prostitutes' rights are similarly characterized by considerable disagreement over the social meaning and appropriate response to prostitution. Most notably, organizations founded by or for prostitutes such as Women Hurt in Systems of Prostitution Engaged in Revolt (WHISPER) maintain that prostitution is premised on enforced sexual abuse under a system of male supremacy that is itself built along a continuum of coercion. As a result, WHISPER claim that no woman chooses prostitution and feminists should fight for its eradication as a form of aggravated sexual assault and a violation of women's rights. In contrast, the International Committee for Prostitutes' Rights (ICPR) defines prostitution as a form of service work that many women freely choose, and often enjoy, and contend that feminists should aim to eliminate the negative aspects of prostitution, while simultaneously guaranteeing its positive aspects, by promoting the rights of women to economic and sexual self-determination, and thus by placing the prostitution transaction under the jurisdiction of commerce and labour rather than criminal laws (Bell 1994: 123–31). Oral testimonies provided by female prostitutes, as well as academic texts produced by women with personal experience of prostitution, are similarly marked by divergent opinions as to whether prostitution is degrading, empowering, or, at the least, no worse than any ordinary job, and hence whether prostitution practices and businesses should be eradicated, left alone, or completely transformed ('Barbara' 1993: 11–22; 'Jasmin' 1993: 33–7; Koureskas 1995: 99–107; Kruhse-Mountburton 1996).

Given the recent polarization of this debate in terms of 'anti-prostitution' versus 'pro-sex work' factions, however, it seems appropriate to ask what intellectual modes of inquiry have characterized feminist responses to prostitution in the late twentieth century, and, perhaps even more importantly, whether they have any practical utility. After all, in recent years, a growing number of scholars have expressed concern that feminist accounts of prostitution, enmeshed as they are within the sexuality debates that began to openly divide the feminist movement during the 1980s, have not only reached a conceptual impasse, but have also failed to generate legally based strategies that can address the problems experienced by women in prostitution. Moreover, despite attracting some popular and governmental support, the prostitutes' rights campaign in the USA has been declared 'a failure' (Weitzer 1991: 23–41), and the international movement for prostitutes' rights based in the Netherlands has been pronounced 'a fiasco' (van der Poel 1995: 42).

Questions concerning the utility of feminist responses to prostitution turn on the vexatious relationship between prostitute discourses and feminist theories of sexuality, and the ensuing elision of the more practical issues associated with the 'good' policing and effective governmental management of prostitution businesses and practices. In consequence, it is useful to outline the predominant feminist approaches to prostitution and highlight some of the problems that are associated with them. Although the subject of China does not feature in this chapter, such an examination is a necessary precursor to indicating how the Chinese response to prostitution might be more usefully read as a theoretical point of departure for rethinking, rather than re-rehearsing, existing debates within the new humanities.

The development of theoretical approaches

Probably the earliest second-wave feminist text to focus exclusively on the subject of prostitution was *The Prostitution Papers*, written by the radical feminist, Kate Millet, and published in 1971. In an amended postscript to the 1975 second edition of this text, Millet notes that the first feminist conference on prostitution was held in December 1971 and it displayed all the hallmarks that have since made prostitution such a difficult subject for feminists. On the second day of the conference, tensions apparently exploded when a panel, which included numerous academics but no 'real experts' (read female prostitutes), was convened entitled 'Towards the elimination of prostitution'. A number of prostitutes who attended the panel subsequently took the floor and accused the speakers of being 'straights' who wanted to remove their livelihood. Heated arguments ensued, and, to paraphrase Millet's words, all the sophistry of the contemporary rhetoric of the women's liberation movement – that all women are prostitutes, that marriage is prostitution, that prostitutes are oppressed and prostitution is a form of female sexual slavery – proved to be of no avail. A chasm had opened between feminists and female prostitutes, with enraged prostitutes putting the well-intentioned (if somewhat naïve) organizers of the conference on the defensive by declaring that prostitutes – not female academics – were best equipped to speak on the subject of prostitution. For Millet (1971: 14–19), this incident turned the women's movement and female prostitute activists into members of opposing camps, a conflict which she hoped would be resolved by the foundation of the North American prostitutes' rights organization COYOTE (an acronym for 'Call Off Your Old Tired Ethics') in 1973.

From its very inception, however, COYOTE promoted a platform that diverged sharply from the radical feminist construction of prostitution as paradigmatic of women's sex-based oppression under the system of hetero-patriarchy. Instead of viewing prostitution as the worst-case scenario along a continuum of gendered, sexual-economic exchange, COYOTE put forward three quite different propositions. First, prostitution is predominantly a voluntarily selected occupation. Second, prostitution should be treated as equivalent in social status to other forms of waged labour, because the fact that it involves sexual activities of some kind does not make it inherently different from any other form of work. Third, legal restrictions on the practice of prostitution constitute a violation of civil rights regarding the freedom to choose employment and therefore should be repealed. By pressing their claims in terms of civil rights and liberal conceptions of 'free contract', 'work', and 'choice', COYOTE did not deny that women in prostitution frequently suffered exploitation and abuse. Rather, they argued that most of the problems associated with prostitution stemmed from prohibitory laws and negative social attitudes towards sex and especially sex work (Jenness 1990: 403–4).

COYOTE's tactical reconfiguration of the female prostitute subject as a sex worker victimized by 'bad laws' and 'sex-negative attitudes' attracted considerable support and ultimately spawned a whole host of affiliate prostitutes' organizations. By initiating national campaigns to highlight the discriminatory nature of prostitution laws, and contending that the 'real victim' of an arguably victimless crime such as prostitution is the taxpayer, COYOTE garnered support from the 'liberal public' and reform-minded government officials. In addition, they cemented significant ties with the women's movement in the USA by aligning themselves with the then existing 'Wages for Housework' campaign, supporting feminist struggles surrounding the Equal Rights Amendment, abortion, domestic violence, rape, and lesbian and gay rights, and developing grassroots services to assist female prostitutes with matters such as legal aid (St. James 1989: xvii–xx).

In retrospect, however, it appears that COYOTE's initial popularity stemmed more from its capacity to generate broad support against the discriminatory nature of prostitution controls than its implicitly celebratory reconfiguration of the female prostitute subject as a sex worker. The predominant focus on prostitution as 'work' rather than 'sex', for instance, meant that feminists could lobby for the decriminalization of prostitution practices as a necessary precondition for improving the working conditions of female prostitutes, by eliminating police harassment and corruption, without comprising their principled objection to prostitution, or even abandoning the long-term goal of abolishing the 'sex industry'. In effect, these issues were 'set aside' (Sullivan 1995: 188).

This inherent duality in feminist thinking about prostitution is most succinctly captured in a slogan put forward by the English Collective of Prostitutes (ECP) – 'for prostitutes, against prostitution' (Hunter 1992: 110). In marked contrast to COYOTE's utilization of the liberal rhetoric of work and civil rights, the ECP furnished an explanation for prostitution that largely concurred with the predominant strand of Marxist-socialist feminism which existed in the UK during the 1970s and early 1980s. As they argued, prostitution was a product of the economic inequality between the sexes. If women had better economic circumstances, then there would be no need for women to engage in prostitution; and, they further insisted, no woman would (ibid.: 110). The ECP basically elaborated upon Engels' critique of the propertied nature of the relation between the sexes, and Marx's metaphorical use of prostitution as a means to underscore the subordinated and alienated nature of wage labour under capitalism, in order to emphasize the hierarchical divisions of gender, class, and race, that both structure prostitution and find expression via the implementation of discriminatory prostitution controls.

The ECP's 'for prostitutes, against prostitution' stance continues to underpin many feminist accounts of prostitution, even though it has since been rejected by prostitutes' rights organizations. This approach initially appealed to feminists of all political persuasions because of its focus on the gendered nature of the sexual division of labour. Such a focus enabled feminists to highlight the exploitation experienced by female prostitutes at the hands of (male) pimps, panderers, and procurers, and due to the gendered, racist, and classist, nature of prostitution controls. It also focused attention on the tendency of law enforcement officials to harass and penalize women in prostitution, especially those at the lower level of the prostitute hierarchy (i.e., those most in economic need), while effectively ignoring the activities of male clients (Chancer 1993: 151; Satz 1995: 79, 83). In short, this approach proved attractive because it enabled radical, liberal, and socialist feminists alike to express solidarity with the female prostitute subject by exposing the double standard inherent in 'state-enforced' prostitution controls, and, subsequently, to offer qualified support for struggles aiming to ameliorate the exploitative conditions experienced by women in prostitution.

According to many prostitutes' rights organizations, however, the notion of 'for prostitutes, against prostitution' is both apologist and outdated. Most significantly, it precludes the claim of many sex workers to have freely chosen and also to enjoy prostitution as a job option, since the moral presumption that no woman would willingly prostitute (or sell herself) renders such claims untenable other than as an expression of 'false consciousness', or as a psychological coping-mechanism for dealing with the emotional damage incurred by their very involvement in prostitution (Alexander 1997: 83; Hunter 1992: 111). Concomitantly, by focusing on the wrongs of prostitution, and thereby searching for causal explanations, this approach ultimately implies that there must be something 'wrong' with sex workers, or, at the very least, that female prostitutes are somehow distinguishable from other women, since not all economically disadvantaged women choose to enter prostitution (see Overall 1992: 705–25; Pateman 1988: 189–218). In sum, many prostitutes' rights organizations contend that the 'for prostitutes, against prostitution' platform ignores the many positive aspects of prostitution as an employment option and keeps intact the very 'sex-negative' attitudes that contribute to the social stigmatization of the female prostitute subject as whore.

The perception that classic feminist approaches are somehow anti-sex, or unwilling to radically engage with the politics of sexual difference, gained increased critical purchase following the establishment of the International Committee for Prostitutes' Rights (ICPR) in 1985. ICPR, whose inception owed much to the founding members and international aspirations of COYOTE, was founded at the First World Whores' Congress in Amsterdam in 1985, and sponsored the Second World Whores' Congress in Brussels in 1986 (Jenness 1990: 410; Pheterson 1989: 3). Prostitutes' rights activists often cite the formation of ICPR as groundbreaking in that it gave birth to a new politics of prostitution, one based on prostitutes' self-representation and the perspectives of prostitutes themselves. This new politics of prostitution demands public recognition of prostitutes' rights as an emancipation and labour issue and opposes any construction of prostitution in terms of criminality, immorality or disease. In addition, it challenges radical feminist constructions of prostitution in terms of 'subordinated sex', and socialist feminist constructions of prostitution in terms of 'subordinated labour', by contending that sex workers are an oppressed sexual minority and thereby linking the fight for prostitutes' rights to the cause of radical sexual liberation.

In contrast, prostitutes' organizations such as WHISPER, which was also founded in 1985, have rejected ICPR's construction of prostitutes as legitimate workers and an oppressed sexual identity. According to WHISPER, the prostitutes' rights movement has constructed a mythology of 'liberal lies' to the effect that prostitution is a 'career choice', that prostitution 'epitomizes women's sexual liberation', and that prostitutes 'set the sexual and economic conditions of their interactions with customers' (Giobbe 1990: 80). For members of WHISPER, nothing could be further from the truth. So far as they are concerned, prostitution is 'nothing less than the commercialization of the sexual abuse and inequality that women suffer in the traditional family and can be nothing more' (ibid.). And in refutation of ICPR's depiction of prostitution as empowering, or, at the very least, no worse than any ordinary job, WHISPER's Oral History Project, a first-person documentation of the lives of women self-described as having been 'used' in systems of prostitution, is replete with accounts of women physically degraded and emotionally traumatized by their experiences. Not surprisingly, members of WHISPER describe themselves as 'survivors' of prostitution and have developed various outreach programmes designed to empower women to escape from the 'victimization' that is prostitution (Bell, S. 1994: 123–31).

The transparent alignment of WHISPER with radical feminist theorizations of sexuality, particularly those that underpin the anti-pornography campaign, and the corresponding alignment of the prostitutes' rights movement with the feminist sex radical position, have meant that feminist responses to prostitution have become polarized on similar lines to those that characterized 'the sex wars'. As discussed in Chapter 2, 'the sex wars' flowed from a fundamental conflict within North American feminism over the meanings of sex and sexuality for women. This conflict has been variously described but revolves around the question of whether female desire is always/already subordinate to male power, and therefore an expression of women's sexual colonization and victimization under the system of hetero-patriarchy (the so-called 'victim' model), or whether women's liberation might be better achieved by rejecting the traditional dichotomization of women into good girls/bad girls, madonnas/whores, and hence refusing to organize one's sexual desire and pleasure in terms of the repressive and passive roles that are traditionally ascribed to female sexuality within dominant discourses (the so-called 'agency' model). Once combined with the kinds of hierarchical divisions that currently condition the poststructuralist academe, this conflict has meant that feminist prostitution debates have become polarized around two diametrically opposed perspectives – the radical feminist versus the sex radical, queer, and/or poststructuralist-feminist positions.[1]

Prostitution and 'the sex wars'

At one extreme of the feminist prostitution debate there is the anti-prostitution lobby, which relies almost exclusively on radical feminist theorizations of sexuality. Following Catharine MacKinnon (1989: 128) radical feminists generally argue that sexuality is 'a social construct of male power defined by men, forced on women, and constitutive of the meaning of gender'. This contention rearticulates the early radical feminist counter to Marxism–socialism, namely, that sex, not economic class, constitutes the primary contradiction in women's lives, and that women *as women* constitute a class in struggle against men as a class. Radical feminists thus oppose the institution of prostitution on the grounds that it arises from a particular system of political oppression – male supremacy – and denies women their full status as human beings by reducing them to the level of objects. In keeping with their ongoing critique of the system of hetero-patriarchy, radical feminists also locate prostitution on a continuum with the forms of sexual abuse and inequality that women frequently experience within the traditional family system, and insist that prostitution will continue to exist so long as existing gendered structures of power and desire remain intact.

Interestingly enough, and contrary to the popular feminist contention that the Marxist canon is irredeemably gender-blind, the radical feminist construction of prostitution as paradigmatic of women's sex-based oppression under the system of hetero-patriarchy owes much to the utopian sexual politics of Friedrich Engels. In his classic text, *The Origin of the Family, Private Property and the State*, Engels (1972) maintains that prostitution is the historic complement of the bourgeois marriage system. This system, he continues, was founded on the open or concealed domestic slavery of women for the purposes of propagation and ensuring patrilineal descent, and thus produced the first class opposition in society, namely, the antagonism between women and men.

Engels further maintained that prostitution would only 'disappear' following the abolition of capitalist property relations, and the institution of monogamous, bourgeois marriage, for three consecutive reasons. First, the transformation of the means of production into social property, the socialization of domestic labour and child-care, and the involvement of women in large-scale social production, would remove the economic conditions which predispose women to enter prostitution. Second, the transformation of these conditions would allow marriage to become a free union between two equals, one based on reciprocity and mutual sexual love, as opposed to being an arranged union based on economic or class considerations. Third, once the conditions supporting a system of marriage based on property relations and the presumption of male supremacy were destroyed, monogamy would finally become a reality for men, not a social demand of women alone. In short, Engels believed that the abolition of property, and hence the material basis for male supremacy, would remove the conditions that have historically enabled men to claim unilateral access to women's bodies as 'wives' or 'whores'.

Radical feminist theorizations of prostitution clearly reiterate the main conceptual parameters of Engels' work, even as they claim to exchange and surpass his (Marxist) emphasis on the economically determined nature of women's subordination with a (feminist) focus on the psychological and socially conditioned aspects of women's oppression as a gendered sex-class (Millet 1971: 49–67). Bearing this theoretical debt in mind, it strikes me that the accusations of biological essentialism and anti-sex prudery, which are so often flung at radical feminism, may be somewhat misplaced. The homogenizing move in most radical feminist theorizations does not follow strictly from an intractable adherence to naturalized conceptions of 'maleness' and 'femaleness'. For even though radical feminists consistently fall back on deterministic readings of the nature of male sexuality and desire, they are equally adamant that the relationship between the sexes is a social and hence transformable product (Rowland and Klein 1996: 9–36). The homogenizing move in most radical feminist theorizations of sexuality stems from their unexamined rearticulation of Engels' suggestion that existing sexual relations have prevented both women and men alike from realizing their full human capacity.

Like Engels, for instance, radical feminist theorists of sexuality have experienced enormous difficulty in articulating what a future and more 'ideal' form of human sexuality will look like. While Engels conjectured that the family of the future would probably be a monogamian, heterosexual family unit, he insisted that his speculations were necessarily limited to the question of what should disappear with the overthrow of capitalist property relations, namely, the assumption of male supremacy and female inferiority, and hence the related institutions of bourgeois marriage and prostitution. As to the question of what socialist sexual relations and/or marriage would look like, Engels replied:

> That will be answered when a new generation has grown up: a group of men who never in their lives have known what it is to buy a woman's surrender with money or any other social instrument of power; a generation of women who have never known what it is to give themselves to a man from any other considerations than real love, or to refuse to give themselves to their lover from fear of the economic consequences. When these people are in the world, they will care

precious little what anybody today thinks they ought to do; they will make their own practice and their corresponding public opinion about the practice of the individual – and that will be the end of it.

(1972: 145)

Radical feminists, however, cannot afford to be quite so 'open-ended' regarding the question of what future sexual relations will look like. Their rearticulation of the Marxist canon, combined with the implicit suggestion that feminism constitutes a more advanced and revolutionary form of politics than Marxism, means that their primary objective is to undermine the related institutions of heterosexuality, marriage, and prostitution, in which men 'use' women's sexuality for their own pleasure and reproduction, rather than to first realize the 'end of capitalism'. Unlike Engels, therefore, radical feminists are more or less obliged to say what they think a more 'ideal' form of human sexuality will look like; and, not surprisingly, none do this very well. Those that try tend to fall back on a normalizing discourse of human sexuality, or the idea that sexual relations should be long-term and take place in conditions of mutual love and reciprocity, rather than replicating the relations of subordination and domination which they associate with male sexuality or patriarchal society and culture.

It is precisely this continued commitment to a totalizing conception of emancipatory politics, one that must inevitably fall back on certain prescriptive assessments regarding what is 'not-feminist' and 'not-revolutionary' sexual-political behaviour in order to project a utopian feminist future, that has opened radical feminism to attack from feminists with different theoretical allegiances. One of the major contributions of poststructuralist-feminist scholarship has been to show that sexuality, in the sense of sexual behaviours, structures, and meanings, has to be theorized independently of its location in male, female, or otherwise gendered bodies. This contention is antithetical to radical and classic gender Feminism, which is grounded in the assumption that all institutions, structures, and concepts have different meanings for women and men. It suggests that there is neither a general global condition of female oppression nor a privileged locus of female resistance, and thereby undermines both the *raison d'être* for the women's liberation movement *and* the claim of radical feminists to speak for all women. It is hardly surprising, therefore, that radical feminists tend to view theoretical approaches of this kind as anti-feminist, male-identified, and apolitical.

The largely polemic opposition of radical feminists to the incursion of theory has proved to be somewhat self-defeating, however, since the radical feminist rendition of 'men' as 'the oppressors' and 'women' as 'the oppressed' – a framework which leads them to construct monolithic representations of women and their needs – has generated considerable controversy among both the lesbian feminist movement and among women of colour. A major argument here is that the radical feminist reification of the political lesbian subject as the quintessential feminist – a tendency encapsulated in the slogan: 'feminism is the theory, lesbianism is the practice' – has made lesbian identity far more important than lesbian sexual practices. Moreover, it has led radical feminists to impose a 'suffocating' form of sexuality on all women via the suggestion that lesbian sexuality is either *naturally* different from heterosexual sexuality, or that it *should not* replicate the relations of subordination and domination which they associate with male-defined sexual practices.

According to the Chicana writer, Cherríe Moraga (1983: 125), for instance, the radical feminist prescription that 'real' lesbian (and hence feminist) sex should be loving, monogamous and nurturing, enacts a form of cultural imperialism by ignoring the specificities of different sexual cultures. Citing the radical lesbian feminist attack on butch-fem role-playing as a case in point, Moraga maintains that the prescriptive assumption that butch-fem role-playing constitutes a gross mimicry of heterosexuality effectively erases cultural and sexual differences. Speaking from her own perspective as both a lesbian feminist and a Chicana, Moraga avers that she experiences butch-fem role-playing as an empowering and subversive 'play' on the commonly understood gender roles within Mexican culture. In a similar fashion, lesbian feminist practitioners of sadomasochism have rejected radical feminist arguments to the effect that sadomasochistic practices replicate and reify the violence associated with male sexuality and patriarchal relations of subordination and domination. As they argue, sadomasochistic sexuality is about disrupting extant gender boundaries and creating a new non-violent organization of bodily pleasures, as indicated by the tripartite mantra that informs the activities of many gay and lesbian s/m organizations, namely, 'safe, sane, and consensual' (Hart and Dale 1997: 344).

Flowing from the effective explosion of Feminism into feminisms, at the other extreme of the feminist prostitution debate there is not so much a 'pro-prostitution' lobby as an anti-anti-prostitution perspective, or an assorted group of feminist scholars and prostitutes' rights activists who are unified primarily by their opposition to radical feminist theorizations of sexuality. This is not to deny that many feminist theorists and prostitutes' rights activists offer full support for the reconfiguration of prostitution as sex work, and some have played an active role in promoting the more contentious construction of the female prostitute subject as a transgressive sexual-political identity. But the fact remains that many of the arguments mounted on the so-called pro-prostitution side of the debate do not constitute an unqualified endorsement of prostitution practices and businesses so much as a direct reaction to radical feminist theorizations of sexuality, especially the informing assumptions of the anti-pornography campaign.

In this respect, Gayle Rubin's 'Thinking sex: notes for a radical theory of the politics of sexuality' has proved seminal, being consistently cited as a key theoretical contribution to the 'sex debates' which have redefined the terrain of North American feminism since the mid-1980s (Rubin 1984: 3–31). In this article, Rubin argues for a radical pluralist theory of sexuality via a critique of radical feminism. Describing radical feminism as more a 'sexual demonology' than a theory of sexuality, Rubin (ibid.: 28–9) castigates the moralistic, 'anti-porn fascism' of radical feminists as indicative of their unremittingly ugly portrayal of human sexuality and concomitant refusal to accept that their 'ideological' prescriptions have produced 'the most retrogressive sexual thinking this side of the Vatican'. Sexology, Foucault, and gay liberationists, she continues, have shown us that sexual variation is infinite, that sexuality is as much a human product as are diets and systems of etiquette, and that it is possible to challenge the sex-negative attitudes which underpin the legal regulation of so-called deviant sexual conduct. Arguing that radical feminists have simply overlaid the conservative valorization of monogamous, heterosexual sex with monogamous, lesbian sex, Rubin contends that progressive sexual liberationists should acknowledge that consensual sexual acts, whether cross-generational, transsexual, sadomasochistic or commercial, are not vices to be prohibited, and thereby kept marginal and distorted. Rather, she maintains that achieving the desired feminist goal of sexual liberation demands a 'pro-sex' approach, one that allows people to engage in what are ultimately consensual, if unconventional, sexual practices, while continuing to oppose systemic, structural inequalities.

The significance of Rubin's text thus lies in its explicit challenge to the former hegemony of radical feminism in the USA and concomitant opening of the theoretical space for what has since become unified under the rubric of lesbian and gay studies, or queer theory. Put crudely, Rubin's main argument is that the radical feminist construction of sexual liberalization as simply an extension of male privilege has effectively ceded sex to men. For like the conservative 'anti-sexual' attitudes of mainstream society, radical feminism has also placed enormous restrictions on female sexual behaviour, by privileging monogamous, lesbian sex as the fullest expression of feminist egalitarianism, and ultimately depriving female heterosexual desire of any legitimacy, agency, or content. Calling for a form of sexual liberation that will work for women as well as for men, therefore, Rubin utilizes the work of sexologists and poststructuralist theorists to suggest that people already organize their desires in terms that far exceed homogeneous conceptions of patriarchy and the homo-hetero binary (the act of defining sexual identity in terms of gender of object choice). In doing so, Rubin's 'Thinking sex' has enabled theorists of sexuality to argue that unconventional sexual practices should be positively re-evaluated because they perform or 'play on' conventional sexual scripts, as opposed to merely replicating them, and thus have the potential to generate a form of sexual politics which transcends the limiting binaries of male/female, heterosexual, and homosexual.

As active proponents of lesbian sadomasochism, both Rubin's work and, in more recent years, the work of Pat Califia (1988, 1994), have helped to promote the celebratory conception of the female prostitute subject as both a sex worker *and* a transgressive, sexual-political identity. To begin with, although Rubin intimates that prostitution practices can be distinguished from those of 'other sexual minorities', in that prostitution refers to an occupation rather than an erotic preference, her coupling of commercial sex workers with other oppressed erotic minorities has proved popular with organizations for prostitutes' rights because it enables them to affiliate with other groups as part of a broader-based movement to destigmatize sex and sexuality. In addition, Rubin's 'Thinking sex' not only offers unqualified support for the demand that prostitutes be granted the right to economic and sexual self-determination, it has also enabled some sex workers, especially prostitute performance artists, to insist that they are 'sex-positive', that is, to claim that they enjoy the sex in their work and are simultaneously engaged in a spiritualistic or carnivalesqe disruption of the conventional division of women in terms of feminist/mother/good girl and male-identified/slut/bad girl (Bell, S. 1994: 137–84). In short, prostitutes' rights activists have utilized poststructuralist and queer theorizations of sexuality to reject both the radical feminist emphasis on prostitution as sexual violence, and the former emphasis of socialist feminists on prostitution as subordinated labour, on the grounds that their joint concern with 'the problem of prostitution' displays an anti-sex/sexual difference position, i.e., they are sexuality-blind.

Somewhat ironically, however, if radical feminists ultimately fall back on deterministic readings of the system of hetero-patriarchy in order to posit an alternative feminist future, the sex radical position also turns on a certain latent sex essentialism. Most notably, although sex radical and queer theorists have done much to problematize popular conceptions of gender and sexual identity, they have signally failed to de-essentialize sex. Indeed, even though queer theorists insist that sexuality is a historical product, and have moved towards an increasing focus on the culturally-conditioned nature of desire, fantasy, and pleasure, their continued appeal to notions of 'sex-negativity' and the transgressive nature of 'doing the forbidden' veers towards reinstating the (most unFoucauldian) repressive hypothesis. More precisely, their valorization of 'the forbidden' reinstates the idea that what mainstream society perceives as perverse sexual acts, while not exactly referring to a fixed sexual identity, exist in a 'natural' state of opposition to the assumed repressive and predatory aims of government. In doing so, sex radicals and queer theorists tend to replicate even as they redefine the utopian sexual politics of radical feminism, in that they are similarly concerned to elaborate what 'kind of sex *counts* as progressive' (Glick 2000: 21).

Concomitantly, although the feminist sex radical position is sympathetic to the prostitutes' rights movement, this sympathy turns on the presumption that prostitution is simply another configuration of sexual desire and pleasure (Zatz 1997: 294). This characterization of prostitution has proved useful insofar as it links the demand for prostitutes' rights to the cause of other oppressed sexual minorities and intimates that prostitution is treated differently from other forms of employment only because of the sex. But the sex radical rendition of prostitution as merely another sexual variable obscures the fact that most women prostitute for money, 'not because sex for money turns them on' (ibid.: 294). In fact, many female prostitutes argue that they do not experience prostitution as sex but rather as sex without desire or a sex act.

The tendency of sex radicals to lump prostitutes together with other oppressed sexual minorities thus has the paradoxical effect of homogenizing prostitution practices and eliding the experiential diversity of sex workers and prostitute clients. Somewhat paradoxically, this move is not always quite so apparent in radical and socialist feminist *empirical* accounts of prostitution because of their predominant concern with the structuring effects of gendered and economic inequalities. For even though the principled objection of radical and other feminists to the institution of prostitution leads them to posit monocausal explanations for the existence of prostitution per se, their concern with the differential effects of gendered social and economic inequalities for women vis-à-vis men has also done much to highlight the diversity of prostitution businesses and practices, as well as to demonstrate that participants in prostitution practices experience their involvement in varying ways. Indeed, the work of feminist anti-prostitution activists in practice – for example, their concern with the differential subjectifying effects of engagement in the 'sex industry' for women and men – often raises precisely the kinds of issues that need to be *theorized*.

Viewed from this perspective, the polarization of feminist prostitution debates in terms of a position that proclaims itself as 'feminist', but is accused of being essentialist, moralistic, and anti-sex, on the one hand, and a position that proclaims itself as 'progressive' and theoretically superior, but is accused of advocating a male-identified, 'anything goes' sexual libertarianism, on the other, constitutes a classic example of two groups talking past each other. Both sides insist that there can be no middle ground, while simultaneously placing the blame for their intractability on the extremist nature of the other 'camp'. However, if radical feminists and supporters of the prostitutes' rights movement hold divergent views on the nature and meaning of prostitution, they tend to concur on one broad point. They both agree that governmental strategies designed either to prohibit or license prostitution activities are problematic and should be altered; and it is to a discussion of why two groups with such differing perspectives should agree on this issue that I now turn.

Feminist legal responses to prostitution

Feminist scholars and prostitutes' rights organizations alike reject the traditional prohibitionist approach to prostitution – a system wherein the prostitution transaction and all prostitution-related activities are deemed illegal – on the grounds that it places the primary burden of responsibility for prostitution on women and enhances the exploitative aspects of prostitution (Shrage 1994: 82). A standard empirical referent here is the high rate of female prostitute arrests vis-à-vis the number of male client arrests in the USA (Chancer 1993: 151). Feminists and prostitutes' rights organizations thus oppose traditional prohibitionist approaches to prostitution on the grounds that they reinforce the gendered, double standard, both by making it a worse crime to sell sex than to buy it, and by exposing female prostitutes to exploitation at the hands of predatory (male) pimps and corrupt (male) police (Millet 1971: 50–1).

A connected line of argument is that, in situations where prostitution is criminalized, female prostitutes cannot alert the police to the existence of dangerous clients, exploitative bosses and violent pimps, since, by the very act of coming forward, they implicate themselves in an illegal trade, and thereby risk summary arrests, fines, penal confinement, and even deportation and confiscation of property (McClintock 1993: 3). It has also been noted that, while the 'typical customers' of (white) 'call girls' who command relatively high prices are predominantly middle-class men between the ages of 30 and 60, those most penalized by the law in both the USA and the UK are young black women who, due to economic hardship, are forced onto the streets and into acts of blatant solicitation where the risk of arrest is highest (Flowers 1987: 129). Prostitutes' rights activists and feminist scholars alike thus reject traditional prohibitionist approaches to prostitution on the grounds that they reinforce the already inequitable hierarchies of gender, race, age, and class, which structure the 'sex industry', while simultaneously functioning to punish, rather than protect, women, particularly working-class women and women of colour (McClintock 1992: 88).

Feminist scholars and prostitutes' rights organizations also oppose conventional systems of legalizing or licensing prostitution (Pheterson 1989: 8–10). Under the German system, for instance, prostitution is legalized and confined to certain metropolitan areas, but pimping and other activities associated with the organization of prostitution remain illegal. Regulationist systems of this kind are premised on the liberal understanding that prostitution is an inevitable and perhaps even necessary social institution, but one that may also entail a certain degree or risk of harm which laws should aim to minimize or prevent (Tong 1984: 47). Hence the policy of licensing prostitution purports to benefit female prostitutes, by removing them from the coercive control of pimps and procurers, and to curb the instance of rape and therefore diminish the risk of harm to women in general, by ensuring that men have an 'affordable' access for their assumed 'innate' and 'natural' sex drive. In a similar fashion, the policy of restricting the presence of brothels and street-walkers to certain fixed locales is intended to minimize the potential 'moral offence' of prostitution to other citizens, while the stipulation that licensed prostitutes undergo regular health checks is meant to halt the spread of sexually transmissible diseases, both within the system of prostitution and throughout society at large (Barry 1995: 228).

Prostitutes' rights organizations, however, ultimately reject government-led attempts to license and prohibit prostitution on the grounds that they are simply the 'flip-side' of the same coin. As they argue, legalized prostitution is the equivalent of legalized abuse since, despite its benign ring, it often renders women in prostitution subject to even greater degrees of 'state' and/or 'male' control, and still locates many aspects of prostitution under the jurisdiction of the criminal code rather than commerce and labour laws. A standard argument here is that, under legalized systems of prostitution, the profits to be made from prostitution go to the predominantly male managers of the 'sex industry', or else to 'the state' in the form of exorbitantly high taxes which are not returned in the usual form of sickness benefits, pensions, etc. Concomitantly, the prevalence of 'bad work practices' in legalized brothels often means that female prostitutes have to work long hours and accept clients who they may personally object to, but whom the management has deemed acceptable. As a result, even in countries where certain forms of prostitution are legalized, many prostitutes prefer to continue working illegally (i.e., outside of government-sanctioned places of prostitution), rather than submit to the diverse rules governing legal businesses (Chapkis 1997: 162–4; McClintock 1992: 89–90).

Feminist scholars similarly object to the governmental regulation of prostitution on the grounds that it subjects female prostitutes to even greater degrees of male control. Unlike the more 'work-orientated' focus of arguments mounted by prostitutes' rights activists, however, feminist scholars often object to the governmental licensing of prostitution in broader theoretico-philosophical terms. Liberal feminists, for example, tend to oppose prohibitory laws on the grounds that they deprive many women of the only means to improve their circumstances. But they are divided as to whether improved governmental management of prostitution practices and businesses would provide better opportunities for women, or simply create another female job ghetto (Shrage 1996: 44). Conversely, radical and socialist feminists usually oppose the governmental regulation of sex work on the grounds that it serves to normalize prostitution by institutionalizing the concept that every man has the right, albeit a monetary one, to gain access to the female body whenever he wants and on his own terms (Barry 1995; Pateman 1988). Classic feminist approaches thus retain either an explicit or latent objection to the phenomenon of prostitution, one that is not apparent in sex radical and queer theorizations, or in the arguments put forward by the prostitutes' rights movement.

Despite such differences, feminists and prostitutes' rights organizations alike concur that 'state-led' efforts to prohibit or license prostitution function to the detriment of the female prostitute subject. Consequently, there is broad-based support for the notion that the activities of female prostitutes should be decriminalized, as in removed from the jurisdiction of the criminal code. Beyond this broad consensus, however, there remains substantial disagreement over the meaning of the term 'decriminalization' and hence the actual form that a feminist policy of decriminalization should take. Used in some contexts, the term 'decriminalization' comprises a demand that the activities of prostitutes and prostitute clients should be removed from the jurisdiction of the criminal code, but the activities of pimps, panderers, and procurers should remain subject to criminal sanctions. This concept of decriminalization basically reiterates the historical response to prostitution known as abolition. As used by the prostitutes' rights movement, however, the term 'decriminalization' means 'total decriminalization' as in the repeal of all laws against consensual adult sexual activity in commercial and non-commercial contexts, including laws against pimping and other non-coercive third-party involvement in prostitution (Prostitutes' Education Network (n.d.)).

The question of what constitutes an appropriate feminist legal response to prostitution is thus largely contingent on whether the term 'decriminalization' is understood in relation to abolition or total decriminalization. Historically, the abolitionist movement against the state regulation of prostitution was led by the nineteenth-century feminist and social purity campaigner, Josephine Butler, and fought for the abolition of the governmental licensing of prostitution, not, as its name might imply, for the prohibition of prostitution per se (Butler 1896; Fisher 1996: 32–8). Briefly, nineteenth-century proponents of abolition argued that the activities of female prostitutes and their clients should be removed from the purview of the law, while pimping, procuring, and trafficking, and third-party involvement in brothels and other places of prostitution, should be made subject to stricter criminal sanctions. This approach was premised on the understanding that those who forced or coerced women into prostitution should be severely penalized, but 'the state' should not intervene either to prohibit or license prostitution because both systems worked to the disadvantage of the female prostitute subject, not the male prostitute client. Expressed in this way, abolition is coterminous with the delimited strategy of decriminalization supported by those who endorse a 'for prostitutes, against prostitution' stance. It appeals to feminists and prostitutes' organizations who wish to ameliorate the exploitation experienced by women in prostitution, but who retain a principled objection to the institution of prostitution.

In keeping with the polarization of feminist prostitution debates, however, arguments concerning the decriminalization of prostitution practices have also diverged along two opposing lines. WHISPER and radical feminist theorists of sexuality contend that the historical strategy of abolition should be reconfigured so as to remove the exploitative conditions experienced by women in prostitution, but also guarantee the eradication of prostitution. In consequence, they oppose the abolition of laws on pimping and procuring, arguing that their repeal would be equivalent to promoting sexual assault, and support the decriminalization of all laws that contain punitive provisions for women in prostitution, while simultaneously insisting that male prostitute clients should be made an explicit target of legal sanctions. Put another way, WHISPER and radical feminist theorists of sexuality want to shift the moral onus and legal burden of criminalization from female prostitutes to those whom they believe create the demand for prostitution in the first place, namely, male clients, but they do so with an eye towards the elimination of prostitution all together (Raymond 1995: 18). This kind of approach has now realized concrete expression for, on 1 January 1999, Sweden became the first country in the developed West to outlaw the buying but not the selling of sex, by decriminalizing the activities of female prostitutes and simultaneously making it an offence to obtain casual sexual services against payment, punishable by a system of fines and up to six months penal confinement (Gould 2001: 437–56).

While the results of adopting this strategy in Sweden have yet to be fully assessed, relocating the moral responsibility for prostitution onto the male side of demand will not necessarily function to ameliorate the exploitative conditions experienced by women in prostitution, or even produce the desired effect of eliminating prostitution. Relocating the punitive emphasis of prostitution controls onto the male side of demand may neither eliminate nor substantially diminish the demand for women in prostitution since the illicit and clandestine nature of participating in prostitutional sex is arguably what makes the transaction desirable for a certain group of men (Sharpe 1998: 123, 156). Furthermore, attempts to redress the gendered bias of prostitution controls have proved remarkably unsuccessful to date. To offer one example, in the interests of gender-fairness and also to appease complaints from the general public, police officers in countries such as Britain and Australia adopted a temporary strategy of targeting the activities of male kerb-crawlers as opposed to female streetwalkers. Women in street prostitution, however, roundly condemned this tactic on the grounds that it exposed them to a higher risk of exploitation and violence. To overcome the increased fear of apprehension on the part of prospective clients, they were obliged to reduce the amount of time normally taken to negotiate services and prices, as well as to assess the general character of a potential client, before getting into a vehicle (Edwards and Armstrong 1988: 209–19; McClintock 1992: 85–6).

As this example suggests, radical feminist theorists of prostitution may be guilty of getting their analyses partially 'back-to-front'. After all, if legally based efforts to deter prostitution actually produce the kinds of problems that give rise to calls for the eradication of prostitution in the first place, then a more appropriate response might be to eliminate those efforts rather than commercial sex (Zatz 1997: 304). This is not to say that the socio-cultural production of prostitution occurs through mechanisms that are exclusive to the law alone. Radical feminists have demonstrated most forcibly that the socio-cultural production of prostitution is linked to the organization of gender and sexuality, just as social feminists have shown its myriad connections to the organization of labour. It is simply to point out, as the work of prostitutes' rights activists suggests, that radical feminist theorists of prostitution tend to underestimate how much of what they identify as harmful in prostitution is a product not of the inherent character of sex work or sexuality itself, but rather of the specific regimes of legal regulation and moral condemnation which function to marginalize and oppress sex workers (ibid.: 290). In any case, if we accept the radical and socialist feminist contention that the overwhelming majority of female prostitutes are forced into systems of prostitution due to personal and economic hardship, then it is difficult to see how criminalizing the male prostitute client is intended to work to their advantage.

Certainly, so far as prostitutes' rights activists are concerned, abolitionist strategies in general constitute a 'calamitous' attempt to liberate the worker by eliminating the work (McClintock 1993; Pheterson 1996: 60). Like WHISPER, the prostitutes' rights movement does not deny that prostitution is the product of a male-dominated consumer society and hence structured by gendered inequalities. Unlike WHISPER, however, they argue that the decision to prostitute is as free a choice as any that can be made in the context of racist, capitalist, patriarchal, Western societies; moreover, it is one of the few 'games' that women can play and win for the cost of being exploited, as most women are anyway. Consequently, the prostitutes' rights movement demands the decriminalization of all aspects of adult prostitution that result from individual decision, namely, in the context of 'voluntary' as opposed to 'forced' prostitution.

This strategy of total decriminalization was first outlined in the 'World charter for prostitutes' rights' – which was issued by ICPR following the First World Whores' Congress in 1985 – and entails two main components (International Committee for Prostitutes' Rights 1993: 183–5). First, it demands the decriminalization of the prostitution transaction *and* the repeal of existing laws against pimping. This is because many sex workers argue that laws against living off the earnings of a prostitute, and/or cohabiting with a prostitute, function to their detriment, rather than presumed benefit, by preventing them from acting as the primary wage earners for their families. A standard argument here is that 'the exploitative pimp' (just like classical conceptions of the 'villainous brothel-keeper') is largely a thing of the past, or else a phenomenon connected with 'forced prostitution'. Hence the continued existence of pimping laws functions to deny female prostitutes the ordinary support of lovers and friends by rendering chosen protectors potentially subject to criminal sanctions (Bell, S. 1994: 129).

Second, the 'World charter for prostitutes' rights' demands the relocation of prostitution practices and businesses from the jurisdiction of the criminal code to the domain of standard commerce and labour laws. Subsequent to this shift, prostitutes should pay taxes on the same basis as other independent contractors, or employees, and receive the same social benefits in return; and, third-party involvement in prostitution should be regulated under standard business codes, with the provision of special clauses to prevent the abuse and stigmatization of female prostitutes. The 'World charter for prostitutes' rights' also demands the implementation of public education programmes designed to promote safe sex practices, change discriminatory social attitudes towards prostitutes, and generate public awareness of the crucial role played by the (historically 'invisible') male client within the phenomenon of prostitution. At the same time, it rejects the implementation of any laws that imply the systematic zoning of prostitution, arguing that prostitutes should be able to provide their services under conditions that are absolutely determined by themselves and no one else (International Committee for Prostitutes' Rights 1993: 183).

One evident problem with this latter statement is that it portrays prostitution as an essentially private matter in which neither the general public nor governmental authorities should have any interest. And, it is precisely this slippage between advocating a policy of decriminalization *with* legal regulations, and what ultimately amounts to a laissez-faire policy of decriminalization, that has brought the prostitutes' rights movement into question. After all, it is quite conceivable that the gradual introduction of worker's rights – 'making the legal position of prostitutes identical to that of workers in other (legal) industries' – will function to alleviate or remove many of the problems currently associated with prostitution (van der Poel 1995: 46). But bringing prostitution businesses and practices under the jurisdiction of commerce and labour laws would necessarily entail the introduction of some system of licensing and/or zoning so that local governments and other relevant authorities could fulfil standard requirements concerning the establishment, the facilities, and, most importantly, the working conditions, of business operations within the social service sector. Furthermore, from the viewpoint of the police – who, lest we forget, have to deal with issues of criminality, as well as complaints of impediment and disturbance from residents in neighbourhoods where prostitution activities occur – a system of prostitution controls is exactly what is needed to guarantee the observance of public order, and effect a working compromise between the interests of sex workers, the men who demand their services, and the broader community.

Despite its apparent yearning for legality and respectability, therefore, the prostitutes' rights movement has a curious tendency to assume that prostitution can be transformed into an acceptable form of employment without having to undergo the inescapable bureaucratic processes associated with the standardization and regulation of any profession. This opposition to the 'administrative normalization' of prostitution stems, in no small part, from the general distrust felt by prostitutes' rights activists and feminist scholars alike towards the so-called male-dominated state. But, once combined with the presumption that the prostitution transaction is essentially a private matter between consenting individuals, this distrust functions to preclude the question of how prostitution businesses might attain an 'acceptable' business-economic, financial, and juridical form, under a woman-centred leadership (Tong 1984: 80; van der Poel 1995: 50).

Opposition to the administrative normalization of prostitution also stems from the fact that many participants in prostitution are not interested in working in legal premises, paying taxes, and so forth. This is particularly the case with regard to occasional prostitutes, incorporating single or married women who want to earn additional disposable income, drug addicts, homeless youth and illegal immigrants, who either do not want the legal status of a prostitute, or who would be ultimately precluded from working legally as a sex worker due to considerations such as age and immigration controls. Unfortunately, although street prostitution is often cited as an independent, profitable, and flexible, form of work, one that avoids the tax liabilities, financial overheads, and regulatory controls, associated with legal and male-controlled forms of prostitution, street prostitutes as a whole are said to experience more physical and emotional abuse than women who work as call girls or in parlours. In fact, the claim that prostitution is merely 'another job' is severely undermined by the multiple problems associated with street prostitution by feminists, governmental authorities, and the public alike, including concerns relating to exploitation and violence, drug addiction, and the maintenance of public health and order (Edwards and Armstrong 1988: 209–19; McCloskey and Lazarus 1992: 233–47; Satz 1995: 78). Viewed from this perspective, street prostitution has to be made open to governmental regulation in order to fulfil the desired feminist goal of ameliorating the exploitative conditions associated with prostitution. Alternatively, the prostitutes' rights movement may have to accept that turning prostitution into a socially accepted form of work might require abandoning the noble platform of solidarity and focusing their demands exclusively on the particular types of prostitution practices and businesses that can be opened to governmental procedures of standardization and professionalization (van der Poel 1995: 61–3).

In sum, the alignment of the prostitutes' rights movement with sex radical and queer perspectives has proved to be a double-edged sword. Arguments to the effect that sex workers are an oppressed sexual minority victimized by 'bad laws' and 'sex-negative' attitudes may have proved useful for the purposes of reconfiguring the prostitute subject as a transgressive sexual-political identity and hence establishing broad-based alliances between prostitutes' organizations and struggles for gay, lesbian and queer rights. But the celebratory reconfiguration of the female prostitute subject as an oppressed sexuality minority is problematic insofar as it winds up associating prostitution with the cause of radical sexual revolution – the libertarian ideal of total freedom from governmental intrusion into the lives of presumably independent individuals – for which it is far from clear that there exists a popular mandate, let alone the practical possibility of persuading governments and local authorities to take the implications of such an association on board. In fact, the contention that prostitution practices comprise a legitimate expression of sexual desire and pleasure not only elides the radical separation which many prostitutes make between their 'sex work' and their 'sex life', it effectively undermines practical efforts to transform the nature of prostitution businesses by suggesting that prostitution is a private matter between individuals, and therefore an inappropriate object for corrective programmes of governmental intervention.

The more popular reconfiguration of prostitution as sex work is similarly rendered problematic by its reliance on generalized conceptions of civil rights and libertarian understandings of sexuality. Most notably, although the use of terms like 'sex worker' and 'sex industry' may avoid many of the negative moral connotations that accrue to the terms 'prostitute' and 'prostitution', it also elides the fact that prostitutes do not form a homogeneous socio-economic 'class' group, and prevents a focus on the different interests of what, in the absence of any agreed upon terminology, might loosely be called 'sex workers' and 'sex capitalists' (Sullivan 1992: 10). Another disadvantage of the popular portrayal of prostitution as 'just work' is that the primary object of analysis continues to be the female sex worker, not the male client. In consequence, 'the sexual desires and aspirations of clients' – and the ways in which these desires and aspirations may 'reflect broader cultural practices and patterns of masculinity – remain unprioritized and assigned to the realm of natural male sexual needs' (ibid.).

Last but not least, while the pro-sex work lobby has quite convincingly shown that prohibitory regimes produce a restructuring of prostitution practices and businesses in ways that disadvantage the female prostitute, they tend to assume that these problems will somehow disappear once 'voluntary' prostitution is decriminalized and recognized as work. In Australia, however, decriminalization policies have resulted in the expansion of legal definitions of prostitution and the development of a new bureaucratic machinery to extend official control over illegal and legal prostitution practices and businesses (Sullivan 1997). Specifically, decriminalization has led to the elaboration of criminal law and harsher police crackdowns on illegal brothels and street prostitutes, often at the behest of legal sex workers, on the grounds that 'illegal operators' are law-breakers who undermine the profitability and/or professional credibility of legitimate providers of sexual and other health/leisure services (Borrack and Davies 1998: 3). This hierarchical restructuring of prostitution practices and businesses, flowing from the adoption of a more tolerant legal response, not only highlights the need for more localized studies of the varied effects of introducing decriminalization policies in different cultural and temporal contexts, it also suggests that prostitution cannot be regarded as a stable or consistent object of law reform. Decriminalization strategies – just like the much maligned systems of prohibition and licensing – may lead to a restructuring of prostitution practices and businesses in ways that exacerbate the very inequalities and problems which the adoption of a more tolerant response is supposed to redress (Sullivan 1997: 12).

Transnational prostitution debates

As the preceding remarks indicate, just as women in prostitution do not speak with a univocal 'voice', there can be no single, politically correct 'feminist' blueprint for realizing the eradication or transformation of the diverse practices and businesses that make up prostitution. But this quandary has not stopped those who oppose the institution of prostitution, or supporters of the prostitutes' rights movement, from taking their conflicting opinions into the international arena in the form of a fight over the human rights status of prostitution in the United Nations (UN). Supporters of the feminist anti-prostitution lobby now contend that prostitution is an issue which relates to matters of inequality, exploitation, and violence; as such, its very existence is contrary to human dignity and constitutes a violation of human rights. Conversely, feminist supporters of the prostitutes' rights movement maintain that prostitution is an issue which relates to matters of work, privacy, and choice, hence the individual rights of prostitute women to economic and sexual self-determination should be recognized by law (Edwards 1997: 74–5).

These two polarized accounts of the nature of prostitution have not only influenced the reformulation of prostitution controls in first-world developed countries, they also have resulted in the formation of broad-based coalitions designed to address the subject of prostitution at a global level. Thus, in recent years, the Global Alliance Against Trafficking in Women has lobbied national governments, the UN's Working Group on Contemporary forms of Slavery, the Council of Europe, and the European Parliament, to acknowledge a new Convention to replace the still-in-force UN (1949) Convention on the Suppression of the Traffic in Persons and of the Exploitation of the Prostitution of Others. Briefly, the 1949 Convention enjoins signatory nations to prohibit all third party involvement in prostitution and advocates a strictly abolitionist approach to prostitution, as the following statement contained in the explanatory preamble to this treaty would suggest:

> Prostitution and the accompanying evil in the traffic of persons for the purpose of prostitution are incompatible with the dignity and worth of the human person and endanger the welfare of the individual, the family, and the community.
>
> (UN 1949)

In opposition to the abolitionist thrust of this treaty, the Global Alliance Against Trafficking in Women contends that the 1949 Convention should be replaced by a new Convention, one which recognizes the right to self-determination of prostitute women and hence differentiates between 'forced' prostitution and prostitution that is 'voluntarily' chosen as a form of work.

In opposition to 'anti-abolitionist' proposals of this kind, the Coalition Against Trafficking in Women (1995), spearheaded by the radical feminist, Kathleen Barry and Evelina Giobbe of WHISPER, among others, has drafted a new Convention Against Sexual Exploitation with the support of UNESCO. This Convention contends that it is a fundamental human right to be free from sexual exploitation in all its forms and argues that the 1949 Convention should be expanded in order to make all prostitution and trafficking violations of human rights. It also includes a new clause designed to penalize the male customers of prostitution, while simultaneously demanding the removal of all punitive provisions for women in prostitution, as well as a clause designed to penalize the producers, sellers, and distributors of pornography, who are seen to be promoting and engaging in sexual exploitation. The Coalition Against Trafficking in Women further advocates the introduction of positive programmes in work, education, and other economic and supportive structures, so as to diminish the economic necessity for women to engage in prostitution.

This controversy has been exacerbated by the recommendations outlined in a 1998 study authorized by the International Labour Organization (ILO), entitled *The Sex Sector: The Economic and Social Bases of Prostitution in Southeast Asia* (Lim 1998). Briefly, the report points out that 'the commercial sex sector' in developing countries such as Indonesia, Malaysia, the Philippines and Thailand, not only provides substantial income and employment for those people who are directly or indirectly involved in prostitution-related activities, it also serves as a mechanism for redistributing incomes (most notably through income remittances from women prostituting in urban areas to their families in underdeveloped rural areas), as a survival mechanism for coping with poverty, and as a method of compensating for the lack of social welfare and income maintenance programmes for large segments of all four societies in question (ibid.: 9–10). In addition, case studies conducted in all of these countries confirm that earnings from prostitution are often more than those from alternative employment opportunities open to women with no or low levels of education. Furthermore, the report intimates that earnings from the 'sex sector' contribute significantly to the national economy of these four developing countries, and the international economy as a whole (ibid.: 207).

Given both the size and significance of the 'sex sector' and the urgency of related problems – such as the threat of HIV/AIDS, the expansion of organized crime and child prostitution, and the pernicious problem of governmental corruption – the report suggests that legal approaches based on a policy of total prohibition are neither realistic nor truly enforceable (ibid.: 206, 211, 214). Instead, the report recommends that policy-makers should implement stricter laws designed to penalize the trafficking in women and children and the exploitation of the prostitution of others, and also to penalize the activities of corrupt law enforcement authorities, as well as the clients of child prostitutes (ibid.: 214–15). Reiterating the demands of the prostitutes' rights movement, however, the report further recommends that adults who have freely chosen sex work should be granted the same labour rights and social protection as other workers.

According to the ILO report, the advantages of legally recognizing 'voluntary' prostitution as work are threefold. First, it would help keep the 'sex industry' above ground and thereby enable relevant authorities to more effectively monitor the criminal aspects of the 'sex sector', including the related problem of governmental corruption. Second, it would enable relevant authorities to ameliorate the exploitative conditions often experienced by women in prostitution, while simultaneously enabling relevant authorities to implement more effective HIV/AIDS prevention strategies, and support programmes designed to assist those sex workers who wish to leave the institution of prostitution. Finally, the report intimates that recognizing prostitution as a legitimate form of work could provide an additional source of government revenue via the extension of the taxation net to cover many of the lucrative activities connected with the 'sex industry' (ibid.: 212–13).

Not surprisingly, these recommendations have ensured that the ILO report has met with a mixed reception. On the one hand, it has been acclaimed for offering a dispassionate account of prostitution, that is, for acknowledging that prostitution is better understood as a labour issue rather than as a moral problem. On the other hand, the study's recommendation that the 'sex industry' should be officially recognized as an 'economic sector' has been condemned by supporters of the feminist anti-prostitution lobby for eschewing ethical considerations and for capitulating to the 'conservative laissez-faire market ideology prevalent in many countries' (Raymond (n.d.)). While not denying that many people in Southeast Asia benefit economically from the existence of prostitution, the feminist anti-prostitution lobby contends that reconfiguring prostitution as a legitimate form of employment can only lead to the expansion of sex tourism in developing countries, allow governments to cash in on the booming profits of the 'sex industry' by taxing and regulating prostitution as a legitimate occupation, and ultimately enable governments to abdicate responsibility for making alternative forms of sustainable employment available to young women.

Given the internationalist nature of these proposed responses to prostitution, it should also come as no surprise that lobbyists on both sides of the anti-prostitution/pro-sex work divide have accused each other of being cultural imperialists. The pro-sex work lobby has condemned the feminist anti-prostitution lobby and supporters of abolitionist strategies in general on the grounds that they contribute to the global stigmatization of the female prostitute subject by viewing prostitution as a 'moral evil', and by defining prostitutes and trafficked women as victims. In doing so, or so supporters of the prostitutes' rights movement argue, the feminist anti-prostitution lobby has adopted a first-world, 'middle-class' attitude towards prostitution, i.e., they treat prostitution as an ethical problem and not as a survival strategy (van der Vleuten 1991: 21, 34).

In response to criticisms of this kind, the feminist anti-prostitution lobby has accused the pro-sex work lobby of attempting to globalize the politics of sexual libertarianism, and hence of failing to address the limitations of Western liberal conceptions of the (male) individual, sexual subject, as well as the ways in which liberal forms of thinking already structure the debate on prostitution within popular discourses and mainstream political theory. Concomitantly, the feminist anti-prostitution lobby insists that the pro-sex work lobby's rendition of prostitution as 'just work', a 'free choice', or a primarily economic issue, denies the extensive human suffering associated with most prostitution practices, whether in developing Asian countries or in developed Western ones (Raymond (n.d.)). Despite its implicit recommendation that policy-makers in Southeast Asian countries should legally recognize the 'sex sector', for instance, even the ILO report admits that 'prostitution is one of the most alienated forms of labour', since in-country surveys of women in prostitution showed that most worked 'with a heavy heart', 'felt forced', and would leave sex work if they could (Lim 1998: 213). While the pro-sex work lobby contends that this 'alienation' is predominantly an effect of moral condemnation and prohibitory legal regimes, the feminist anti-prostitution lobby maintains that reconfiguring prostitution as 'just work' will not  necessarily function to ameliorate the exploitation experienced by women in prostitution, since 'bad work practices', as well as illicit prostitution practices and businesses, continue to flourish even in first-world countries where prostitution is legally recognized by various governments (Raymond 1995: 17).

As the polemic and disputatious nature of this debate would suggest, choosing between the feminist anti-prostitution lobby and the pro-sex work lobby is more a matter of personal, ethico-political preference than a matter of succumbing to the inescapable logic of one or the other argument (Jolin 1994: 77). While the arguments mounted by both sides are rhetorically persuasive, they are also flawed in a number of crucial respects. Most notably, although it is practically de rigueur to criticize the radical feminist stance on prostitution for being universalizing and essentialist – that is, for failing to recognize the differences between prostitution practices across time and between cultures, as well as the differences between different forms of contemporary commercial sexual practices – it is equally important to note that neither the sex radical position on prostitution nor the more popular reconfiguration of prostitution as work is problem-free. Like the radical feminist rendition of prostitution as violence against women, the queer and sex radical construction of prostitution as merely an unconventional configuration of 'private sexuality' also functions to homogenize prostitution practices and to elide the experiential diversity of sex sellers and buyers. What is more, even though the more popular reconfiguration of prostitution as work has functioned to provide the prostitution transaction with an imprimatur of acceptability, it remains the case that the concept of sex work is fraught with problems, not the least of which is the question of what is meant by the terms 'sex' and 'work' and hence the very rendition of prostitution as *sex work* (Prestage and Perkins 1994: 6–21).

Putting these problems temporarily aside, the pertinent point to note here is that the subject of prostitution has emerged as a controversial focus of debate within the metropolitan academy and within the arena of international law. And given the continued efforts of feminist activists on both sides of the anti-prostitution/pro-sex work divide to expand or repeal existing UN conventions with regard to the subject of prostitution, and the trafficking in women, the broad parameters of these debates look set to exert an influence on the shape of legally based governmental responses to prostitution for the foreseeable future. I have therefore highlighted the morally invested and disputatious nature of feminist prostitution debates, not as a precursor to adjudicating between the feminist anti-prostitution and pro-sex work lobbies, but rather to indicate how current debates surrounding the legal regulation of prostitution have been produced and what they entail. Having done so, the issue I now want to broach is whether metropolitan discourses on the subject of prostitution have any relevance for the study of China or not.

4 Prostitution debates and a changing China

Prostitution as a 'new' object of discourse in reform-era China

The subject of prostitution in the PRC offers a useful vehicle for questioning the utility of travelling theories, chiefly because the emergence of prostitution as a renewed object of metropolitan concern has coincided with the emergence of prostitution as a 'new' object of discourse in China. Prostitution comprises a new object of discourse in the PRC in the sense that, following their assumption of political power in 1949, the Chinese Communist Party embarked upon a series of campaigns which purportedly eradicated prostitution from the mainland by the mid to late 1950s. The extraordinary nature of this feat, irrespective of its actual validity, meant that the eradication of prostitution was (and still is) vaunted as one of the major accomplishments of the Maoist regime ('Duanping jiefang jinü' 1949: 1; Information Office of the State Council of the PRC 1994). Since the early 1980s, however, governmental authorities in China have acknowledged that the phenomenon of prostitution has not only reappeared on the mainland, it also constitutes a widespread and growing problem. In fact, it is now considered that new laws and regulatory measures have proved unable to curb the prostitution business (Kwan 2000).

In saying that prostitution comprises a new object of discourse in the PRC, I want to indicate that the resurgence of prostitution in China is generally perceived as being historically coincident with the introduction of Deng Xiaoping's economic reforms and the Open Door policy in December 1978. Although recent studies have challenged the popular construction of prostitution in the PRC as something that was 'gone' and is now 'back' by demonstrating that the disappearance of prostitution under the Maoist regime was far from complete (Hershatter 1997: 331–3; Shan Guangnai 1995: 353), it remains the case that the subject of prostitution did not exist as a serious object of governmental and intellectual concern in China for a period of nearly three decades. The prostitution transaction only became a distinct object of legal classification in the PRC in September 1991, following the promulgation of the *Decision on Strictly Forbid-*

ding the Selling and Buying of Sex (hereafter the 1991 Decision),[1] which was issued in conjunction with the *Decision on the Severe Punishment of Criminals Who Abduct and Traffic in or Kidnap Women and Children* (Quanguo renda changweihui *et al.* 1991).

In any case, statistics released by the Chinese police indicate that governmental authorities in the PRC are grappling with a new social phenomenon, since the rate of prostitution on the mainland is burgeoning relative to the rate of prostitution during the Maoist era. According to incomplete statistics composed on the basis of nationwide crackdowns, the rate of prostitution in China has been rising every year since 1982. In 1983, as part of the nationwide 'strike hard' (*yanda*) against crime, 46,534 people were apprehended for involvement in prostitution-related activities. Between 1989 and 1990, as part of the nationwide campaign against the 'six evils' (*liuhai*), this figure rose to 243,183 (Xin Ren 1999: 1414); and, in 1996–7, as part of a nationwide campaign against illegality, 250,000 people were detained for involvement in prostitution-related activities (O'Neill 1999). A further 189,972 people were detained in 1998 and 216,660 people were apprehended in 1999 ('1998 nian quanguo gongan jiguan li'an de xingshi anjian fenlei tongji biao' 1999: 95; '1999 nian...' 2000: 95). Although these figures are difficult to assess – because they are incomplete, and often comprise an aggregate number of those detained for prostitution-related activities over varying periods of time – they nevertheless suggest that the phenomenon of prostitution is now rampant in the PRC. Indeed, policing scholars contend that these figures are highly conservative, estimating that they only account for around 25–30 per cent of the total number of people who are actually involved (Zhang Ping 1993: 27).

Investigations conducted by the Chinese police further suggest that prostitution-related activities are not only widespread throughout the PRC, but also that they are characterized by a proliferation of types, venues, prices, and labour migration patterns, that alter along with changes in patterns of policing (Ouyang Tao 1994: 15–18; Quanguo renda changweihui *et al.* 1991: 12–13). The transparent revival of prostitution in China during the early 1980s was initially associated with China's eastern, open, coastal cities, and thus somewhat tenuously linked to the influx of foreign investment and 'Western ideas'. Following the implementation of nationwide campaigns against prostitution in the late 1980s and early 1990s, however, it was revealed that the phenomenon of prostitution could be found throughout urban and rural China, incorporating such remote and economically underdeveloped regions as Guizhou and Tibet (Poole 1999: 11; 'Tibet anti-pornography, drugs, prostitution campaign' 1996: 7–8). Police investigations also demonstrated that prostitution-related activities took place in all manner of venues, including high and low grade hotels, karaoke/dance venues, health and fitness clubs, cinemas, teahouses, hairdressing and beauty salons, truck stops and temporary work camps, and in public spaces such as beaches, parks, and the unlit spaces beneath overpass bridges, to name but a few (Beijing dongcheng ... 1993: 14–17). Additionally, police investigations intimated that the prices women could command for engaging in a single act of prostitution varied from as little as the cost of a simple meal (10 *yuan* or less) to several hundred and even several thousand *yuan* (Shan Guangnai 1995: 359, 374; Zhao Qinggui 1994: 12).

Hence, just as the initial understanding that prostitution existed primarily in China's open cities has altered, so too have popular conceptions of the Chinese prostitute subject. In the 1980s, mainland commentators tended to portray the typical 'seller of sex' as a young, poorly educated woman who had relocated from an underdeveloped rural area to a major urban centre to look for work, and who had been somehow lured, tricked or forced, into prostitution. Nowadays, while issues pertaining to the relationship between prostitution and the use of deception and force continue to receive widespread publicity in the PRC,[2] mainland commentators routinely note that the majority of women who enter prostitution do so of their own free will, primarily as a means to realize a higher standard of living than would be afforded to them by more conventional forms of employment. In fact, Chinese policing scholars consistently cite the benefits to be realized from engaging in prostitution – in terms of more disposable income and improved access to upwardly mobile social circles and lifestyle options – as one of the major reasons why urban residents with socially sanctioned forms of employment, including university-educated women, have not only chosen to prostitute in their original city of residence, but also have proved just as willing as their rural counterparts to travel elsewhere in the PRC for the explicit purpose of engaging in prostitution (Quanguo renda changweihui *et al.* 1991: 12–13; Shan Guangnai 1995: 416–17).

The perception that many Chinese women now choose to engage in prostitution is the benchmark used to distinguish prostitution in present-day China from that of the 1950s. Whereas women in the pre-liberation period and early 1950s were viewed (in accordance with Marxist theory) as being literally forced into prostitution in order to survive, it is now argued that many women voluntarily engage in prostitution so as to fulfil their hedonistic desire for expensive consumer goods and an individualistic, high consumption life-style. Thus, while acknowledging that the decision to prostitute is not necessarily an autonomous choice (since actual and relative poverty, combined with unequal opportunity structures, are still viewed as the main factors which predispose women to enter prostitution), policing and other scholars in China have become increasingly concerned with sociological and criminological issues of personal motivation and deviancy, and ultimately with establishing a socio-economic, and psychological, profile of the 'typical' prostitute and client (Beijing dongcheng ... 1993: 14–17). Accordingly, the identity of the Chinese prostitute subject has become increasingly problematized, with female sellers of sex being variously constructed as 'wilful perpetrators' of harm and as 'victims' of economic inequalities and gendered societal norms.

Nonetheless, in the process of categorizing prostitution practices and businesses, policing scholars have drawn attention to the demand side of the prostitution transaction. Following the original depiction of prostitution as a phenomenon associated with China's open coastal cities, mainland commentators initially portrayed the typical 'buyer of sex' as an overseas businessman, and, to a somewhat lesser extent, as a 'decadent' mainland bureaucratic entrepreneur[3] with experience of a 'disreputable' Western lifestyle, or else as a member of China's new class of relatively affluent but not very 'cultured' private business entrepreneurs (Li Shi and Gao Ling 1993: 10–13; Zhang Yanshang 1993: 12–19). Nowadays, policing and other scholars readily admit that the demand for prostitution in the PRC is generated by mainland Chinese men in order to fulfil various 'natural' or socially constructed desires, but 'desires' that are generally perceived as both stemming from and reinforcing the secondary status of women. Investigations conducted by the Chinese police further indicate that male buyers of sex come from a wide range of occupational backgrounds, including the unemployed, factory workers, taxi drivers, transient and agricultural labourers, private business entrepreneurs, teachers, university academics, and government employees, including high level cadres (Beijing dongcheng . . . 1993: 14–17; Wang Jinling *et al.* 1998: 53–9).

Last but not least, policing scholars have pointed to the developing links between prostitution and crime. On the one hand, they have expressed concern over the growing number of criminal acts that are directed at women who sell sex. Apart from incidences of violence associated with the prostitution transaction per se, policing and other reports indicate that as presumed high income earners, an increasing number of women who sell sex have been physically assaulted, and even murdered, in the course of attempts to steal their money and property (Song Zhenyong 1996: 69–70; Xin Ren 1999: 1423; Zhou Wenhui and Wang Dekang 1993: 34–7). On the other hand, policing scholars have expressed concern over the growing number of criminal acts, especially incidences of theft, bribery, and fraud that are directed at men who buy sex. For example, apart from incidences of straightforward theft perpetrated during the course of the prostitution transaction, police reports indicate that some women pose as sellers of sex in order to entice a prospective client to a given venue, only once they are behind closed doors, the unsuspecting 'client' is accosted by the woman's awaiting accomplices, who threaten to physically assault him, and/or publicly expose him, unless he hand over all his available money (Pan Suiming 1996b: 55; Wang Shouzhi 1995: 47).

These kinds of activities, as mainland scholars readily admit, are intrinsically related to the PRC's official policy of banning prostitution, with offenders capitalizing in multiple ways on the unwillingness of participants in the prostitution transaction to report such activities and thereby bring themselves to the attention of public security officials. While these problems point to the potential benefits of legally recognizing the prostitution transaction, mainland commentators often suggest that such a shift is unfeasible because it would not receive public support (Zhang Zhiping 2000: 32–3). Moreover, given the underdeveloped nature of the Chinese economy and legal system, other commentators contend that it would further complicate the already difficult task of establishing the legal responsibility for third-party involvement in 'forced' prostitution and the traffic in women (Flores, in K. Peratis and J.R. Flores 2000).

In a similar vein, policing scholars have expressed growing concerns over the links between prostitution and problems such as governmental corruption, trafficking in women, and organized vice. Although the Chinese police have been associated with numerous instances of high and low level corruption – most notably, they have been implicated in the running of high grade hotels where prostitution activities occur, and countless public security officials have been accused of accepting bribes or demanding sexual favours to ignore the existence of prostitution activities (Malhotra 1994: 32–9) – police-led anti-prostitution campaigns have nonetheless done much to expose the entrenched corruption and enormous sums of public money that go into sustaining the diverse recreational venues where prostitution activities occur (Chang Xumin 1994: 1; 'Cheats pay for fun with company cash' 1994: 3; Chen Siyi 1995: 2).

Police investigations have also revealed that an increasing number of women are entering the PRC from bordering countries for the explicit purpose of engaging in prostitution, and that organized crime rings are trafficking women into and out of China for the sex trade (Chen Yanni 1996: 2; 'Cruel trade hard to end' 1995: 7; Li Rongxia 2000: 13–19). Such investigations indicate that some women have consented to being trafficked for the purposes of prostitution, but others have been tricked into being trafficked and engaging in prostitution, and even kidnapped, drugged and subjected to multiple incidences of rape, before being forced to engage in prostitution either within or outside of China's territorial boundaries ('Jinyibu ba jinchang gongzuo tuixiang shenru' 1992: 7–11; Zhang Ping 1993: 25–9). Apart from the problems of trafficking and forced prostitution, policing and other scholars have noted that the PRC not only has a growing number of 'heroin hookers', but, as in the West, China's burgeoning sex and drug industries are connected to international and domestic crime rackets in multiple, nefarious ways ('Jinyibu . . .' 1992: 7–11; Wang Xingjuan 1996: 27–8).

In consequence, if the phenomenon of prostitution has emerged as a new and complex object of policing in present-day China, as with many other countries, the potential threat of the spread of HIV/AIDS through commercial sex has prompted public debate on prostitution and generated calls to review existing prostitution controls. Like prostitution, sexually transmissible diseases (STDs), including HIV/AIDS, constitute a new object of discourse in the PRC in the sense that, following their accession to power in 1949, the CCP set in place a series of programmes designed to cure an estimated 10 million people of venereal diseases (VD); and, in 1964, the acting director of the Research Institute of Dermatosis of the Chinese School of Medicine and Sciences announced to the world, on behalf of the communist government, that China had basically eliminated VD (Hershatter 1997: 348–9). Since the late 1970s, however, public health authorities have expressed growing concern over the obvious recurrence and escalating rates of STDs in China. In January 1988, the PRC reported its first case of a sexually transmitted HIV infection in a mainland person. By the end of September 1999, HIV infections in China had grown to a reported 15,088 cases, with the World Health Organization (WHO) estimating that the actual level of infection stood at around 400,000 cases. Internal and external projections suggest that this number will rise to 10 million cases by the year 2010 ('China among Asian countries most seriously plagued by AIDS' 1999: 8–9).

While China's health authorities attribute the now widespread incidence of STDs to a range of factors, including changing sexual mores and increased population mobility, the spread of HIV/AIDS has been explicitly linked to intravenous drug use and prostitution. Such concerns reflect the standard if problematic portrayal of participants in prostitution as 'high risk groups' by WHO and various other NGOs who are involved in developing AIDS prevention strategies in Asian countries. For instance, unlike 'Pattern 1' countries, meaning countries such as North America, Australia, and those in Western Europe, where HIV infection is presented as being concentrated in subpopulations of men who have sex with men and among intravenous drug users, in 'Pattern 3' countries, such as those in South-east Asia, where HIV has been relatively recently introduced, preventative strategies have emphasized the potential link between prostitution and the spread of HIV/AIDS, on the understanding that individuals who sell sex are more likely to encounter clients who could 'import' the virus from abroad, and thereby transmit the infection to local populations (Murray and Robinson 1996: 43–59). Reiterating such concerns, Chinese health officials and interested academics alike insist that it is not beyond the realms of possibility that prostitution will become the main route of HIV transmission in the PRC as it has in developing countries such as Thailand and India. In consequence, 'the development of a cross-disciplinary and cross-sectorial approach to the social, ethical and legal issues surrounding HIV and prostitution' is viewed as a matter of pressing concern ('Consensus and recommendations on HIV and prostitution' 1996: 104–6).

Similarly reiterating the concerns of international health organizations, some mainland commentators now contend that the PRC's policy of banning prostitution is problematic because it hinders the task of developing measures to prevent the spread of HIV (Li Dun 1996: 16–17; Zhang

Heqing 2002: 313–44). Most significantly, the official ban on prostitution is seen to complicate attempts to establish outreach programmes designed to promote safe sex practices among sellers and buyers of sex. Likewise, existing prostitution controls are viewed as a major impediment in attempts to investigate the prevalence of STDs/HIV among participants in the prostitution transaction and also to assess their knowledge of and attitude towards such diseases. Adding to these difficulties, mainland health officials and interested academics alike suggest that it is virtually impossible to gauge the extent of STD/HIV infection in the PRC, because the vast majority of urban residents with an STD can now seek treatment at one of China's new private health clinics, rather than going to government-run hospitals and clinics, where relevant officials are obliged to notify China's public security forces of anyone found with a sexually transmitted infection (Gil *et al.* 1996: 143–4; Qiu Renzong 1996: 42–4). Concerns over the possible links between prostitution and the spread of STDs/HIV have thus led to suggestions that the PRC's policy of banning prostitution is impractical and should be revised.

Responses to prostitution in reform-era China

If the phenomenon of prostitution has emerged as a new object of governmental and intellectual concern in reform-era China, questions pertaining to the most appropriate nature of its regulation have also become the focus of controversy. For example, the 'Consensus and recommendations on HIV and prostitution' (hereafter the Consensus Recommendations), a document that ensued from the 'Expert workshop on HIV and prostitution: social, ethical and legal issues' (hereafter the Expert Workshop) held in Beijing during October 1996, explicitly states that the situation in present-day China is quite different from that of the 1950s and 1960s. Consequently, the Consensus Recommendations note that, even though the official policy of banning prostitution stems from 'a good will', the desired goal of eliminating prostitution is unrealistic. Instead, like Lin Lean Lim's (1998) ILO-sponsored report on the 'sex sector' in Southeast Asia, the Consensus Recommendations state that prostitution in the PRC has now developed to the extent that it comprises an industry, one that involves a great number of people and produces a considerable economic output. Given the size and entrenched nature of the 'sex sector' in China today, the Consensus Recommendations suggest that the existence of prostitution is a reality (albeit perhaps an unhappy one) that governmental authorities are obliged to acknowledge.

As with the ILO report, the Consensus Recommendations stop short of explicitly stating that acknowledging prostitution could entail legalizing the 'sex sector' in some fashion or another, the former because such a recommendation lies beyond the brief of the ILO, and the latter because central guidelines laid down by the CCP do not permit the public advocacy of the legalization of prostitution in China. However, in keeping with general concerns to ameliorate the exploitation of women in prostitution, the Consensus Recommendations (1996: 106) note that the official policy of banning prostitution constitutes a double-edged sword. For while prohibitive policies may function to deter the buying and selling of sex, they also have the documented effect of placing an already marginalized group of women in a more vulnerable position. Hence in a manner that should prove pleasing to supporters of the feminist anti-prostitution lobby, the Consensus Recommendations conclude that the punitive emphasis of China's prostitution controls should be directed towards those who buy sex and organize prostitution, especially government officials and law enforcement agents who do so.

But the Consensus Recommendations' conclusion that China's prostitution controls should target 'the buyers and organizers of sex' owes more to a combination of (Marxist-informed) concerns regarding the classist and gender-biased nature of the enforcement of existing controls than the abolitionist arguments of the feminist anti-prostitution lobby. For instance, in 'The prohibition of prostitution: whom does it serve?', Pan Suiming (1996a: 20–1) contends that, while the phenomenon of prostitution in the PRC can be compared to the situation in other developing countries, China has a specific type of prostitution that entails a 'bargain' between those who use their power and authority to obtain sex (*yiquan moxing*) and those who use sex to obtain the privileges that accrue to those in positions of power (*yixing moquan*). Specifically, Pan argues that, during the 1950s, the CCP only managed to eradicate 'visible' prostitution and that 'invisible' prostitution – in the form of women providing sexual services to cadres in exchange for certain privileges and cadres using their privileged positions to obtain sexual services – became a distinctive feature of Mao's China, particularly towards the end of the Cultural Revolution period (1966–76).

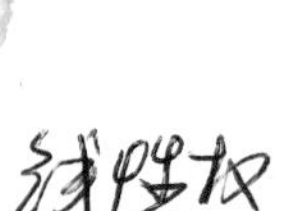

According to Pan, the continued existence of this invisible type of prostitution in present-day China demonstrates that existing prostitution controls reflect and reinforce the vested class interests of China's privileged elite, i.e., corrupt Party officials. In keeping with the incisive humour that characterizes much of his work, Pan (1996a: 20) maintains that many cadres have reinterpreted Deng Xiaoping's 'Four Cardinal Principles' – cadres must show commitment to Marxism–Leninism and Mao Zedong thought, Party leadership, socialism, and the existing state structure – in the following manner: 'I rarely need to buy food and drink, I rarely need to buy any items of clothing or personal accessories, I rarely need to touch my pay-packet, and I rarely need to use my wife'.

In other words, Pan suggests that corrupt officials seldom need to touch their personal salary because most of their living and entertainment expenses will be reimbursed via recourse to public funds, or they will be met by other people in the form of gifts provided with the expectation of returned favours. Pan further implies that, unlike 'ordinary' Chinese men, corrupt officials are not restricted to monogamous, marital sex, because the opportunities for them to have sexual relations with women other than their wives in exchange for various forms of patronage and recompense are so plentiful.

Given the entrenched nature of this particular form of prostitution, Pan avers that existing prostitution controls discriminate against men and women from the lower levels of Chinese society. Briefly, Pan maintains that the practice of 'using one's position to get sex and using sex to obtain the privileges that accrue to those in positions of power' is neither viewed nor handled as prostitution, hence participants in this particular prostitution practice are not only exempted from legal penalties, they are also not tarred with the negative identity that accrues to those who are categorized as buyers and sellers of sex. Instead, the moral censure that is directed at 'the problem of prostitution' affects ordinary people and keeps intact the divisive hierarchies of class and gender that have traditionally organized Chinese society, via the 'un-Marxist' dichotomization of women into 'chaste women, wives and mothers' versus 'bad women', and via the 'un-Marxist' dichotomization of men into 'upright gentlemen' versus 'shameless hooligans'. Pan (1996a: 21) thus criticizes the PRC's prostitution controls on the grounds that they constitute an expression of bourgeois right, i.e., they retain the privileges that accrue to China's new bourgeoisie (read government officials and bureaucratic entrepreneurs), while penalizing certain subpopulations of 'the people' who already (as a collective labouring class) have unequal access to the social distribution of goods and resources.

In view of these problems, Pan somewhat obtusely concludes that he does not understand why the policy of banning prostitution is being pursued on such an unprecedented scale in the current era of 'market-socialism'. That is to say, apart from the suggestion that China's prostitution controls do not concord with Marxist theory, the question of whether Pan is calling for the official ban on prostitution to be lifted, or simply asking the CCP to resolve the long-standing problem of bureaucratic/governmental corruption, is left open to interpretation. In any case, apart from the suggestion that efforts to eradicate prostitution are severely undermined by the actions of corrupt officials, Pan's argument is purely rhetorical. The forms of prostitution that existed in the Maoist era cannot be equated with the types of prostitution practices and businesses that exist in present-day China, because they are radically different in nature and scale. Contemporary prostitution practices in the form of cadres using their privileged positions to obtain sexual services, and women providing sexual services to cadres in return for certain privileges, cannot be equated with the forms of prostitution that existed in the Maoist era, since the mutual obligations and social conditions that inform such practices would be significantly altered by the changed and commercialized nature of the reform period.

Although Pan and other contributors to the Expert Workshop stop short of suggesting that the PRC's policy of banning prostitution should be abandoned, this does not mean that arguments concerning the legalization of prostitution are absent from China. On the contrary, some commentators explicitly refer to prostitution as work and contend that legally recognizing the 'sex industry', in conjunction with further economic development, will ultimately reduce the number of women in prostitution (Zhang Beichuan *et al.* 1996: 73–5). This contention flows from the Marxist informed, albeit empirically erroneous, assertion that the legalization of prostitution in various first-world countries has been accompanied by the virtual disappearance of prostitution due to the existence of better economic and social opportunities for women. Conversely, other commentators have rebuked an unspecified group of cadres, including government officials, law enforcement officers, and bureaucratic entrepreneurs, for allegedly supporting the legalization of prostitution, either by failing to implement prostitution controls in the required manner, or for suggesting that the existence of prostitution is good for China's developing hospitality and tourism industries, and that taxing sex workers will generate a significant source of revenue for local governmental authorities. In fact, rebuttals of the pragmatic and economistic philosophy that 'prostitution is an inevitable feature of a developing economy so we might as well tax it' feature regularly in statements on prostitution authorized by the Ministry of Public Security and the All-China Women's Federation (ACWF) (Bo Xu 1994: 4; 'China abhors calls for legal prostitution' 1994; 'Jinyibu . . .' 1992: 11; Kwan 1995a; 1995b: 6).

Ding Juan's contribution to the Expert Workshop, entitled 'A case study on female prostitutes, sexual exploitation and violence', suggests that calls to acknowledge the 'reality' of prostitution in China do not necessarily translate into an implicit call for government toleration of the 'sex industry'. Speaking as a researcher for the ACWF, Ding (1996: 9–10) concurs that the phenomenon of prostitution in reform-era China is different from that of the 1950s and has much in common with the situation in other developing countries. As she argues, the vast majority of Chinese women who engage in prostitution do so on a voluntary basis, often as a means to escape actual or relative poverty. Given the 'voluntary' and economically motivated nature of prostitution in China today, Ding contends that many mainland scholars and bureaucratic entrepreneurs (people whom she genders as being predominantly male) have advocated the setting up of 'red light districts', in order to turn prostitution into an open and acceptable component of the hospitality and tourism industries. Concomitantly, Ding notes that some Chinese women have argued that their bodies are their own capital and they should have the right to use their bodies as they see fit, and yet others have argued that prostitution is a private affair in which the government should not interfere. So far as Ding is concerned, the existence of prostitution cannot be condoned with reference to essentially liberal and economistic arguments, because prostitution not only stems from and reinforces gendered social and economic inequalities, it also has specific and deleterious consequences for the physical and mental health of women.

Ding therefore concludes that the ACWF and international NGOs should continue to support the Chinese government's policy of suppressing prostitution, while encouraging the development of supportive strategies on the understanding that prostitution constitutes a violation of women's rights. Briefly, Ding (1996: 10) argues that, although China has specific laws designed to promote and guarantee equality between the sexes, these laws are virtually useless once located in the domain of sexual relations. In the early 1980s, she continues, the Chinese government abolished rulings that problematized 'illicit sexual relations', i.e., sexual relations other than monogamous, marital sex. Consequently, engagement in the prostitution transaction is treated as a misdemeanour in Chinese law, not as a crime, and offenders are handled according to the Chinese system of administrative punishments, not on the basis of the penal code. Ding's broader if implicit argument here, and one that runs counter to the emphasis of many Anglophone China scholars on notions of individual rights, is that the Chinese government's more relaxed stance on non-marital sexual behaviours constitutes something of a 'step backward' in that it has opened more spaces wherein Chinese men can sexually exploit Chinese women.

What Ding's reference to the administrative system means, however, is that even though mainland Chinese citizens who are classified as sellers and buyers of sex may be physically detained for varying periods of time, and even obliged to undergo rehabilitative education and labour, the practice of detaining such people cannot be viewed as equivalent to penal incarceration as in the West.[4] This is because detention for rehabilitative education and labour is defined as the maximum administrative punishment that can be imposed upon those who have committed illegal acts, but whose criminal liability is not deemed sufficient to bring them before the courts. In theory, therefore, the activities of those who participate in the prostitution transaction are not criminalized in China. Rather, they are viewed as undesirable forms of social behaviour that can be opened to governmental programmes of corrective intervention ('Criminal reform in China' 1992; Information Office of the State Council of the PRC 1992: 9–24; Xu, S. 1999).

Hence contrary to the feminist maxim that prohibitionist policies – and thus the Chinese response to prostitution – are inherently objectionable because they criminalize *all* aspects of prostitution, the prostitution transaction is not criminalized in Chinese law. In this respect, as mainland scholars suggest, the PRC's response to prostitution can technically be described as abolitionist not prohibitionist in that the Chinese penal code, in accordance with UN conventions, is primarily concerned to penalize those third parties who seek to benefit from the prostitution or sexual exploitation of others (Shan Guangnai 1995: 592). This is not to deny that the Chinese police often handle female sellers of sex in a quasi-criminal fashion, but rather to highlight the theoretically ameliorative origins of the administrative system as a means of transforming those who have committed acts that are deemed to be neither a 'crime' nor an 'accepted' social practice. Doing so helps to explain why representatives of the ACWF tend to view rehabilitative education as a positive support measure, albeit one that needs to be revised in order to realize its stated goals.

Given the theoretical emphasis in Chinese law on the reform, as opposed to the criminalization, of participants in the prostitution transaction, Ding (1996: 10) offers full support for the Chinese government's policy of banning prostitution. However, she adds that the implementation of China's prostitution controls, as with many other countries, has been conducted in a gender-biased fashion; and this bias, which contradicts the legal emphasis on reforming *all* participants in the prostitution transaction, needs to be redressed. The most transparent problem, and one that mainland police have acknowledged since the early 1990s, is that women who are apprehended as sellers of sex are more likely to be detained for rehabilitative education than men who are apprehended as buyers of sex. As with many other countries, male buyers of sex are detained less often than female sellers of sex in China because little or no stigma attaches to 'the male prostitute client', and due to the difficulties associated with policing their activities as migrants or 'sex tourists'. According to Ding and policing scholars alike, addressing this bias means ensuring that male participants in the prostitution transaction also undergo re-education (Wang Dazhong 1995: 57; Wang Jinling *et al.* 1998: 53–9).

Although Ding does not raise the following issues, it bears noting that male participants in the prostitution transaction are detained less often than female sellers of sex due to the limited number of centres, trained staff and funding currently available for the specific purpose of re-educating participants in the prostitution transaction. Moreover, and contrary to the implication of many Anglophone accounts of prostitution in present-day China, it is equally important to note that the overwhelming majority of men *and women* who are apprehended for involvement in the prostitution transaction are released with a caution and fine. According to mainland policing scholars, the tendency to fine less serious prostitution offenders stemmed originally from a general proclivity towards leniency. However, this practice was rendered increasingly problematic because it not only contradicted the spirit of the 1991 Decision, but also had serious implications for the development of police accountability and professionalism. Put simply, the practice of fining participants in the prostitution transaction, rather than detaining them for police-funded re-education, had become a way in which the Chinese police could generate much needed finances, while conserving their limited resources, and it had simultaneously contributed to the pernicious problems of police corruption and arbitrariness. The PRC's Law on Administrative Punishments (1996) thus establishes strict guidelines regarding the issuance and management of fines in an effort to enhance police accountability, a move that has abetted calls for stricter sentencing practices with regard to sellers and buyers of sex.

Returning to the problem of gender-biased law enforcement practices, however, Ding maintains that Chinese women who are detained as sellers of sex are often unfairly discriminated against upon their release. As Ding (1996: 10) argues, the fact that women who sell sex are more commonly detained for rehabilitative education than men who buy sex can impinge negatively on their future prospects. For despite their supposedly reformed status, such women are frequently subjected to social disapproval upon their release due to the continued existence of the sexual double standard. According to Ding, this negative attitude – which can be summarized as 'once a prostitute, always a prostitute', whereas male buyers of sex seldom if ever accrue a negative and fixed identity – even informs the approach of the very people who are meant to ensure that women who have been transformed via rehabilitative education are successfully reintegrated into society and do not return to prostitution.

In view of these problems, Ding (ibid.: 10) calls upon the Chinese government to maintain its policy of suppressing prostitution, while simultaneously introducing a comprehensive range of programmes designed to raise the social status of women and transform the cultural values that encourage men to treat women as sexual objects or 'playthings'. To do so, she argues that relevant authorities need to adopt a stricter approach with regard to the apprehension and forced detention of male buyers of sex. Ding further calls on China's public health authorities to implement sexual health and education programmes especially for women, on the basis that STDs/HIV are more easily transmitted via sexual contact from men to women than vice versa. She also calls upon 'society' to adopt an ethic of care with regard to the recovery and reintegration of women in prostitution, and contends that the media should be used to promote the positive value of female involvement in productive labour, rather than valorizing images of feminine youth and beauty, and thereby encouraging the objectification and sexualized commodification of women. In short, Ding recommends that the PRC's response to prostitution should be revised on continued abolitionist lines as constituting a violation of women's rights.

If researchers with the ACWF support an abolitionist approach to prostitution as constituting a violation of women's rights, arguments in support of decriminalization as a means to improve the position of women in prostitution have begun to emerge in China. Li Yinhe, for instance, maintains that decriminalization constitutes a preferable response for two reasons (cited in Zhang Heqing 2002: 313–14). First, Li contends that the PRC's policy of banning prostitution hinders the task of disease prevention and prevents female prostitutes from becoming self-employed, by reinforcing their dependency on exploitative brothel-keepers to evade policing controls. Second, she draws on Engels' (1972) assertion that the only difference between the prostitute and the (bourgeois) wife is that the former lets out her body on piece-work as a wage-worker, whereas the latter sells it once and for all into slavery, to maintain that the sexual-economic relationships between men and women in prostitution and marriage are indistinguishable. Li thus concludes that the social valorization of marriage and corollary moral condemnation of prostitution in China is nonsensical. Therefore, as with marital relations, the exchange of sex for money between consenting adults is an inappropriate object of governmental concern.

In broaching this conclusion, Li apparently favours decriminalization as a potential means of empowering women in prostitution by removing the stigma that attaches to their body and person, and liberating them from exploitation at the hands of third parties. However, like early radical feminist re-articulations of the Marxist canon, Li's equation of prostitution with marriage functions more to condemn all heterosexual relations than to diminish the whore stigma. The rhetorical basis of Li's argument is underscored by her failure to outline what a policy of decriminalization might look like and how it might be implemented in China. Indeed, given that Li previously has dismissed Western discussions of sexual rights in relation to the subject of prostitution as 'gibberish' with no applicability to the Chinese setting (Li Yinhe 1997, trans. Sigley 1998: 31), it is difficult to ascertain precisely what she is promoting, other than registering a general objection to inequity.

Nonetheless, arguments in support of decriminalizing the prostitution transaction undoubtedly will develop in China, even though Li suggests that persuading the Chinese public and policy-makers of the benefits of such an approach will be a slow and difficult task (cited in Zhang Heqing 2002: 317). Such arguments are likely to develop because some of China's new social scientists are now engaged in collaborative work with international NGOs and pro-sex work organizations such as Zi Teng in Hong Kong (Zhang Heqing 2002: 313–44). As discussed in Chapter 2, however, we need to be wary of automatically valorizing the emergence of such debates as a sign that China is becoming 'just like us'. Quite apart from the problem of assuming that intellectual and political positions progress in a linear and teleological fashion, it is necessary to recognize that the existence of seemingly familiar debates in different cultural contexts may be grounded in different concerns from those in which they were originally formulated. Certainly, the arguments put forward by Li Yinhe and Pan Suiming would suggest that domestic criticisms of the PRC's current prostitution controls might owe more to the ongoing (Maoist) critique of class-based discrimination and privilege than liberal conceptions of human-cum-sexual rights.

In sum, if the phenomenon of prostitution has appeared in reform-era China, so too have a wide array of mainland professionals who are keen to analyse the phenomenon and propose solutions to it. While such commentators have focused predominantly on the 'conventional' prostitution transaction, they have also broached the subject of male sellers of sex and highlighted the relationship between prostitution and a diverse array of sexual practices ('Law faces sex problems – Sichuan teahouse case' 1999; Liu and Wu 2000; Wan Yanhai 1996: 28–30; 'Wu ge nanji de zaoyu' 1995: 37–47). Furthermore, as with Western discourses on prostitution, Chinese prostitution discourses are far from unified. Different accounts of prostitution are inevitably linked to particular understandings of the nature of gender, sexuality, class, commercial exchange, specific sexual acts, and modes of STDs/HIV transmission, and these understandings generate different conceptions of what constitutes the most appropriate governmental response.

Unlike Euramerican prostitution debates, however, Chinese discourses on prostitution have not been historically organized in relation to a developing and now divided independent feminist movement, nor formulated in relation to advocacy groups founded by or for prostitutes. Consequently, they are not articulated in relation to the radical feminist quest for a politically correct 'feminist' sexuality, the queer and sex radical valorization of unconventional sexual practices as politically subversive, or the equally utopian (albeit masquerading as practical) suggestion that prostitution practices will somehow be made 'good' via their legal reconfiguration as 'not-sex/just-work'. Instead, they tend to be framed in terms of broader public health and order concerns, and, in those instances where class and gendered inequalities are a primary concern, in terms of criticisms or reconfigured conceptions of the historical accomplishments and future promise of Chinese Marxism. What this genealogical difference implies is that Chinese prostitution discourses may not be translatable in terms of the underlying concerns with issues of sexual/identity politics that inform metropolitan prostitution debates.

The fact remains, however, that just as the phenomenon of prostitution has become a renewed object of controversy in metropolitan circles, it has also emerged as a renewed object of governmental and intellectual concern in present-day China. This convergence affords Anglophone China scholars a rather unique opportunity to engage in topical mainstream debates, both by virtue of their ability to show how the subject of prostitution has been constructed as an object of discourse in the PRC, and their ability to interrogate the explanatory capacity of metropolitan prostitution debates with regard to the study of China. Put another way, practitioners of China studies have the opportunity to make mainstream debates as much the object of analytic attention, as they are a means for analysis, by pursuing the critical imperative to reveal the difference of China. The question that remains to be asked, therefore, is: how has the subject of prostitution in the PRC been generally presented – and hence translated – for consumption by an Anglophone readership?

Prostitution in reform-era China as an object of metropolitan discourses

The revival of prostitution in the PRC, after nearly three decades of apparent absence, has inevitably attracted the interest of Western commentators. During the late 1980s, foreign correspondents in China eagerly reported the presence of female prostitutes in hotels and other venues that catered primarily to non-Chinese. One of the major motivations for such reports, as Gail Hershatter (1996a: 205) suggests, was the desire to alert Anglophone audiences to perceived discrepancies between what the Chinese government had to say about socialist society and what could be observed in everyday life. Briefly, these reports intimated that the process of reform had not only resulted in economic development, it had also introduced much-needed social change. The resurgence of prostitution, or so they implied, indicated that the Chinese people, if not the Chinese government, had finally thrown off the shackles of Maoist (read puritanical) socialist morality and embraced the joys associated with notions of sexual liberation and individual freedom as in the West (Burton 1988: 65; 'China rediscovers the joy of sex' 1997; Gargan 1988: 4).

While more recent commentators seem less eager to herald the existence of prostitution as a 'healthy' sign that sex is 'back' in China, they have tended to express reservations about its re-emergence primarily in order to criticize the CCP. Put simply, they have criticized the CCP either for failing to guarantee social and economic equality for women, or else for continuing to condemn prostitution on moral grounds, and thereby subjecting prostitutes to additional legal harassment, when Chinese law enforcement agencies themselves are 'busy making good money in the "red light district" sector of socialism' (McElroy 1998, 1999: 13; 'Three escorts' 1994: 6). The subject of prostitution thus features in such accounts less as an object of analytical inquiry in itself and more as a vehicle to highlight the perceived shortcomings of the Chinese (communist) government.

Since the 1990s, the subject of prostitution in reform-era China has also emerged as a focus of debate in metropolitan academic and activist circles. A growing number of expatriate mainland Chinese intellectuals, Anglophone scholars with a diverse array of disciplinary trainings, and various advocacy groups for human rights, have focused their attention on issues relating to prostitution in China (Gil 1994; Gil *et al.* 1994, 1996; Gil and Anderson 1998; Hershatter 1996b, 1997; Human Rights in China *et al.* 1998; Ruan 1991; Xin Ren 1993, 1999). As with the work of their journalistic counterparts, however, many of these accounts are marred by the desire to demonstrate that there is something intrinsically wrong with the way the Chinese government has chosen to respond to the phenomenon of prostitution.

Saying that Western accounts of prostitution in contemporary China are problematic does not mean that the PRC's prostitution controls cannot be called into question. The absurdity of making such a claim is highlighted by the fact that mainland professionals – whether policing and public health officials, sociological sexologists, women's studies scholars, or researchers for the ACWF – quite readily admit that the official policy of banning prostitution is imperfect. It is to suggest that Western accounts of prostitution in the PRC – that is, accounts which are intended for consumption by an Anglophone readership – offer particular ways of reading prostitution practices, and also the politics of the CCP, that fail to adequately explain what they claim to account for, namely, the nature and effects of the governmental regulation of prostitution in China today.

The failure of metropolitan academics to adequately account for the PRC's response to prostitution owes much to their unreflective deployment of the commentary-principle-as-translation. As discussed in Chapter 2, the activation of the commentary-principle-as-translation enables Anglophone scholars to reiterate endlessly the work of mainland commentators on subjects such as gender, sexuality and power, while simultaneously pointing to the impoverished nature of Chinese discourses vis-à-vis the masterful language of the Anglophone new humanities. Once activated in relation to the subject of prostitution, the commentary-principle-as-translation effectively turns the Chinese response to prostitution into a *known* phenomenon. It becomes a focus for empirical research that fleshes out an established theoretical skeleton by exposing the difference of China, simplistically understood as the failure of mainland Chinese intellectuals and governmental authorities to address the subject of prostitution in terms of some idealized transnational response.

A popular writing strategy, for instance, is to note that new conditions of openness in the PRC have allowed mainland Chinese scholars significantly more freedom to write about previously 'taboo' subjects such as sexuality and prostitution. As an Anglophone readership, however, we are immediately cautioned that this 'openness' does not mean that mainland Chinese scholars are no longer constrained in their writing – there are still matters pertaining to such 'sensitive' issues that mainland intellectuals cannot talk about for fear of governmental reprisals. While official guidelines indubitably shape the parameters for what is considered to be acceptable scholarship in the PRC, this appeal to traditional conceptions of 'the repressive Party state' translates in practice into asymmetries that render any notion of a mutual dialogue between mainland Chinese and metropolitan commentators redundant. It intimates that the task of the metropolitan intellectual-cum-activist remains what it always has been, namely, to reveal to an Anglophone readership that which cannot – but under different political conditions *would* – be said by 'them'.

Accordingly, the expatriate mainland Chinese physician and medical historian, Fang-fu Ruan (1991: x), informs us that the aim of his book *Sex in China* is:

> to outline the great contributions of the Chinese people to sexology and sexual literature, to elucidate the processes by which an open, sex-positive culture became negative and repressive, and to demonstrate the ineffectiveness of repressive governmental policies, whether practiced by imperial regimes or the current [CCP-led] dictatorship.

Noting that the 'thoughtful reader will wonder how it is possible to develop an accurate portrait of a nation whose government, consistent with a general denigration of sexuality, fails to provide nationwide statistics on sexual matters',[5] Ruan avers that his own personal experience as a physician and sexologist in China enables him to 'read beyond' the limited data available and hence to reach some conclusions about major social trends. In case we have any remaining doubts about his sincerity and ability to pronounce on the repressive nature of the relationship between power and sexuality in China today, Ruan adds that a text such as *Sex in China* – one that exhorts the Chinese government to adopt more open policies towards sex-related issues – could not have been written if he had stayed in the PRC.

Flowing from his unexamined commitment to the repressive hypothesis, Ruan subsequently positions himself as an authoritative, authentic cultural spokesperson on the governmental regulation of sexuality in China and his claim to be engaged in 'real' academic-cum-activist labour is endorsed by two prominent Western scholars. The noted sexologist and writer on prostitution, Vern L. Bullough (in Ruan 1991: vii), points out that Ruan is not only the author of a best-selling Chinese-language text on sex but that prior to his relocation to the USA, he was also 'a leader in attempting to change the repressive attitudes of the [Chinese] government toward human sexuality'. Confirming Ruan's status as an assumed dissident intellectual, Richard Green (in Ruan 1991: v–vii) informs us that, speaking from his own experience of lecturing in the PRC, the Chinese themselves are sorely in need of a candid account of human sexuality, since physicians who attended his lectures told him that there were no homosexuals in China. But, if a quarter of the world's population appear doomed to remain in the darkness with regard to their own sexual history and behaviours, Green happily concludes that, due to the publication of Professor Ruan's text in 1991, we in the West need no longer have a blind spot in 'our' view of Eastern sexuality.

In this way, Ruan lays claim to, and is accorded, what Michel Foucault calls 'the speaker's benefit' – that is, the claim to a certain moral authority flowing from the courage displayed in breaking the rules and daring to speak out against oppression.[6] Recourse to the speaker's benefit operates as a legitimating device in that it confers an almost palpable ethico-political authority upon 'the author' and 'the text'. This actuality notwithstanding, it bears noting that the basis of the speaker's benefit is rendered irretrievably problematic due to its reliance on the repressive hypothesis, or the assumption that sexuality constitutes an inevitable target of power because of its natural and inherently liberatory capacity. As Foucault (1978: 3–13) explains, although repression is a concept used above all in relation to sexuality, the positing of a purely negative conception of power in relation to sexuality is not only empirically and theoretically unsustainable; it also elides the positivity and effectivity of the diverse techniques and practices that make up governmental programmes of intervention.

Since I will discuss the positivity of Chinese governmental practices in the following chapters, it will suffice to say here that Ruan's deployment of the repressive hypothesis, and subsequent activation of the speaker's benefit, enable him to provide a popular yet limited account of the PRC's response to prostitution. Briefly, while praising the Maoist regime's efforts to rehabilitate female prostitutes and eradicate VD in the 1950s as laudable historical goals, Ruan (1991: 75) argues that the same cannot be said of China's current controls. For Ruan (ibid.: 82), public health concerns over the possible relationship between prostitution and the spread of STDs could offer some support for the Chinese government's continued efforts to eradicate prostitution, but these legitimate concerns do not constitute the primary basis of China's current anti-prostitution policies. Instead, he maintains that prostitution controls in the PRC today are indicative of little more than the CCP's determination to stay in power by suppressing the private lives and sexual desires of the Chinese people (ibid.: 84; see also Massonnet 1999: 67–72).

Like many journalistic and neo-liberal readings of China in the post-1989 era, therefore, Ruan employs a purely negative conception of power and a wholly positive conception of sexuality to tie the perceived popular movement for Western-style liberal democracy in China to the alleged need for even the most basic of individual/sexual freedoms. Viewed in this context, any objections to the prostitution transaction become simply 'tired' expressions of out-dated conceptions of socialist-cum-puritanical morality. Concomitantly, government-initiated campaigns to control the spread of prostitution become nothing more than ideologically motivated attempts to retain a monolithic degree of social control. Indeed, if it were not for recourse to the assumption that the interests of 'the Chinese state' and 'the Chinese people' are fundamentally opposed, articulated in relation to a liberatory conception of the sexual and a juridical conception of power, how else could Ruan and other commentators forward the apparent ineffectiveness of campaigns against prostitution and pornography (issues, I might add, that are highly contentious even in Western societies) as proof that the CCP has failed to suppress 'the Chinese people's' desire for a more 'humanitarian and normal sex life'?[7]

Ruan (1991: 170) subsequently claims that vocal opposition to prostitution in China stems largely from political struggles within the CCP itself, with conservative and reform factions alike condemning the 'new problems' of the reform era in order to effect social control, and deflect attention away from the 'real' problem of governmental (as opposed to 'spiritual') corruption. For Ruan, the hypocrisy of the CCP's continued abolitionist stance on prostitution is evidenced by the fact that even the revered former Premier, Zhou Enlai, acted as a procurer for the equally revered yet libertine Chairman, Mao Zedong. Given the ongoing existence of what allegedly amounts to two rules of sexual conduct – permissiveness for those in positions of authority and repression for the 'ordinary' Chinese people – Ruan (ibid.: 83–4) contends that the implementation of 'draconian' anti-prostitution/anti-pornography campaigns, such as the late 1989 campaign against the 'six evils', is indicative of nothing more than the CCP's determination to maintain political power and suppress the common people. As a result, the fact that this campaign actually helped to restore the tarnished legitimacy of the Dengist regime, not by crushing popular will, but rather by responding to student accusations of moral turpitude on the part of the Party, and demonstrating a renewed political will to combat problems that were (and are still) widely perceived to require remedial action, is elided. Instead, we are enjoined to believe that prostitution in China would be accepted as an unremarkable expression of human sexuality if not for the repressive and puritanical CCP (ibid.: 69–84).

Vincent Gil *et al.* (1994) reiterate Ruan's suggestion that the punitive nature of China's prostitution controls is a function of intra-party conflicts. While acknowledging that the Chinese prostitute subject is viewed by the Chinese government predominantly as a redeemable and not a criminal entity, Gil *et al.* (ibid.: 330) aver that the need for high level cadres 'to convince others of their own moral purity', combined with fears that 'China's moral soul is being lost to modernization and corruption from outside influences', has resulted in the implementation of harsher prostitution controls (meaning the 1991 Decision). The problem here, or so Gil and his co-authors (ibid.: 320) imply, is that China's prostitution controls are premised on ideological grounds, as opposed to an objective understanding of '*who* the contemporary prostitute is' and the 'rationales and pressures that motivate her into the trade'.

Drawing on the time-honoured combination of fieldwork and ethnographic observation, Gil *et al.* claim to expose the out-dated rationales of the Chinese government by revealing *who* prostitutes in China and *why*. As they argue, 'official representations' of the 'typical' prostitute – a young, impoverished and poorly educated ruralite, with a personal history of family and relationship problems, who flees the countryside in search of new opportunities and winds up prostituting in a large urban centre – are inaccurate (Gil *et al.* 1994: 332; Gil *et al.* 1996: 149). Their own analysis of police records for 'convicted prostitutes' in Chengdu City and four counties in Sichuan Province showed that, while this particular sample group of prostitutes came from rural backgrounds, they were not poor, and they had a standard education and a stable home environment. Additionally, although the primary motivation offered by these women for entering prostitution was financial (50.7 per cent), 'a strong secondary motivation was stated to be "for sexual enjoyment"' (41.4 per cent) (Gil *et al.* 1994: 324–5). Here, Gil *et al.* imply that some Chinese women have departed from 'the strictures of normative female roles in the socialist environment', and voluntarily chosen to enter prostitution, in order to combine sexual adventure with economic gain (see also Gil and Anderson 1998: 133). It bears noting, however, that this suggestion is undermined by their more recent admission that the meaning of 'for sexual enjoyment' might be more accurately interpreted as referring to increased access to consumer goods and a more flamboyant life-style, not sexual pleasure per se (Gil *et al.* 1996: 144).

Claiming to further highlight the inadequacy of so-called official explanations, Gil *et al.* (1994: 142) point out that there is a 'higher class' of prostitutes in China who operate from 'hidden environments' and, as in many Western societies, they are 'virtually immune' from police harassment and 'woefully underrepresented' in arrest records.[8] One way to meet such women, they continue, is to visit 'select' dance clubs in most urban centres in China, as they did on a number of ethnographic forays. After observing and conversing with such women, Gil *et al.* (ibid.: 327–9) note that, contrary to official explanations, Chinese prostitutes are often highly educated urban women, including university students, who have no qualms about prostituting in their own metrocities in exchange for money, and the various pleasures (finer clothes, dancing, partying, personal attention, etc.) that involvement in prostitution can bring. Moreover, many candidly confessed that they found the life-style addictive.

Quite apart from the fact that the women to whom Gil *et al.* spoke would probably have stated that they were well-educated even if they were not,[9] what should be apparent by now is that Gil and his co-authors' empirical observations do not so much expose the inadequacy of official representations as the arbitrary and reductive nature of what we choose to call 'official'. After all, a Chinese-language commentary explaining the Clauses of the 1991 Decision explicitly states that police-led investigations conducted between 1986 and 1990 had rendered previous assumptions about the nature of prostitution obsolete (Quanguo renda changweihui *et al.* 1991: 12–13). These investigations demonstrated that the 'typical' prostitute subject could not be characterized as an impoverished, unemployed, poorly educated ruralite, because female and male participants in the prostitution transaction included: employees from state, collective and private enterprises; Party and state cadres; intellectuals; science and technology personnel; and even university students and researchers. They also demonstrated that, whereas prostitution activities had previously taken place in a limited number of underground locations, such activities had become 'visible' or 'open' and took place in a wide array of recreational venues, including high-class hotels and 'select' urban dance clubs. Therefore, contrary to the suggestion of Gil *et al.* that China's 'harsher' prostitution laws stemmed from intra-party conflicts and reflect the CCP's limited, ideological understanding of who prostitutes and why, the 1991 Decision was clearly formulated to enable the Chinese police to regulate the new kinds of prostitution practices and businesses that were officially acknowledged to have emerged from the interstices created by the processes of economic reform itself.

These inaccuracies notwithstanding, Gil and his co-authors' contention that the Chinese government is too caught up with intra-party conflicts and consequent ideological posturing to recognize the 'true' nature of prostitution in the PRC is integral to the major implication of the text, namely, that due to their scholarly objectivity and astute use of sociological-cum-ethnographic data, they are telling us the 'real' story. Gil *et al.* (1994: 321–2, 332–3) thus conclude by stating that the resurgence of prostitution in China is not adequately explained by the CCP's one-dimensional rationales. Nor, they continue, can it be entirely explained as the product of new socio-economic opportunities for a marginalized group of women. While hinting that this latter suggestion might prove attractive to feminists, Gil *et al.* add that the resurgence of prostitution in China cannot be contextualized with reference to Western conceptions of prostitution as simply paid labour, because the earning potential of each and every woman in prostitution is structured by sexist frameworks, or the diverse culture processes whereby men come to place a commodified value on particular female attributes (youth, beauty, the ability to charm, non-threatening intelligence, etc.) as opposed to others. Hence Gil *et al.* (1994: 333, 335, fn 9) suggest that Western conceptions of the sex worker as an independent economic and sexual actor may not be entirely appropriate for the analysis of 'more-patriarchal-than-us' China. This is because Chinese women in prostitution are still used and exploited by men, even if they manipulate patriarchal values to their own advantage. The authors therefore somewhat lamely conclude that analysis of the subject of prostitution in the PRC requires a multi-factorial rationale (ibid.: 332). But the implication remains that they have provided an objective and multi-faceted account, whereas the Chinese government adheres to an out-dated and ideological one.

In discussions relating to the subject of prostitution and HIV in China, Gil (1994) and Gil *et al.* (1996) further aver that the inadequacy of the Chinese government's approach to prostitution owes much to the CCP's (limited) Marxist understanding of human sexuality. As they argue, the development of HIV/AIDS prevention strategies in China is hindered not only by a severe shortage of funding, but also by the fact that official perspectives of sexuality – read the socialist veneration of monogamous marital sex and condemnation of all other expressions of human sexuality – conflict with the actual sexual practices of the population (Gil 1994: 215). Sexual experimentation and cohabitation, they continue, are no longer considered moral wrongs amongst most of China's youth, the drug and sex trades are booming, and homosexuality is becoming increasingly visible. Yet condom usage remains low and mainland Chinese people remain in a relative state of ignorance about the nature of STDs and HIV transmission. If the PRC is to develop comprehensive sex education and HIV prevention programmes, therefore, Gil *et al.* (1996: 150) conclude that the Chinese government will have to change the way it thinks about and deals with sexual expression as a whole, and move away from a moralistic and punitive perspective to one that values saving the lives of people at risk, regardless of their sexual behaviours.

Interestingly, Gil (1994: 216) maintains that 'modest' but 'consistent "sex research"' by mainland Chinese scholars is placing a 'novel pressure on the Chinese leadership to shift, epistemologically, how they think about sexuality in general and about sexual practices in the population in particular'. I say 'interestingly' because, in contrast to earlier suggestions that the CCP cannot think outside of its own puritanical, socialist strictures, we now have a government that is potentially open to pressure from specific interest groups. Rather than disrupting conventional wisdom regarding the repressive nature of 'the Party police state', however, the suggestion that the work of some 'enlightened' scholars has literally forced the CCP to change its moralistic, socialist stance on sex-related matters simply functions to valorize the specific knowledge skills of a particular group of mainland intellectuals who are arbitrarily and temporarily reified as 'non-state commentators'. The ongoing problem here is that 'non-state commentators' are presented as active, oppositional voices who have the capacity to resist the rigid, ideological, outlook of the CCP-led 'dictatorship' only when they speak the same language or disciplinary 'truths' as us. When they do not, they are relegated to the status of Party hacks.

Similarly highlighting the assumed ideological rigidity of 'the Chinese state', in *Women and Sexuality in China*, Harriet Evans (1997: 188) argues that the Chinese government 'has consistently ignored the gender issues present in the commercial and violent abuse of women, defining them instead as social, economic or moral issues'. Adding to this contention, Evans (ibid.: 187, 168) maintains that the official ban on prostitution in China is part of a 'discourse that is moulded more by moralistic assumptions about sexual propriety, women's in particular, than by an understanding of gender hierarchy'. For example, she continues, the dominant construction of the Chinese prostitute subject either as a victim of patriarchal structures of power and resurgent feudal practices, or else as a 'malicious perpetrator' of disease and bourgeois degeneration, not only ignores the 'reality' of women's lives and offers no space for 'women's own voices', it also perpetuates traditional conceptions of the 'ideal woman' as chaste, a wife, or a mother. Hence, Evans (ibid.: 188, 178) concludes that, '[w]hile a rhetoric of gender equality continues to establish the parameters within which discussion about women takes place', mainland accounts of prostitution and other commercial practices that exploit women focus on 'generally articulated ideological injustices' and 'neglect the crucial function of gender hierarchies of power'.

In this way, Evans dismisses official and most non-official Chinese accounts of prostitution for adhering to a gender-blind Marxist framework, rather than utilizing the insights made available by recourse to poststructuralism–feminism. This style of argumentation, despite its evident popularity amongst feminist sinologists, is merely a form of 'argument-by-absence'. The rhetorical persuasiveness of such a claim rests on little more than the reactivation and subsequent elision of the early (radical) feminist insistence that Feminism comprises a more politically correct and all-encompassing 'Theory' than that of the male-dominated Left, due to its focus on gender rather than socio-economic issues alone. This initial privileging of the category of gender proved useful in that it offered a much-needed legitimacy to feminist theory in the 1970s. In the current era of *feminisms* and non-adherence to totalizing conceptions of emancipatory politics, however, it should be patently clear that the positing of a separation between a focus on gender and socio-economic issues is completely artificial. Moreover, it should be equally clear that, even though the Marxist canon has never privileged the category of gender, it has always opened the space for women's issues to be raised and continues to do so in numerous, unforeseen ways. Nevertheless, Evans' overlaying of Feminism's historical claim to legitimacy with the kudos that currently accrues to those who 'do theory' embodies the suggestion that her conclusions are more intellectually rigorous than those who adhere to old-fashioned, gender-blind Marxism or to superseded, sexuality-blind radical feminism.

As per the work of Gail Hershatter, for instance, Evans' underlying premise is that 'our Chinese interlocutors' have a limited understanding of prostitution because they do not acknowledge autonomous expressions of female sexuality and agency (i.e., they lack a poststructuralist-feminist understanding of sexuality as a key site of women's emancipation). In consequence, Evans (ibid.: 177) similarly intimates that the PRC's response to prostitution is flawed because governmental authorities in China have failed to acknowledge that '"sex work" might be a legitimate form of employment that should enjoy the same legal and social status as any other'. One *could* argue that such may well be the case. But, like Hershatter, Evans (ibid.: 220) fails to demonstrate why the Chinese government *should* recognize prostitution as work, or to indicate in what ways legitimating prostitution as sex work *will* function to advantage Chinese women, and enable them to reposition themselves as sexual subjects in a manner which truly subverts what she calls the Chinese 'belief in an originating gender hierarchy fixed by nature'. She simply relies on the academic popularity of the term 'sex work' to prove the difference (understood as inadequacy) of Chinese discourses on prostitution, namely, their failure to conform to some idealized metropolitan response.

However, Western commentators on prostitution in reform-era China might have to start considering the implications of the political agenda they are helping to set in place. According to a recent article by the expatriate mainland scholar, Xin Ren (1999: 1434), the Chinese government has long since abandoned its historically bequeathed goal of eradicating prostitution and is now focusing on how to control, regulate, or *even capitalize on* the existence of prostitution. To support this contention, Xin (ibid.: 1427–31) argues that governmental authorities in China have freely admitted the impossibility of eradicating prostitution in the immediate future and have therefore moved towards the regulation of prostitution businesses and practices, via the implementation of improved management controls over the hospitality and service industries, and via the introduction of measures designed to tax and license women who work in the 'sex sector'. In other words, she suggests that the Chinese government has started to tolerate, even if it has not yet formally legalized, prostitution practices and businesses.

Xin's contention that the Chinese government has shifted from a focus on eradicating prostitution to controlling, then regulating, and now towards possibly legalizing the 'sex industry', is somewhat overstated. I say this because she not only confuses terms such as 'control', 'regulation' and 'legalization', she also equates localized governmental initiatives, such as the decision of certain municipal authorities to tax the earnings of women who work as 'hostesses' (an income-generating activity that is widely construed as a 'front' for prostitution in China) with central government initiatives. Furthermore, I cannot accept that the CCP is quite so free to abandon what Wang Zheng (2000: 69) describes as that 'powerful signifier of modernity and socialism', namely, its perceived commitment to the realization of gender equality, including the elimination of prostitution. If the arguments of researchers with the ACWF are anything to go by, this is demonstrably not the case.

Nonetheless, Xin usefully points out that governmental authorities in China *are* trying to manage the phenomenon of prostitution in new and diverse ways. This observation challenges most Anglophone scholarship on the subject of prostitution in the PRC. To begin with, it undermines the basic argumentative thrust of all the above-mentioned literature by drawing attention to the potential pragmatic flexibility, as opposed to the assumed ideological intractability, of the current regime. In addition, it suggests that theory-minded scholars, especially those who claim feminist allegiances, might want to reconsider the political consequences of presenting the arguments of the pro-sex work lobby, albeit by default, as a superior model to which the PRC must necessarily aspire.

Scholars with feminist allegiances might want to consider the political consequences of implicitly upholding the arguments of the pro-sex work lobby as the only legitimate response to prostitution, because the Chinese government is currently being pressured to revise its official policy of banning prostitution in different directions. On the one hand, female researchers with the ACWF have explicitly called on the Chinese government to retain its current policy of suppressing prostitution, while simultaneously introducing a comprehensive set of programmes designed to combat the various cultural and socio-economic factors that encourage both prostitution and male/female inequality. On the other hand, numerous health officials, local tax officials, bureaucratic entrepreneurs, and people whom Xin Ren describes as 'liberal Chinese scholars' (a collective group which the ACWF genders as being predominantly men), are pushing the Chinese government to recognize and legally regulate the 'sex sector'. This proposed shift is justified on the conventional liberal grounds that it will minimize the health threat of prostitution, reduce prostitution-related crime, enable government authorities to tax prostitution businesses and practices, help promote China's developing hospitality and tourism industries, and permit a 'natural' expression of human sexuality, while simultaneously ameliorating many of the exploitative conditions experienced by women in prostitution.

Adding to this mixed domestic pressure, the Chinese government is now under pressure from international human rights organizations to legally recognize prostitution as sex work. In a recent report on the PRC's implementation of the UN (1979) Convention on the Elimination of All Forms of Discrimination Against Women (CEDAW), various NGOs have criticized China's governmental authorities for failing, amongst other things, to tackle the domestic and intra-country trafficking in women for the purposes of 'forced' prostitution, and for refusing to recognize 'voluntary' prostitution as a legitimate form of work (Human Rights in China *et al.* 1998: 9–12, 27). Drawing on the work of Gil *et al.*, and various contributors to the Expert Workshop, the report somewhat erroneously castigates law and government officials in China for targeting only the poorest and most vulnerable of female prostitutes, for penalizing women who sell sex while exonerating men who buy sex, for ignoring the ongoing problems of police and governmental complicity in the running of prostitution businesses, and for refusing to acknowledge the problems associated with the policing of the traffic in women (Human Rights in China *et al.* 1998: 24–7). While admitting that the PRC's prostitution laws are designed to penalize those who organize prostitution, rather than participants in the prostitution transaction per se, the report concludes that China has failed to meet international human rights standards as stipulated by the UN with regard to the regulation of 'workers in the sex industry'. Specifically, the report concludes that the PRC has failed to recognize sex work as a legitimate form of labour as advocated by Li Lean Lim's (1998)

ILO-sponsored study on the 'sex sector' in Southeast Asia. This conclusion could gain some support in China as mainland commentators develop arguments in support of decriminalization.

In sum, there is something akin to an international and domestic consensus that the Chinese government has to revise its official policy on prostitution so as to satisfy certain conditions relating to the provision of women's rights, as well as the maintenance and improvement of public health and order. Contrary to the impetus of the above-mentioned NGO report, however, the Chinese government does not have to legally recognize prostitution as work in order to meet existing UN stipulations. This is because the ILO's recommendations do not bind state parties to any course of action and they remain highly contested. In any case, the PRC's prostitution laws are quite in keeping with the abolitionist thrust of the UN (1949) Convention for the Suppression of the Traffic in Persons and of the Exploitation of the Prostitution of Others, and they also concord with Article 6 of CEDAW, which calls upon signatory nations to suppress all forms of traffic in women and exploitation of prostitution of women. Furthermore, many of the revisions to the PRC's prostitution controls proposed domestically share certain surface commonalities with the abolitionist platform currently advocated by the feminist anti-prostitution lobby, the Swedish government, and socialist anti-prostitution campaigners within the Council of Europe, all of whom insist that the very existence of prostitution is contrary to the principles of human rights ('Campaign against prostitution: motion for a recommendation' 1997).

To admit the possibility that the PRC might possess a 'legitimate' response to prostitution, however, requires a rejection of the popular assumption that the operation of power in China can be defined solely in terms of state repression of the individual, and therefore a different *translational practice*. Given the different genealogical underpinnings of metropolitan and Chinese prostitution discourses, recourse to the liberal language of individual rights/identity politics can only offer a dyslogistical translation of the Chinese response. Instead of measuring the imperfections of the PRC's response to prostitution by way of reference to its apparent lack of conformity with some idealized transnational response, it might be analytically more productive to turn to modes of theorization that offer a different way of translating the relationship between 'sex' and 'government'. The critical necessity of doing so is underscored by the problematic nature of the recent feminist turn to international human rights law, as the next chapter shows.

5 Re-situating the Chinese response to prostitution

The feminists turn to human rights law

Although the feminist anti-prostitution and pro-sex work lobbies employ different understandings of prostitution as a matter of women's human rights, they nonetheless operate on the basis of a common rationale. They similarly assume that the international legal system can be used to hold individual governments responsible for failing to prevent, prosecute, or punish, individuals and organizations that violate the rights of women, irrespective of how those rights may be defined. This point is demonstrated by the fact that certain NGOs have used existing UN frameworks to criticize the Chinese government for failing to acknowledge the rights of sex workers to self-determination, and thus for failing to place the prostitution transaction under the jurisdiction of commerce and labour laws (Human Rights in China *et al.* 1998). Yet if governmental authorities in China were to adjust their policies and recognize prostitution as work, they would no doubt be taken to task by the All-China Women's Federation, and presumably by NGOs that support the feminist anti-prostitution lobby, for condoning sexual exploitation, and thereby contravening UN frameworks concerning the human rights of women to physical and mental integrity.

Rather than automatically endorsing the platform of either lobby, therefore, a fundamental issue that needs to be addressed is: what do metropolitan feminist theorists and activists have invested in the recent turn to international law? As Coomaraswamy (1996: 18) explains, the language of women's rights was catapulted on to the human rights agenda during the 1990s with a speed and determination that have seldom been equalled in the history of international law. The rapid ascendancy of the language of women's human rights, she continues, owes much to the fact that the discourse of human rights offers a recognized vocabulary for framing political and social wrongs, and carries with it an air of universality and legitimacy. Recourse to the discourse of human rights has thus enabled feminist theorists to challenge 'the state's' lack of attention to practices that harm and discriminate against women (flowing from the historic relegation of women to the 'private' domain), and, subsequently, to gain greater public visibility for issues such as domestic violence, sexual abuse, sexual harassment, trafficking, and prostitution, by translating them in terms of internationally accepted norms concerning the right to life, and the right to economic and social self-determination (Cook 1994; Mahoney and Mahoney 1993; Peters and Wolper 1995). Additionally, it has enabled women's rights activists to claim access to the diverse machinery set up at the international level for the promotion of human rights and for taking action against nations that fail to meet international requirements.

By claiming the *right* to enter into and redefine the 'masculinist' terrain of international law, however, women's human rights activists have effectively revitalized the once beleaguered claim of Feminism to speak for all women, albeit this time in the name of multivocal, transnational feminisms, as opposed to univocal, 'White-Western-Feminism' (Howe 1995: 63–91). This is not to deny that most feminist theorists are wary of the false universalism inherent in the notion of human rights, especially given the long-standing rendition of human rights as the rights of the autonomous male individual (Charlesworth 1995: 103–13). Nor is it to deny that many feminists have questioned the universal applicability of international human rights law in Western and non-Western settings alike by intimating that the international legal community operates like a 'blown-up liberal state', legislating in accordance with (post-)Enlightenment humanistic values (Romany 1994: 285). It is simply to point out that the language of women's rights has been catapulted onto the international human rights agenda with a speed and urgency that have left little space for reflexivity, especially when it comes to the vexed question of how to specify or 'think-together' both the differences among women *and* issues pertaining to cultural diversity.

Most notably, despite repeated admonitions to the effect that transnational strategies must be viewed as interim measures, based on the provisional tactic of 'thinking globally, while acting locally', metropolitan women's rights activists evince an inordinate faith in the universal efficacy and transformatory capacity of *feminist* legally based strategies. This faith is invariably justified by referring to the urgent need for remedial action regarding issues that harm and discriminate against women, and the unavoidable necessity of using the language of human rights because it is the only language that works or has the capacity to set legal remedies in operation. While these justifications may ring true, the underlying appeal to notions of an oppressed universal sisterhood, and hence to commonsensical understandings of 'real politics' or 'the way things are under patriarchy', has had the corollary effect of functioning to preclude theoretically informed attempts to disassemble the language of human rights, by intimating that such endeavours are purely academic, or even non-feminist, in the final analysis. The recent turn to international law has thus lured many feminist human rights theorists into 'the trap of arrogant perception' (Gunning 1992: 189–99). This is the trap of assuming that metropolitan feminist concerns can and *should be* translated into a universally applicable set of policy recommendations, a replication of the masculinist and ethnocentric binary logic of Western humanist discourse which subordinates or erases the difference of non-Western peoples and social formations.

Assessed from the purview of postcolonial-feminist scholarship, therefore, the preoccupation of feminist human rights theorists with developing legal strategies on behalf of women globally is problematic because it implies a generality and universality of experience that are incongruous with a recognition of 'difference' and the global range of feminisms. Certainly, while metropolitan women's rights activists routinely concede the need to acknowledge 'other' points of view, their turn to international law is ultimately grounded in the assumption that 'feminists from all worlds share a central concern: their domination by men' (Charlesworth 1995: 103). Hence feminist human rights theorists tend to fall back on such time-honoured and overarching analytical categories as 'patriarchy', 'the family', 'the sexual division of labour', and 'the public/private distinction', in order to create a sense of commonality among women globally. In the process, they are inclined to forget that the private/public distinction may not exist cross-culturally, and that their concern with the issue of 'male domination' has to be substantiated in different contexts (Howe 1995: 84).

The recent preoccupation of metropolitan human rights theorists with developing international legal strategies on behalf of women has thus been accompanied by a marked reluctance to examine the *interested* nature of feminism's political agenda on a global scale (ibid.: 69–70). I use the term 'interested' in the sense that feminist human rights theorists appear loath to acknowledge the extent to which their claim to be speaking on behalf of all women, and hence the authorizing claim of NGOs lobbying for women's rights, is enabled by the process of 'othering' non-Western cultures. Indeed, rather than attempting a fundamental reconceptualization of the analytical categories that 'make up' international law, feminist human rights theorists have tended to collude with the colonizing 'master discourse' of Western humanism, by universalizing the experience of first-world women across cultural and national boundaries, and by portraying third-world women as a homogeneous group who lead more truncated lives and are ultimately less empowered than their Western counterparts, by virtue of their 'more patriarchal' traditions, cultures, and beliefs. They also often wind up justifying this homogenizing strategy (and thereby explaining away its problematic political effects), via a circular appeal to the practical necessity of using the language of human rights (given the universality of male domination and female subordination), and, subsequently, by intimating that taking on board the issues raised by postcolonial theorists would mean throwing the 'women's rights baby' out with the bathwater, and accepting an apolitical, 'anything goes', position of absolute cultural relativism (Rao 1995: 167–75; Winter 1994: 939–74).

The effect of adhering to this circular form of argumentation has been to render the newly configured terrain of 'feminist international law' impervious to deconstructive interrogations of its own foundational premises. This apparent resistance to 'internal critique' is anachronistic not only because the feminist turn to international law has entailed effects that are incongruous with the postcolonial goal of reconceptualizing difference in ways that 'are not complicit with Western humanism's always already "disinterested" imperialist tradition' (Howe 1995: 76), but also because it implies an optimism with regard to 'the law' and 'the state' that runs counter to the traditionally pessimistic, feminist construction of both entities as, at best, 'paternalistic', and, at worse, irretrievably 'male' (Heath 1997: 45–63). In fact, the assumption that the international legal system can be used to realize feminist goals implicitly reinforces the classic liberal rendition of 'the state' as a neutral arbiter capable of promoting justice for all, albeit in this instance due to the development of what are perceived as properly feminist (read truly human) laws.

The ultimately 'illiberal' nature of feminist efforts to speak legally on behalf of women globally can be highlighted with reference to NGO activism concerning the PRC's response to prostitution. As discussed in Chapter 4, certain NGOs are currently lobbying the Chinese government to recognize 'voluntary' prostitution as a condition of being in compliance with the UN (1979) Convention on the Elimination of All Forms of Discrimination Against Women. Actions of this kind are explicitly premised on the understanding that international law possesses a symbolic as well as a regulative function, and that claims couched in the language of human rights carry an emotional and moral legitimacy which can exert a powerful influence for change. Drawing on the popular portrayal of CEDAW as the 'women's human rights treaty', various NGOs have cited the PRC's failure to place the prostitution transaction under the jurisdiction of commerce and labour laws as yet another example of the Chinese government's substandard record with regard to the observance of basic human rights.

The irony of this well-intentioned attack on China's human rights record, especially given the sloganistic justification of such criticisms as 'bringing CEDAW and Beijing home' (so as to underscore the UN's renewed commitment to the understanding of women's rights as human rights at the 1995 Fourth World Conference on Women in Beijing), is precisely the failure of metropolitan theorists to adequately consider: where is the place that enunciates our world-travelling, activist itinerary? After all, China's implementation of CEDAW – the first rights treaty applying to the domestic situation that has been ratified by the PRC – indubitably leaves room for improvement. Even the Chinese representatives at the UN Review Committee admitted that 'Chinese women had "a long way to go" before realizing full equality' ('International scrutiny in action' 1999). However, the strategy adopted by the NGOs in question – to dismiss the Chinese delegates' allusions to broader structural problems and entrenched cultural values as 'political face-saving' designed to obscure the PRC's refusal to empower Chinese women via the implementation of a rights-based approach – simply underscores the Eurocentric bias of human rights activism in general.

In addition, the NGO report on the PRC's implementation of CEDAW, entitled 'Can dialogue improve China's human rights situation?' (Human Rights in China *et al.* 1998), highlights the Eurocentric predisposition of metropolitan activists to selectively focus on perceived instances of third-world resistance to positive feminist-political change, while eliding the fact that most developed countries were slow to ratify CEDAW and the USA still has not done so. In doing so, it demonstrates the problematic ways in which the hyperreal space of 'Euramerica' is naturalized and reified as the most progressive model, to which developing nations must aspire. Since prostitution is prohibited in most North American states, and the legal recognition of prostitution in other developed nations has not resulted in a significantly more woman-centred (or even a more equitable) restructuring of the 'sex industry', it shows how developing nations are expected to live up to an idealized standard that few, if any, first-world nations have attained.

Proponents of the understanding of prostitution as sex work, for instance, maintain that the Chinese government has failed to meet its obligations as a signatory to CEDAW; by failing to place the 'sex sector' under the jurisdiction of commerce and labour laws, it has denied women the right to control their own bodies and lives, as well as the right to migrate and to decide for themselves whether or not to work in the 'sex industry'.[1] This line of argument is persuasive insofar as it appeals to liberal conceptions of civil rights and the popular conviction that the operation of power in China functions predominantly to repress. By adhering to this mode of argumentation, however, metropolitan activists fail to register that the apparent failure of mainland Chinese commentators to define prostitution as a legitimate form of work is indicative of more than the presumed moralistic and authoritarian intractability of the CCP-led regime. It indicates that the specific amalgam of interests and forces that has enabled metropolitan intellectuals-cum-activists to categorize prostitution as work has not coalesced in quite the same fashion in China. Hence, placing the prostitution transaction under the jurisdiction of the PRC's labour laws may not produce the empowering effects that the introduction of a more 'enlightened' response is assumed to guarantee.

One way of illustrating this latter contention is to note that the NGO report itself points to the multiple problems associated with female employment, the lack of independent trade unions and the limited access of individuals to civil redress vis-à-vis occupational health and safety issues, in China. In view of these structural and legal limitations, it is difficult to see how recognizing prostitution as work is supposed to empower Chinese women in prostitution, or even enable the more effective administration of the 'sex sector', in the immediate future. In fact, if the arguments of the ACWF are given any credence, it could well lead to the creation of another female job ghetto, while simultaneously generating more profits for the predominantly male-run hospitality and tourist industries. This is because, as with many other countries, prevailing social mores will continue to militate against female sex workers being treated as equivalent to any other wage labourer. For example, surveys conducted in China suggest that clandestine forms of prostitution will continue to proliferate alongside the establishment of legalized prostitution businesses, since survey responses indicated that 'virtually no one would like to openly work in a red-light district', and virtually no one would have the temerity to patronize a 'red-light district' (Pan Suiming, cited in Zhang Zhiping 2000: 32–3). Bearing these considerations in mind, and given the virtual absence of sophisticated and recognized prostitute unions in developed first-world countries,[2] metropolitan human rights activists might be better advised to focus on the kinds of changes that can be rendered both 'thinkable' and 'operable' in China for improving the situation of women in prostitution, rather than attempting to turn the PRC into a replica of our own 'idealized self'.

At any rate, it is somewhat curious that the NGO report draws on the work of mainland Chinese professionals, including those who contributed to the Expert Workshop, to indict the Chinese government for failing to protect the rights of women in prostitution, while never acknowledging that these same professionals outline a provisional response to prostitution that could garner considerable support both in China and abroad. The recommendations of this particular workshop, as noted in Chapter 4, veer between implicitly calling for the legal recognition of prostitution – so as to facilitate the introduction of improved STD/HIV prevention strategies and ameliorate the exploitation of women in prostitution – and explicitly calling for the continued suppression of prostitution businesses and practices – by recommending that the punitive emphasis of China's prostitution controls should be directed at those who buy sex and those who organize prostitution, especially government officials and law-enforcement agents who do so ('Consensus and recommendations on HIV and prostitution' 1996: 104–6). Given that many of the concerns outlined at the Expert Workshop replicate those of the NGOs in question, even though they do not admit the liberal construction of the prostitute subject as an oppressed sexual minority, a delimited version of the legal response advocated by the feminist anti-prostitution lobby might offer a more effective means to agitate for women's rights in China. That is to say, if the NGOs in question are truly concerned with achieving immediate improvements in the lives of Chinese women in prostitution, they might be better advised to recognize the existing parameters and *domestically acknowledged* limitations of the PRC's prostitution controls, and offer interim support for the recommendation that the Chinese government provide supportive programmes for women in prostitution, while simultaneously directing official attention towards those who create the demand for and organize prostitution.

Even more curiously, if supporters of the NGO report appear unwilling to accept anything short of the immediate legal recognition of 'voluntary' prostitution in the PRC, the feminist anti-prostitution lobby appears oblivious to the fact that China's prostitution laws enunciate many of their demands. This omission partly reflects the recent nature of feminist interest in prostitution as an object of international human rights law, and the different organizing concerns and structural imbalances that determine the nature of NGO activism. Organizations such as Human Rights in China, for instance, have an established interest in issues of policing and legal accountability, which would enable them to 'matter-of-factly' incorporate the governmental regulation of prostitution as yet another area in need of remedial action. But the feminist anti-prostitution lobby's lack of attention to the Chinese case clearly owes much to the popular feminist conviction that Marxism is gender-blind, ergo 'China' has nothing to offer feminist theorizations except as an object example of socialism's signal failure to realize women's liberation. Certainly, Kathleen Barry's effective dismissal of the Chinese response to prostitution as a paternalistic, socialist variant of the much denigrated 'male-capitalist-prohibitory' approach is quite in keeping with the general tenor of feminist sinology, and it also concords with broader feminist criticisms of the perceived 'masculinist' nature of 'the state' and 'the law', and the even more paternalistic nature of such entities in most developing countries (see Barry 1995: 222–7). Indeed, the feminist anti-prostitution lobby's elision of the Chinese case offers yet another illustration of the problematic ways in which the 'non-West' is rendered subordinate to the sovereign theoretical space of 'Europe', in this instance primarily reflecting a transcontextual concern with the subordinate status of women viewed as a collective sex-class, rather than issues of identity politics viewed through the universalizing lens of liberal individualism.

In short, the recent feminist turn to international law has generated yet another space wherein the subject of prostitution in the PRC could be admitted into a transdisciplinary dialogue. Like the bulk of Anglophone China studies scholarship on issues of sexuality and power in the PRC, however, feminist interventions into and within the international legal community have been constructed and conducted in a manner that poses no serious challenge to the traditional dichotomy between Euramericans as 'theory makers' and developing nations/third-world women as 'objects of theory'. Put crudely, the Chinese response to prostitution cannot be included in a broader feminist conversation because it is always already excluded by the logic of classic gender Feminism, and by the fact that 'difference feminisms', particularly in their legal or rights-based manifestations, appear to have jumped out of the frying pan of essentialized gender politics only to have landed in the fire of classic liberalism (Valverde 1999:

345–61). To resituate and thereby admit the Chinese response to prostitution into a metropolitan debate requires a different way of interpreting the relationship between 'sex' and 'government', one that avoids the problems associated with classic liberal *and* classic feminist analyses of power and 'the state'. In this respect, I can think of no mode of theorization more suited to translating 'China' against the grain of existing 'China-watching' conventions than the Foucauldian concept of governmentality.

Governmentality: getting rid of 'the Chinese State'

Michel Foucault (1979: 5–21) contends that all modern forms of political thought and action are grounded in a particular way of *thinking* about the kinds of problems that can and should be addressed by various authorities, which he calls 'governmentality'. Since the overthrow of absolutist monarchies in the eighteenth century, he explains, governmentality has become the common ground of all modern political rationalities insofar as they similarly construe the tasks of authorities in terms of the calculated supervision, administration, and maximization, of the forces of society, rather than in terms of the maintenance of power per se. That is to say, they all construe the ultimate aim of 'government' in terms of improving the condition of a population, via the effective management of the processes that regulate its wealth, health, longevity, its capacity to engage in labour, to reproduce and wage war, etc., and the means that authorities use to achieve these goals are all in some sense immanent to the population itself. The concept of governmentality thus refers to 'the ensemble formed by the institutions, procedures, analyses and reflections, the calculations and tactics, that allow the exercise of this very specific albeit complex form of power, which has as its target population' (Foucault 1979: 20).

As such, Foucault's concept of governmentality refers to government in the broadest sense of the word. It does not draw attention to the actions of a calculating political subject (a State or heads of state) or to the operations of bureaucratic mechanisms and personnel. Instead, it *describes* a particular way of attempting to realize social and political objectives by acting in a calculated manner upon the forces, activities, and relations of the individuals that comprise a population. It therefore signifies a general form of organized reasoning, embracing practical ways of thinking and acting upon what are posited as social and economic problems, and how the conduct of individuals or groups of individuals may be structured and directed. Hence governmentality can also be defined as a particular method of understanding 'the conduct of conduct' – a way of acting on the actions of individuals, taken either singly or collectively, so as to shape, guide, correct and modify the ways in which they conduct themselves (Gordon 1991: 2).

This way of conceiving the exercise of political rule usefully resituates conventional, i.e., juridical, understandings of the nexus between 'government' and 'power'. Briefly, Foucault's method of examining government rationalities avoids 'the problem of the State', namely, the tendency to reduce the operation of political power to the actions of a state, understood as a relatively coherent and calculating political subject. Instead of defining political rule in terms of a state that extends its sway throughout society by means of a ramifying apparatus of control, the concept of governmentality draws attention to the diversity of forces and knowledges involved in efforts to regulate the lives of individuals, and the conditions within particular national territories, in pursuit of various goals. In doing so, it suggests that 'the state' does not give rise to government: rather, the state is an artefact or a particular form that government has taken (Miller and Rose 1990: 3). Put another way, it intimates that power relations refer to the state not because they derive from 'the State', but rather because they have been 'progressively elaborated, rationalized and centralized, in the form of, and under the auspices of, state institutions' (Foucault 1982: 793).

This debunking of the importance traditionally ascribed to 'the problem of the State' flows from Foucault's demonstration that the historically constituted matrix of government has entailed the establishment and development of forms of power that are *not* exercised through simple prohibitions or the extension of control apparatuses (Rose and Miller 1992: 175). Quite the opposite, the 'governmentalization' of society has been achieved via the administering and fostering of life itself, that is, through the establishment and deployment of forms of power (collectively known as 'biopower') that directly and materially penetrate the body. This background helps to explain the importance assumed by 'sex' as a political issue. As a means of access to both the life of the body and the life of the species, 'the problem of sex' is located at the point of intersection between questions pertaining to the discipline of the body and the management of populations. It therefore constitutes a crucial target of a power or biopolitics that is organized around the management of the life of the individual and society as a whole (Foucault 1978: 145–7).

Once the productive nature of this form of power is acknowledged, the concern of those who desire positive political change to limit 'the reach of the State' appears somewhat misdirected. I say 'productive' in the sense that, contrary to the popular construction of 'the modern state' as an entity which was developed above individuals, by ignoring or denying their 'true' nature, the main impetus of Foucault's work has been to expose the diverse ways in which the personal and subjective capacities of citizens have been both shaped by and incorporated into the scope and aspirations of public powers. Concomitantly, although Foucault contends that power is an omnipresent dimension in human relations, he demonstrates that the operation of power in modern societies is an endless and open strategic game, not a fixed and closed regime. This recognition implies that statist-based analyses are not so much unwarranted as over-valued. A far more important focus for political analysis and action is the non-reducible relationship between government and the manifold technologies through which we have been historically constituted and, in turn, come to constitute ourselves (Burchell 1993: 268).

In this way, the Foucauldian concept of governmentality also decentres the founding tenets of classic liberal philosophy by intimating that a political vocabulary structured by divisions such as state/society, public/private, government/market, and sovereignty/autonomy, is unable to adequately capture the diverse ways in which political rule is exercised today. Briefly, liberalism is usually portrayed as a political doctrine or ideology that is concerned with the maximization of individual liberty and with the defence of that liberty against the state, in particular. It is thus marked as a political philosophy by the assumption that civil society – a community of autonomous individuals who tend to be presented as given – places 'natural' limits on the legitimate exercise of power by political authorities. Yet liberalism simultaneously posits that one of the obligations and tasks of the state is to foster the interests and self-organizing capacities of the very citizens that are supposed to provide a counterweight and limit to its power (Hindess 1993: 300).

Within the discourse of liberal politics, therefore, power is confronted, on the one hand, by a community of individuals 'equipped with rights that *must not* be interdicted by government' (Rose and Miller 1992: 179–80). On the other hand, government is charged with the task of addressing a realm of processes which it is theoretically disbarred from acting on via the exercise of sovereign will, because it *cannot know* the 'natural' rules and processes, or internal forms of regulation, that structure civil society, the private domain and economic activity. This contradictory framing of the 'role of government' underpins the traditional concern of political scientists with the question of 'the State' viewed either as a *monstre froid* confronting and dominating us, or else as a privileged and essentially 'neutral' entity fulfilling a number of necessary socio-economic functions. Likewise, it fuels the conventional framing of policy failures and successes in terms of 'unjustified/unjust' versus 'justified/just' governmental interventions.

Following Foucault's work on governmentality, however, a number of scholars have argued that liberalism is better understood as referring to a mode of government, not simply a doctrine of *limited* government (Burchell *et al.* 1991; Minson 1993; Rose 1989). They contend that the elaboration of liberal doctrines of freedom, which demanded the constitutional and legal delimitation of the powers of political authorities, went hand in hand with projects designed to make liberalism operable by creating the subjective conditions in which realms designated 'private', and therefore 'beyond' the reach of political power, could 'learn' to govern themselves. In making this claim, governmentality scholars do not aim to redefine liberalism as an ideology disguising the state annexation of freedom. Rather, their objective is to show that the celebrated sphere of individual liberty, whether defined in terms of the autonomous individual, civil society, or the private domain, should be understood, not as reflective of the 'natural' liberty of the individual, but as a governmental product – that is, as an effect of a multiplicity of interventions concerned with the promotion of a specific form of life.

In short, embracing Foucault's emphasis on the positivity of power, governmentality scholars have been concerned to show that the operation of political power in advanced liberal democracies is 'not so much a matter of imposing constraints upon citizens' as a matter of '"making up" citizens capable of bearing a kind of regulated freedom' (Rose and Miller 1992: 174). Instead of restricting their analyses to 'the problem of the State', therefore, governmentality scholars have been concerned to explore the *problematics of government*. They have been concerned to investigate the complex interaction between the changing discursive field in which conceptions of the proper ends and means of government are articulated, the amalgam of mundane programmes and technical procedures of inscription through which authorities seek to embody and give effect to governmental ambitions, and the diverse ways in which individual subjects acquire self-regulatory capacities that help to align 'personal choices' with the ends of government (Miller and Rose 1990: 1–31; Rose and Miller 1992: 113–205).

Although most governmentality studies to date have focused on what has been called the liberal mode of government, a number of scholars have argued that the form of government highlighted by Foucault is by no means unique to advanced liberal democracies. Barry Hindess (1993: 300–13), for example, extrapolates from Foucault's contention that there is no distinctively socialist technology of government to argue that much the same can be said of liberalism. As Hindess notes, the difference between socialist and liberal political traditions is often presented as clear-cut. Liberal-democratic 'governments' recognize the natural liberty of the individual and aim to defend it against external obstacles, whereas socialist and communist 'regimes' variously undermine that liberty in the name of collective interests and priorities. This easy distinction begins to fall apart, however, if one acknowledges that the founding subjects of liberal and socialist discourses – a community of autonomous individuals in the former, a community of workers or 'the people' in the latter – both have an ambiguous ontological status. In some contexts, these collective subjects are treated as 'objective' realities producing effects in the present and possessing interests that can or should be represented. However, in other contexts, they are treated as artefacts that do not properly exist (at least in their 'ideal' form); hence the task of 'authorities' is to create or re-create the conditions in which they can. In effect, both political traditions adhere to the view that government should work through, and consequently must aim to realize, a community of persons who, for the most part, can be left to regulate their own behaviour. And, in order to produce a suitably calculable population of citizens whose existence can be largely taken for granted, both traditions have relied on the more or less successful workings of the diverse governmental devices that comprise the so-called liberal mode of government. In consequence, Hindess (ibid.: 311) concludes that what these apparently competing rationalities of government have in common may be far more significant than the obvious doctrinal points on which they differ.

Adding to Hindess' argument, it bears noting that the founding subjects of feminism, 'Woman' and 'women', are marked by the same ontological ambiguity that characterizes the collective subjects of liberal and socialist discourses. This makes the absence of sustained feminist analyses of governmentality surprising for several reasons. To begin with, feminist activism itself is arguably engendered by governmentality. Governmental concerns with improving the condition of a population have clearly resulted in women being conceptualized and targeted as 'mothers', 'wives', and 'child-rearers'; and, it is precisely in the interstices created by such programmes that feminist strategies aim to intervene. In addition, feminist strategies themselves, particularly in their legally based manifestations, are premised on the same kind of totalizing logic that informs governmentality. They similarly presume that women possess 'objective' interests that can and should be represented via the correction of erroneous laws and policies. Conversely, they similarly presume that people can be re-created in the image envisaged by 'good' feminist laws. This imbrication may help to explain why feminist interventions in the arena of international law are so bound up with what they seek to contest, insofar as they tend to replicate, even as they aim to redefine, the kinds of distinctions between the 'public' and 'private' realms, and between 'ideology' and 'real practice', that structure statist-based analyses.

Although there is little work regarding the utility of governmentality studies for rethinking transnational feminist approaches, scholars such as Bray (1999), Dutton (1992), and Sigley (1996a), have brought the conventional twinning of statist-based analyses and international human rights activism into question by demonstrating that the basic conceptual parameters of governmentality can be fruitfully applied to the analysis of government in the PRC. All these scholars eschew the conventional sinological framing of 'the problem of the Chinese State' in terms of communist totalitarianism-cum-authoritarianism. Instead, by providing genealogies of the diverse knowledges and organizational practices that 'make up' the Chinese work-unit system, the Chinese policing and penal system, and Chinese reproductive and health programmes, they reveal that Chinese socialist governmentality has much in common with the mode of government described by Foucault, even as the combined weight of traditional knowledges and practices, Maoist techniques and practices, and the imperatives of economic reform, has meant that government in China has been operationalized in different localized forms. In doing so, they intimate that

Western criticisms of the Chinese government for suppressing individuality, endorsing oppressive policing practices, and enforcing draconian reproductive and sex-related policies, are not so much unfounded as analytically misdirected.

Bray (1999), for instance, rejects the popular assumption that the Maoist regime's promotion of collective orientated policies and practices reflected an official and institutional disregard for the sanctity of the individual. By tracing the genealogical links between traditional forms of social organization in China, various urban planning and social reform projects conducted in eighteenth- and nineteenth-century Europe, and the development of the Chinese socialist work-unit, Bray demonstrates that the collective forms of organization promoted during the Maoist era did not flow solely from the CCP's Marxist proclivities. Instead, they drew on, even as they drew away from, the collective mode of subjectivity generated by the hierarchically organized Confucian family. Rather than viewing this connection as indicative of Chinese socialism's reliance on (and subsequent contamination by) feudal social forms, Bray proceeds to show how this traditional mode of subjectivity was transformed via the effective displacement of 'the (patriarchal) Confucian family' as the primary unit of social organization and governmental calculation in favour of the work-unit and its constituent households. After investigating the ways in which the work-unit functioned to promote collective forms of organization *and* give effect to Chinese socialist governmentality, he concludes that the individual is both present and an acknowledged bearer of rights in the PRC, albeit in a form not recognized by the discursive conventions of liberal political philosophy. The example *par excellence* of this right-bearing individual-cum-citizen is the worker who enjoyed life-long benefits and welfare through the work-unit system, such as access to schools, housing, and health care, provided she or he devoted themselves to the collective labour ethos of socialism.

Likewise, Sigley (1996a: 141) dismisses the organizing claim of much Anglophone scholarship on 'sex' and 'power' in the PRC, namely, that the Chinese government 'has refused to confer any rights to pleasure upon individuals'. While conceding that, since 1949, governmental concerns to manage the population for the purposes of socialist production have entailed incorporating 'the family' and individuals into tight social networks, via the regulation and development of the household registration and work-unit systems, Sigley contends that the extension of this network has not intruded on the personal autonomy of Chinese subjects, at least not in the way we like to think. By examining the procedures through which issues such as 'sex', 'marriage', and 'the family', have been problematized and interconnected as objects of governmental intervention in traditional and communist China, Sigley (ibid.: 20) demonstrates that, in contrast to Western societies, 'the Chinese state' and 'the Chinese family' tend to be viewed as interconnected, not as separate entities (jiaguo *tonggou*). As a result, mainland scholars are far more concerned to enhance rather than limit governmental interventions into areas that are deemed 'natural', or 'private', and thereby beyond the legitimate reach of 'the state' in liberal discourses.

Sigley then proceeds to demonstrate that the absence of a clear-cut distinction between the public and private realms cannot be read as proof that 'the individual' is repressed in China, or that Chinese scholars who are concerned to improve governmental interventions in sex-related arenas are Party hacks. For, in marked contrast to the historical experience of Western societies, Chinese governmental concerns with managing the sexual and reproductive conduct of the population have not been organized around the biopolitics of sexuality. Rather than viewing sexuality as a means of interiorizing or expressing 'the self', Sigley suggests that the government of sexual conduct in contemporary China is better understood as being linked to a more mechanistic 'techniques of existence', incorporating the dissemination of a whole body of literature on the technical 'know-how' of sex and 'an economy of pleasure'. He therefore concludes that the Chinese governmental view of sex may paradoxically allow for more privacy than its Western counterparts, because Chinese subjects have not been obliged historically to 'spiritualize' or ethically intensify their relationships (ibid.: 176–7).

In a similar vein, Dutton contends that Western criticisms of the arbitrary and extra-legal nature of many forms of detention and policing in present-day China basically 'miss their target' (Dutton and Lee 1993: 316–36). As he explains, most of the abuses associated with Chinese campaign-style policing flow from economic liberalization, not political authoritarianism. To be successful, economic reform demanded the loosening of state controls over the flow of resources, and the mobility of the population, so that goods and labour could be more freely exchanged on the market. But the loosening of these controls also had two unexpected and antithetical consequences. It led to an upsurge in crime and simultaneously undermined the basis of all forms of policing in China since 1949, i.e., the static and stable population (ibid.: 330). Faced with popular and governmental demands that they redress the deteriorating law and order situation, the Chinese police responded to what amounted to a 'crisis in policing' by implementing a series of concentrated assaults against certain targeted forms of crime and illicit conduct. The first (and most notorious) of these nationwide policing campaigns was the 1983 'strike hard' campaign against criminal activity. This campaign drew on many of the tactics and procedures associated with the now denigrated mass political movements of the Maoist era, and different strategical versions of this original anti-crime campaign continue to be implemented to this day.

While apparently appeasing public concerns over the deteriorating law and order situation, the campaign-style tactics adopted by the Chinese police have attracted trenchant criticism from international human rights activists *and* from within the ranks of the Chinese public security organs. These criticisms turn on the fact that the strategy of deploying short, sharp strikes against particular types of people and places has made extensive use of the Chinese system of administrative sanctions. This system offers the police a greater degree of legal flexibility than the criminal code and has encouraged many of the abuses noted in metropolitan human rights accounts, such as easier arrests and detentions, and harsher sentencing. However, in contrast to the argumentative thrust of most Anglophone commentators, who tend to cite these abuses as evidence of the Chinese government's refusal to abandon the oppressive, overly politicized control apparatus of 'the Maoist Party police state' and establish a 'modern rule of law' (Tanner, H. 1995: 277–303), an examination of the work of Chinese policing scholars reveals a rather different story.

Put simply, Chinese policing scholars themselves are highly critical of campaign-style policing since they are not only aware that it undermines efforts to improve standards of police accountability and professionalism, but also that the periodic channelling of resources into specialized, and somewhat glamorized 'struggles' undercuts attempts to develop a more comprehensive mode of policing (Dutton and Lee 1993: 330–1; Huang Jingpin *et al.* 1988: 42–6). Nevertheless, they also acknowledge that faced with the consequences of rapid social and structural change, and a serious lack of human, financial and technological resources, campaign-style policing offers one of the few interim measures available if low crime levels – and hence *public confidence* in policing efforts – are to be maintained. In view of this domestically acknowledged 'dilemma', Dutton concludes that any discussion aimed at resolving human rights abuses in China would have to start with these pragmatic and specific considerations in mind, rather than attributing the problems of Chinese law and policing to communist totalitarianism or Chinese despotism (Dutton and Lee 1993: 332–3).

The conclusion to be drawn from the preceding remarks is that discussions of human rights that commence with absolute notions of the inalienable, and thereby frame their criticisms in terms of 'the problem of the State', are premised on idealized versions of liberalism. Consequently, they fail to grasp the historically and governmentally constructed nature of the particular mode of sexualized individual subjectivity that they present as 'natural', and therefore universal. That said, I do not intend to promote a position of absolute cultural relativism and insist that all social formations are characterized by differing modes of subjectivity, and associated conceptions of rights, that are equally legitimate given their fundamental difference. Nor do I wish to imply that we need to counterpoise idealized versions of liberalism with a revitalized vision of socialism. Rather, I am suggesting that we should take Foucault (1988c: 37) seriously when he insists that what different forms of political rationality offer as their necessary being, and hence our variously embodied sense of self or 'right-full' being, 'reside on a base of human practice and human history; and that since these things have been made, they can be unmade, as long as we know how it was that they were made'. This means that any constructive discussion of rights must be grounded in relation to the particular amalgam of knowledges and practices through which different governmental programmes have been rendered 'thinkable' and operationalized, not upon abstract notions of the inalienable rights of the individual, and/or the collective rights of women construed as an oppressed sex class that has yet to realize its 'true', unalienated form.

In sum, recourse to the Foucauldian concept of governmentality suggests that it is necessary to examine the institutionalized siting and operation of alternative modes of governance, rather than lamenting China's lack of an individual subject, a feminist understanding of sexual politics, or a modern rule of law. Contrary to the defensive tenor of recent feminist interventions in international law, the aim of conducting such an investigation is not to reify these alternative forms as culturally unique and beyond reproach. It is to show on what basis different institutionalized rights and regulations have been formulated, and thereby move towards calculations of a viable and workable alternative. One distinct advantage of adopting such an approach is that it allows us to admit the numerous issues that mainland Chinese professionals themselves have raised in relation to China's prostitution controls, without automatically treating them as subordinate to the organizing concerns of the Anglophone humanities. Accordingly, the next section further highlights the diversity of forces and groups that have sought to make prostitution a governable form of conduct in China, by outlining the body of laws and regulations aimed at specifying participants in prostitution businesses and practices.

The body of Chinese prostitution law

The phrase 'the body of the law' is generally understood as referring to a determinate corpus – legal codes, statutes, and the rulings of common law, etc. However, as recent interventions into legal studies have shown, the body of the law can also be understood as referring to 'the subjected body that belongs to and is part of the law as the condition of possibility of the law' (Cheah *et al.* 1996: xvii). A basic contention here is that in order for the law to function at all, it must first and foremost have a hold over bodies. But, rather than viewing the body as an object which is always prior to or external to the law, it is important to recognize that laws and legal rulings do not function 'just to produce generalized and to a certain extent abstract bodies of legal subjects'; they also act more concretely to create specific body types in particularized ways (ibid.: xviii). To critically 'think through' the body of the law thus requires an examination of the provisional network of power–knowledge relations that have coalesced to produce a calculable politico-legal subject which can be acted upon in certain strategical situations, while never forgetting that the law is merely one regulatory vehicle among myriad others that comprise a general strategy of government, or governmentality.

If various types of bodies as objects are produced by legal stipulations and their dissemination through non-legal bodies and structures, then the identity of those classified as prostitution offenders has become increasingly complicated in post-Mao China. In 1979, when the National People's Congress enacted the PRC's first Criminal Law and Criminal Procedure Law, the subject of prostitution evidently was not viewed as a major concern for China's legislature. Only two Articles in this particular Law dealt directly with the subject of prostitution. Article 140, under Chapter 4 of that Law, entitled 'Crimes of infringing upon the rights of the person and the democratic rights of citizens', stipulated that whoever forced women into prostitution should be punished by not less than 3 years and not more than 10 years fixed-term imprisonment. And Article 169, under Chapter 6 of that Law, entitled 'Crimes of disrupting the order of social administration', stated that whoever for the purpose of reaping profits, lured women into prostitution or sheltered them in prostitution, should be sentenced to not more than 5 years imprisonment, criminal detention or administrative control, with additional provisions for more serious offences (*Criminal Law and the Criminal Procedure Law of the People's Republic of China* 1984: 58). Hence the PRC's first criminal code banned prostitution for abrogating women's 'natural' and legally created rights to personhood, and it banned all third-party attempts to profit from the prostitution of others as being incompatible with the task of building 'socialism with Chinese characteristics'. But it made no explicit reference to the activities of first-party participants in the prostitution transaction, or those who are generally referred to in the English-speaking world as prostitutes and prostitute clients.

While echoing the abolitionist thrust of the UN (1949) Convention for the Suppression of the Traffic in Persons and of the Exploitation of the Prostitution of Others, the limited reference to prostitution in the PRC's first criminal code owed much to the perception that prostitution had basically been eradicated from mainland China by the Maoist campaigns of the 1950s. Following the visible resurgence of prostitution in the early 1980s, therefore, the legal control of 'women who sold sex' (*maiyin funü*), and 'men who bought the services of illicit prostitutes' (*piaosu anchang*),[3] was effected on the basis of provincial rulings and localized policing initiatives until the introduction of the 'Security administration punishment regulations' in January 1987 (hereafter the Regulations). The Regulations replaced an earlier 1957 version and addressed the behaviours of those who have committed illegal acts but whose criminal liability is not deemed sufficient to bring them before the courts. Article 30, in Chapter 3 of the Regulations, states that it is strictly forbidden to sell sex (*maiyin*) and to have illicit relations with a prostitute (*piaosu anchang*), to introduce others into prostitution, and to provide accommodation for the purposes of prostitutional sex. Depending on the particular circumstances and seriousness of such cases, suspected offenders could be held in custody for a period of up to 15 days while investigating officials determined the particular circumstances of the case, and then given a warning and ordered to make a statement of repentance. Or, in accordance with other administrative regulations, they could be detained for rehabilitative education and/or reform through labour for a period of between 6 months to 2 years, and fined up to 5,000 *yuan* (*Criminal Law and the Criminal Procedure Law of the PRC* 1984: 695–6). This meant that the vast majority of prostitution-related offences and the processes of investigating, determining guilt, and suitably penalizing, the activities of sellers and buyers of sex, were (and are) dealt with by the Chinese public security organs, with only serious cases, such as those relating to the organization of prostitution, forced prostitution, and traffic in women and children, being handled through the courts and criminal justice system.

At the start of the 1990s, however, following various reports and requests from the Ministry of Public Security and the All-China Women's Federation, the National People's Congress passed three pieces of legislation that significantly expanded the range and scope of China's prostitution controls. These were the 1991 Decision on Strictly Forbidding the Selling and Buying of Sex (hereafter the 1991 Decision); the 1991 Decision on the Severe Punishment of Criminals Who Abduct and Traffic in or Kidnap Women and Children; and the 1992 Law on Protecting the Rights and Interests of Women (hereafter the Women's Law) (Quanguo renda changweihui *et al.* 1991; *Zhonghua renmin gongheguo funü quanyi baozhangfa* 1994). The explicit aim of the two Decisions, which were issued in conjunction with each other, was to supplement the 1979 criminal code by giving a formal legal basis to police-led campaigns against the spread of domestic prostitution and the growing traffic in women and children. Adding symbolic weight to these enhanced law enforcement controls, the Women's Law, which was formulated by the ACWF and various other mass organizations, was designed to reaffirm the CCP's perceived historical commitment to realizing women's emancipation in the changed era of economic reform.

Using the same rationale that informs feminist interventions in international law, the Women's Law was formulated to express the Chinese government's commitment to advancing the position of women and taking action against practices that are seen to harm or discriminate against women. Accordingly, Article 36 of the Women's Law, under the heading 'Rights of person', states that it is prohibited to abduct, sell or kidnap women, and to buy women who have been abducted or kidnapped. And Article 37 stipulates that it is forbidden to sell sex and to patronize a prostitute; to organize, coerce, lure, or introduce women into prostitution; and to hire or keep women to engage in obscene activities with other people

(*Zhonghua* ... 1994: 19–20). The Women's Law thus links trafficking, prostitution, and other forms of commercial sex-related activities, by defining them as social practices that abrogate the inherent rights of women to personhood, by reducing them to the status of objects, chattels, or commodities. Certainly, in accounts of prostitution and trafficking that are authorized by the ACWF, the rights of the woman-as-person tend to be presented as something that cannot be given up voluntarily. For instance, it is suggested that a person cannot consent to being sold, or to engage in prostitution as a matter of individual choice, because to do so not only causes broader social harm, but implies a failure to acknowledge one's 'human dignity and worth' and therefore entails harm to the self (Ding Juan 1996: 10; Dong Yunhu and Zhang Shiping 1995).

Although the Women's Law bans prostitution as being incompatible with women's 'natural' and legally created rights, the PRC's revised Criminal Law of 1997 retains the abolitionist thrust of UN Conventions in that it is primarily concerned with criminalizing third-party involvement in prostitution. Reiterating the provisions contained in the 1991 Decision, Section 8 of the new Criminal Law establishes penalties for what are defined as the crimes of organizing, forcing, inducing, sheltering, and introducing others into the practice of prostitution (*1997 Criminal Code of the PRC* 1998: 186–8). Article 358 makes the act of organizing or forcing another person to engage in prostitution punishable by 5–10 years fixed-term imprisonment. And, in cases involving additional circumstances – such as repeated offences, raping and then forcing another person to engage in prostitution, causing serious bodily injury or other harm to a person forced to engage in prostitution, and forcing a girl under the age of 14 to engage in prostitution – it renders these crimes punishable by a fixed-term imprisonment of 10 years to life, or, in exceptionally serious circumstances, by the death penalty. In a similar vein, Article 359 states that anyone who induces, shelters, or introduces, other people to engage in the practice of prostitution, shall be punished by no more than 5 years fixed-term imprisonment, criminal detention or public surveillance, with the possible addition of a fine.

Hence, while the 1997 penal code registers a strong objection to the institution of prostitution, it does not actively criminalize the behaviours of first-party participants in the prostitution transaction – with two notable exceptions. Codifying provisions contained in the 1991 Decision, Article 360 of the new Criminal Law states that anyone who sells or buys prostitutional sex in the full knowledge that they are infected with syphilis, gonorrhea, or any another serious sexually transmittible disease, shall be sentenced to no more than 5 years fixed-term imprisonment, criminal detention, or public surveillance, with the possible addition of a fine. And the same Article further stipulates that anyone who has prostitutional sex with a female child under 14 years of age shall be sentenced to not less than 5 years fixed-term imprisonment, with the possible addition of a fine (*1997*

Criminal Code of the PRC 1998: 187). The first of these stipulations reflects the growing concern of China's health and other authorities over the potential link between prostitution and the spread of STDs/HIV in China, a concern that has been influenced and actively promoted by UN organizations. Likewise, the second stipulation, which aims to criminalize certain behaviours on the part of male prostitute clients, reflects the growing domestic (and, once again, UN-sponsored) concern with issues pertaining to the rights of the child, in particular, the rights of children to freedom from sexual abuse and rape in the form of child prostitution (Jeffreys, S. 2000: 359–79; Jin Jushin 1997; Kristof 1996; United Nations 1995). Apart from these two exceptions, the activities of first-party participants in the prostitution transaction continue to be regulated in practice according to the Chinese system of administrative measures and sanctions.

Viewed in this context, and contrary to the critical impetus of most Anglophone commentaries, the 1991 Decision is not so easily dismissed as a draconian by-product of 'irrational', ideological infighting within the upper echelons of the CCP. This is because it constituted a practical response to requests from China's public security forces and the ACWF that the State Council clarify the legitimate range and scope of their investigative and remedial powers with regard to the control of prostitution activities.[4] Most notably, the provisions contained in the Decision were designed to allow for the more effective management of the new kinds of prostitution practices that had been identified as emerging from the interstices created by the process of reform itself, particularly the rapid spread of prostitution throughout China's newly developing hospitality and service industry. The Decision was also clearly intended to meet the new imperatives of reform era policing, insofar as it enabled the Chinese police to respond to public and governmental demands that they 'strike hard' against the perceived 'high tide' of criminal activities and social problems that had accompanied the reform process, while doing so in a manner prescribed and legitimated by law.

Also contrary to the suggestion that China's prostitution controls are explicable predominantly in terms of some peculiarly Marxist, ideological approach, the 1991 Decision and the revised criminal code turn on the same rationale that informs governmental attempts to manage 'the problem of prostitution' in Western societies. In most Western societies, authorities aim to contain or eliminate prostitution by confining such activities to fixed or delimited sites. In contrast, the principal means that prostitutes use to counter and evade governmental controls is mobility, that is, by effecting changes in the manner of doing business (becoming a call girl instead of a streetwalker) or by moving into other business settings, like bars and cafés, where they can operate beyond the clear purview of the law (Symanski 1981: 26). As such, 'the problem of prostitution' does not relate solely to questions of morality; it is a problem that relates to the ordering of social space.

The PRC's prostitution laws similarly aim to control the development of a 'sex industry' via the policing of social space and, consequently, the ordering of targeted groups of people within specified places. Codifying provisions contained in the 1991 Decision, Articles 361 and 362 of the new criminal code are designed to restrict the conditions which contribute to the formation of a 'prostitution industry' by introducing a system of controls over places of leisure and entertainment, and the people who own, manage, or work within them. Hence Article 361 stipulates that anyone who takes advantage of their work-based location in the hotel, restaurant, entertainment, taxi, or any other service-orientated business, to organize, force, induce, shelter, or introduce, other persons to participate in prostitution practices, shall be convicted and sentenced to fixed terms of imprisonment. And Article 362 states that hospitality and service industry personnel who leak information about prospective police investigations into the existence of prostitution activities in their work-unit will be convicted for obstructing the course of justice (*1997 Criminal Code of the People's Republic of China* 1998: 187–8).

In other words, both the 1991 Decision and the revised criminal code are concerned with regulating the new kinds of recreational habits and venues that have accompanied the economic reform process, that is, to manage hitherto ungoverned, previously nonexistent, social spaces such as karaoke/dance venues, health/fitness centres, and hairdressing salons. In doing so, the ultimate goal of such legally based strategies is to stop managers and workers within the predominantly male-run and male-patronized hospitality and service industry from profiting from and/or encouraging the prostitution of others. As a result, the 'spirit' of the 1991 Decision has been complemented and reinforced by the introduction of more localized measures which aim to transform individuals into 'good citizens', by equipping them with a knowledge of the law and simultaneously encouraging them to abide by and actively enforce the law. For instance, local licensing regulations now require the owners and personnel of hotels, karaoke/dance venues, taxi depots, and so forth, to hold or attend training sessions on the nature of Chinese law with regard to issues such as prostitution, pornography, gambling, and drugs. Regulations concerning the licensing of places of leisure and entertainment also aim to limit the scope of prostitution activities by combining legal education and regulation with a particular kind of responsibility system. This system encourages individuals who work in a wide range of social milieux to report, rather than ignore, the existence of prostitution activities, or else risk losing their licence to operate or manage and work in a particular business enterprise, and/or risk becoming subject to the system of administrative sanctions themselves ('China's crusade against prostitution, gambling successful' 1999).

The PRC's legally articulated goal of halting the development of a 'sex industry' has been further reinforced via the introduction of localized licensing measures that bear directly on the interior spatial organization of recreational venues. For example, the small private rooms in karaoke/dance venues, where commercial sexual activities have been known to occur, are now obliged to contain large, uncurtained windows with transparent glass, to use bright lighting of a fixed wattage, to contain seating of a fixed and restricted size, and to have doors that cannot be locked from the inside. Likewise, venues that offer recreational massage services are now subject to a whole series of regulations regarding who they can legitimately employ and under what circumstances employees can legitimately provide such services. Unqualified or non-professional masseuses and masseurs cannot provide massage services to members of the opposite sex, unless such services are restricted to certain specified venues, and the service provided is limited to a massage of the face, scalp, neck, hands, arms or feet. Moreover, these restricted services must take place in rooms that are arranged according to detailed specifications, and be permanently open to public view ('Chinese police trying to improve situation at massage parlours' 1999; 'Jingcheng qudi yixing anmo' 1996: 5–7; Wang Huanju 1995: 44–9). If enforced, these kinds of regulations will obviously help to undermine the system of social relations that has enabled those who demand the services of women in prostitution, and those who own or profit from businesses that tacitly condone or actively encourage prostitution, to evade being punished for doing so.

Also contrary to received opinion, the PRC's legally articulated concern with regulating the new kinds of recreational habits and venues that have emerged in the reform era is directed at the conduct of government officials, not simply the activities of 'ordinary' participants in the prostitution transaction. In 1988, the Discipline Inspection Commission of the CCP issued a set of regulations designed to penalize Party members for involvement in prostitution-related activities (Shan Guangnai 1995: 698–9). These measures have since been incorporated into the 'Communist Party discipline regulations' (hereafter the Disciplinary Regulations), which were issued for trial implementation in April 1997. Article 132 of the Disciplinary Regulations, under the heading 'Mistakes that seriously violate socialist ethics', states that any Party member who has sexual intercourse with others by 'using their powers, their superior or senior positions, seduction, cheating, or other means, shall be dismissed from their Party posts' ('Communist Party discipline regulations' 1997: 15–16). This stipulation is clearly directed at the forms of invisible prostitution so trenchantly criticized by Pan Suiming (1996a: 20–1), namely, the practice of using one's power and authority to obtain sex and using one's 'sex' to obtain the privileges that accrue to those in positions of power. In doing so, the Disciplinary Regulations signify that the CCP's much-vaunted goal of tightening up Party discipline and wiping out corruption intimates that government officials and bureaucratic entrepreneurs are not above the law. They demonstrate that the conduct of government, not just the conduct of the governed, has become a renewed object of concern in present-day China.

Accordingly, Article 134 of the Disciplinary Regulations, under the heading 'Mistakes that violate social administrative procedure', states that any Party member who engages in prostitutional sex; who forces, introduces, urges, entices, allows, or harbours others to engage in prostitutional sex; or who purposely provides convenient conditions for others to engage in prostitutional sex, shall be dismissed from the Party. Article 135 stipulates that any cadre who engages in sexual intercourse with masseuses or masseurs will be dismissed from the Party in accordance with Article 134; and, any cadre who accepts other forms of sexualized massage shall be given serious warnings or dismissed from their Party posts. In keeping with broader concerns over the existence of prostitution in public places of leisure and entertainment, Article 136 stipulates that cadres in charge of poorly managed work-units where prostitution activities repeatedly recur shall be given warnings or serious warnings, or be dismissed from their Party posts. Similar penalties are laid out in Articles 137 and 138 for cadres who engage in the manufacturing, duplicating, selling, leasing, promulgating, and/or viewing of pornographic movies, television programmes, books and pictures ('Communist Party discipline regulations' 1997: 15–16). Following the introduction of these measures, the Chinese media has publicized numerous cases of government officials being convicted and disciplined for abusing their positions and using public funds to keep 'mistresses', to patronize prostitutes and to buy the 'company' of women in entertainment venues ('Guangdong court judge sacked for hiring prostitutes' 2000; Wu Yaonong 2000; 'Zhifa renyuan baoyang "sanpei" yishen diudiao "wusha"' 1999).

The fundamental objective of the above-mentioned pieces of legislation, namely, to render the new kinds of recreational habits that have emerged in reform-era China open to governmental programmes of corrective intervention, has now found concrete expression in the form of the 'Regulations concerning the management of public places of entertainment' (hereafter the Entertainment Regulations), which came into effect on 1 July 1999 (Zhonghua renmin gongheguo guowuyuan 1999). As the introductory Articles to this new piece of legislation explain, the Entertainment Regulations aim to strengthen the management of public entertainment venues and ensure that such businesses operate to serve the task of building 'socialist spiritual civilization' by promoting civil or mannered recreational practices.[5] Consequently, the provisions contained in the Entertainment Regulations reiterate the basic parameters of the criminal code by proscribing activities relating to prostitution, pornography, gambling, and drugs. However, in response to requests from the Ministry of Public Security and the ACWF that the State Council clarify the legal status of 'hostesses', or paid female companions, they further proscribe a range of commercial practices that rely on the commodification of 'female' attributes and the female body ('Voice from women' 1999).

Most notably, Article 25, in Section 4 of the Entertainment Regulations, forbids the owners and personnel of leisure and entertainment venues from profiting from and encouraging prostitution practices, as well as from profiting from and encouraging the provision of 'accompaniment' or 'hostess-style' services (Xue Jing 1999). It also bans people who enter places of leisure and entertainment from engaging in such activities. In a similar vein, other Articles aim to ban the more recent emergence in China of commercial sex-related activities such as striptease, 'topless' and 'bottomless' waitressing, table dancing, and lap dancing, by prohibiting licentiousness and practices that can be construed as defaming or humiliating people. Although couched in gender-neutral language, this latter stipulation refers to the commercial sexual objectification of the female body in particular, since female jurists and lawyers in China have expressed growing concern over the limited attention paid to the incorporeal rights of women, or the perceived rights of women not to be portrayed in a manner which suggests that they are inferior to or the 'playthings' of men (Ding Juan 1996: 10; Xia Yinlan 1996: 165–9).

The Entertainment Regulations thus signify a provisional halt to various attempts (whether intentional or not) to legally characterize the activities of female 'hostesses' in terms of work. Between 1997 and 1998, for example, the subject of taxing 'female service workers' attracted considerable controversy in the Chinese media. This controversy centred on the decision of certain municipal authorities to levy individual income tax on women who derived an income from 'tips', service fees, or informal consumption taxes, in recreational venues. Representatives from local tax departments justified their actions by arguing that they were obliged by the PRC's taxation laws to levy individual income tax on citizens who met the tax threshold criteria. However, they were not required to determine whether that income was generated legally or not. The analogy reportedly used by various tax authorities was that they were obliged to levy individual income tax on those who derived a living from the sale of tobacco and alcohol, but it was not their responsibility to determine whether the goods sold were counterfeit products ('A taxing question of hostess earnings' 1998; 'Prostitution tax' 1999: 3; 'State never collects "Miss taxes"' 1998; Wang Fengbin 1998: 1).

As far as China's public security forces were concerned, these actions complicated the already difficult task of policing the 'grey area' between 'hostessing' and prostitution, because it granted a quasi-legal status to the activities of 'hostesses' by treating them as equivalent to any other citizen-as-worker. At the same time, some local policing authorities added fuel to this controversy by issuing work-related identity cards to the same kinds of 'female service workers' local taxation departments had 'legally' identified as tax-paying citizens. While local police defended this practice on the grounds that it would enable the standardization and stricter policing of China's recreational market by making such women 'visible' and 'open' to existing regulatory measures, their actions attracted criticism for potentially legitimizing commercial sex ('Eastern Chinese city giving ID cards to karaoke girls' 1998; 'Karaoke women to get cards' 1998; Wu Zhong 1997).

In the face of such debates, the ACWF submitted a report to the State Council requesting stricter controls over commercial recreational enterprises, and clarification of the duties of all relevant departments with regard to the control of prostitution. While ACWF representatives originally maintained that these proposed initiatives would not directly affect 'hostesses' (i.e., women who merely accompanied male patrons of recreational venues), they also insisted that new initiatives were necessary to deter women from engaging in sex-related (*sanpei*) activities by leading to a renewed crackdown on prostitution (Kwang 1999; 'Women's lobby tackles bar sex' 1999). The ACWF's request for stricter controls on recreational business operations was supported by similar requests from the Chinese police, on the grounds that the indeterminate nature of 'hostessing activities', combined with the emergence of new kinds of commercial sex-related practices, had made the task of policing prostitution virtually impossible. In fact, as far as China's public security forces were concerned, the quasi-acceptance of 'hostessing' abetted prostitution by encouraging the practice of 'accompanying first and engaging in prostitution later', a practice that simultaneously evaded official prostitution controls while financially benefiting the owners of recreational business enterprises.

The State Council responded to these requests by issuing the 1999 Entertainment Regulations. These regulations forbid all forms of commercial sex-related activities in places of leisure and recreation by stipulating that anyone who participates in, promotes or profits from and/or fails to report the existence of such activities, will be made subject to criminal or administrative sanctions. To support this ban, the regulations aim to restrict the available pool and turn-over of labour within the hospitality and service industry by reinforcing the long-standing stipulation that all personnel must possess a residency permit, or a temporary work and residency permit, and hence be 'known' to the local police. The Entertainment Regulations further aim to control the existence of corrupt and illegal management practices by reinforcing a system of commercial licensing and fair-pricing procedures; by banning sole foreign ownership of recreational businesses; and by stipulating that any member of a relevant government department who is found to be directly or indirectly involved in the running of such enterprises will face disciplinary charges. Like the larger body of Chinese law, therefore, the Entertainment Regulations are concerned to modify the conduct of government, not just the conduct of the governed.

The heterogeneous range of bodies, behaviours, and social spaces, that are targeted by the PRC's prostitution laws makes a mockery of the generalized feminist critique of 'the state' as masculinist, if by the latter term we are enjoined to believe that the law is ultimately designed to serve male interests. China's prostitution laws do not aim simply to repress the already marginalized female prostitute subject. They aim to shape, guide, and modify, the conduct of all Chinese citizens in what are construed as socially desirable directions. An examination of the body of China's prostitution laws also reveals that the government of prostitution is construed in terms of the corrective management of the new kinds of recreational spaces and habits that have emerged in the reform era. This concern is not directed solely at squashing autonomous expressions of female agency and sexuality. It is directed at closing the specific 'loop-holes' through which men have either sought, come to expect, or have been provided with, the sexualized commercial services of women.

This latent yet central organizing concern with what are deemed to be inappropriate behaviours on the part of men – the prostitute client who fails to respect the inalienable human dignity of women, the corrupt cadre who abuses his position to 'dally' with women, and the exploitative business practices of the 'profit-by-any-means' entrepreneur (Li Shi and Gao Ling 1993: 10–13; Mao Lei 1993: 2–6; Zhang Yanshang 1993: 12–19) – brings into question the viability of recent metropolitan attempts to have prostitution in China reconfigured as work. The act of legally recognizing prostitution as sex work would not only require the Chinese government to introduce (in truly totalitarian fashion) a construction of the sexual-political subject that has limited social substance in China, it would also require the Chinese government to forego a wide range of measures aimed at guaranteeing formal equality between the sexes and eradicating corruption. Precisely for these reasons, metropolitan women's rights activists might be better advised to offer *interim* support for the domestically generated recommendation that the punitive emphasis of China's prostitution controls be relocated away from women in prostitution towards those who organize and create the demand for prostitution.

Viewed in this context, the Chinese response to prostitution offers an imperfect replica of the platform of the feminist anti-prostitution lobby. This surface similarity could easily feed into liberal criticisms of 'the repressive and moralistic Chinese State', and even offer support for the implicit suggestion that radical feminists themselves desire nothing less than the establishment of a totalitarian 'nanny State'. Yet if China's prostitution controls epitomize the eternally optimistic and totalizing dream of governmentality – the dream of a totally administered and well-ordered society – they also remind us that 'government' is a congenitally failing operation. The world of governmental programmes is heterogeneous and rivalrous even in China, as the contested legal specification of the body of the prostitute subject, and ongoing attempts to modify China's prostitution controls, including new calls to either legalize or decriminalize the prostitution transaction, so as to minimize the threat of STDs/HIV would suggest (Lin and Wu 1999: Zhang Heqing 2002: 313–17). In consequence, the introduction of new legally based strategies designed to manage more effectively 'the problem of prostitution' will inevitably open new spaces wherein that goal will be brought into question, not least because the responsibility for governing the spread of prostitution throughout China's recreational market has been placed on the already over-loaded public security forces.

The PRC's response to prostitution thus contains a mixed message for feminist attempts to turn prostitution into a homogeneous and stable object of international human rights law. On the one hand, it illustrates that obliging governments to legally enshrine their objection to prostitution as a violation of women's human rights offers no guarantee of 'feminist' outcomes. To comprehend and thereby remedy the perceived 'failure' of China's prostitution laws in practice, however, does not require further discussion of the Chinese government's so-called hypocrisy, its alleged lack of genuine commitment to eradicating prostitution, or even a more detailed analysis of the supposedly patriarchal underpinnings of Chinese law. The will to govern prostitution in China needs to be understood less in terms of its 'flawed' ideological bases and more in terms of how that 'will' has been operationalized, and with what anticipated and unforeseen consequences.

On the other hand, an analysis of the heterogeneous range of bodies and spaces that are targeted by the PRC's prostitution controls suggests that NGO efforts to pressure the Chinese government into legally recognizing prostitution as work are premised on a disregard for the specificity of the Chinese case. After all, arguments to the effect that the PRC has failed to recognize the rights of sex workers garner all the moral kudos that accrues to those who claim to speak for the truly 'downtrodden', without the accompanying burden of demonstrating how the PRC might go about overturning its existing controls and still address issues that require remedial attention, such as the problem of forced prostitution and the relationship between prostitution and governmental corruption. Even the broader public health argument that recognizing prostitution will empower women by enabling the introduction of more effective HIV/AIDS prevention strategies is undermined by the fact that safe sex programmes assume that women everywhere conceive of themselves as autonomous individuals possessed of a sexualized personhood that can and should be safeguarded. Indeed, it strikes me that just as feminist criticisms of prohibitionist and abolitionist approaches in the West have produced a rather factitious construction of the female prostitute subject as a transgressive sexual-political identity, the objections of human rights activists to issues of law enforcement and 'government' in China have encouraged certain NGOs to treat this factitious subject as a universal one. To further redirect criticisms of the Chinese response thus requires a consideration of what 'the problem of prostitution in China' means to those who are responsible for governing it, i.e., the Chinese police, and the manner in which they have sought to give practical effect to China's prostitution laws, namely, through campaigns.

6 Policing change

Changing disciplinary technologies

Policing change: changing police

I began this book with Michel de Certeau's contention that every story is a travel story (1984: 115); and, in order to bring this text full circle, I want to conclude with reference to the work of Michel Foucault. Like de Certeau, Foucault also intimates that the act of reading and writing can be metaphorically configured in terms of travel, but the journey he proposes is of a qualitatively different kind. Whereas de Certeau is concerned to explicate the kinds of technical procedures through which we seek to ground our different spatial narratives, Foucault implies that the act of writing can be likened to a journey of the most intimate kind. Equating the act of writing with a willingness to enter into a love relationship, or even a willingness to engage in life itself, Foucault (1988b: 9) asks: 'If you knew when you began a book what you would say at the end, do you think that you would have the courage to write it?'

Foucault's suggestion that intellectual work comprises an experiential engagement with different possibilities is apposite. When I started this book, I did not expect to finish by offering a partial defence of the Chinese governmental response to prostitution vis-à-vis mainstream feminist and extant China studies scholarship. Nor did I anticipate concluding that the most 'silenced' voice in Anglophone commentaries on prostitution in the PRC may not be that of the female prostitute subject, but rather that of the Chinese police.[1] However, if Foucault's reference to the term 'courage' implies merely a willingness to pursue an alternative reading, as opposed to staying within the safe parameters of the already known, then this is precisely the conclusion that needs to be broached.

After all, feminist criticisms of the perceived masculinist nature of 'the state' and 'the law', like prostitute discourses on the discriminatory nature of existing prostitution controls, turn on a fundamental disdain for the police. I use the term 'disdain' in the sense that, until recent years, there has been surprisingly little feminist work produced on the relationship between prostitution and localized policing practices. This remains the case even though the police (as the generic 'long arm' of 'the state') have long been singled out for feminist criticism as the corrupt and abusive enforcers of patriarchal laws, and even though prostitutes' rights activists have consistently argued that deleterious changes in prostitution practices are intrinsically related to changes in patterns of policing.

Contrary to the popular rendition of 'the police' and 'female prostitutes' as irreclaimable antagonists, however, those studies that have been conducted on the nexus between prostitution and localized law enforcement practices reveal a far more complicated picture. Such studies indicate that the police are acutely aware of the problems associated with their attempts to negotiate between the competing demands of local residents and participants in the prostitution transaction, and the not always coterminous imperatives of national vis-à-vis international legislation (McCloskey and Lazarus 1992: 233–47). Moreover, while not denying that government officials often participate in discriminatory law enforcement practices, many of these studies suggest that the relationship between local police and older female prostitutes, in particular, is surprisingly amicable. Indeed, one study indicates that although most women in street prostitution support a policy of total decriminalization, they incorrectly assume that the adoption of such a policy will oblige and legally empower the police to patrol the streets so as to provide them with protection and surveillance (Sharpe 1998: 142–69). These anomalies suggest that total decriminalization may not be the panacea propounded by many prostitutes' rights activists.

Metropolitan criticisms of the PRC's prostitution controls are similarly marked by a fundamental disdain for law enforcement practices, especially when considered in relation to Chinese campaign-style policing. Briefly, police-led crackdowns on crime and prostitution have been variously portrayed as periodic, military-style campaigns designed to enforce policy directives in the most punitive and draconian manner (Bakken 1993: 29–58; Gil and Anderson 1998: 129–42); as redeployed Maoist strategies serving to further the self-interested political goals of different factions within the Chinese Communist Party (Gil *et al*. 1994: 329–30; Ruan 1991: 9, 83, 103); and, last but not least, as indicative of the CCP's repressive approach towards sex-related issues and effecting social control in general (Ruan and Bullough 1989: 198–201). Western commentators further aver that the erroneous nature of police-led campaigns against crime and prostitution is underscored by their evident failure to halt the spread of such phenomena (Hershatter 1997: 363–8). Campaign-style policing is thus held up as proof that the CCP has not only failed to combine economic reform with political liberalization, but also that it has refused to abandon the now denigrated, Maoist 'rule of man' in favour of a modern 'rule of law'.

Yet for all the condemnation of campaign-related human rights abuses – hence trenchant criticisms of the CCP's failure to transform the PRC into an acceptable member of the post-modern, global community – the question of what campaign technologies mean to the Chinese police has attracted scant attention. While it is practically *de rigueur* for Western China scholars to note that economic reform has led to profound social change in the PRC, and even to acknowledge that two of the most unwelcome side-effects of the reforms include growing crime rates and a resurgence of prostitution, the question of what economic reform has meant to the Chinese police is seldom considered. Only a handful of scholars have examined the nature and effects of the internal reforms that the Chinese police have been obliged to carry out in order to respond to the changes that economic development has brought in tow.[2]

This lack of interest is undoubtedly related to the popular perception that the Chinese public security forces can be viewed as an unreflexive instrument of the CCP, a perspective encapsulated in the use of expressions like 'the Party police state'. But it has resulted in a general failure to recognize that the Chinese police, like any modern, and, in this case, rapidly professionalizing police force, are engaged in an ongoing struggle for the power to influence the contexts and conditions of their own work, and that innovations in the practice and theory of policing not only do not necessarily serve to legitimate existing governmental policies, they may also lead to the creation of new ones. The title of this section is thus intended to highlight the fact that the Chinese police are simultaneously the objects and agents of social change (Marenin 1996).

Certainly, the implementation of the economic reforms and the Open Door policy in 1979 effectively transformed the *raison d'être* of the Chinese public security forces, while simultaneously undermining the basis of all forms of policing in China since 1949. Unlike the history of professionalized police forces in Western societies, a lineage which is usually traced back to community responses to crime or 'state' attempts to rule, the history of the Chinese police is located in the period of civil war prior to the founding of the PRC. Born before the invention of 'the modern Chinese state', the organizational predecessors of the Chinese police pledged their professional allegiances not to protecting 'law and government', but rather to protecting 'the Party and the revolution'. This early organizational commitment continued to influence the nature of Chinese policing even after the establishment of 'New China' in 1949. For although the Chinese police became a government, not a Party, organ with the founding of the Ministry of Public Security, their allotted tasks were not strictly to 'keep the peace', but also to defend the 'democratic dictatorship', and hence to guarantee their own political loyalty. The result was a highly politicized police force or a government organ that was virtually an organizational replica of the CCP. This situation changed when both the Party and the police came under attack as 'class enemies' during the Cultural Revolution; and, following the proclaimed disaster of this latter event, Deng Xiaoping overturned the Maoist logic of politics in command by setting China on its current course of modernization, thereby making the logic of the economy coterminous with that of government (see Dutton forthcoming).

In keeping with the new governmental rationale of the reform era, and the growing conviction that 'the market economy is a legal-system economy' (Chen, A.H.Y. 1996: 4), the Chinese public security forces had to transform themselves from an integral component of the 'revolutionary vanguard' into a professional law enforcement agency. But internal reform was a tall order for the Chinese police. One of the continued structural legacies of the Maoist era is that China still has a very low ratio of police to population, approximately 7 police per 100,000 people, in contrast to a ratio of between 25 to 70 police per 100,000 people in Western societies (Wang Zhimin 1993: 127). During the Maoist period, professional police numbers were kept deliberately low due to budget constraints and to ensure that China's public security organs would remain 'red' in orientation, rather than becoming overly bureaucratic, professionally discrete, or a force unto themselves. The effect of adhering to this policy was that the Chinese police were forced to augment their numbers by relying on the help of mass-line organizations like the work-unit security system, the urban street and neighbourhood committee system, and the various small groups that came under the umbrella of such organizations (Dutton and Lee 1993: 327). This coordinated system, combined with the household registration system, produced a static and stable population that was permanently open to public surveillance, and contributed to the extremely low crime rates of the early liberation period. In fact, China of the 1950s is often nostalgically recalled as a country where 'nobody appropriated another person's lost belongings and nobody had to lock their doors' (*lu bu shiyi, ye bu bihu*).

With the introduction of economic reform, however, the basis of all crime prevention strategies since 1949, namely, the territorially fixed and 'see-through' population, was undermined (ibid.: 316–36). This system of policing was viable only so long as the central government planned the economy and allocated work. Following the opening up of China's labour and commodity markets, and the subsequent flow of people and goods into developing areas, it was neither possible nor desirable to maintain such a static system of social control. Yet one of the most significant effects of the introduction of market-based reforms, and the concomitant loosening of former controls over population mobility, was an upsurge in rates and types of crime. This upsurge in criminal activity was so dramatic when compared to previous periods in the PRC's history that it was soon identified as a criminal 'high tide' and a matter of pressing governmental and public concern. Consequently, the Chinese police were charged with the difficult task of demonstrating their newfound organizational ethos as law enforcement officers and 'crime-stoppers' at a time when previous modes of policing were falling apart.

The Chinese public security forces responded to this dilemma with the only immediate solution that seemed feasible: they opted for internal reform in the sense of reconfiguring tried-and-tested methods of security work rather than radically reconstituting the regime of policing (Dutton 1995: 415–47). Hampered by an ongoing lack of adequate human, technical, and financial resources, they attempted to recapture previous high levels of public order by revitalizing the former bulwarks of crime prevention in China, i.e., the mass-line security organs. This recuperation of Maoist-style methods of populist policing has demanded the continued leadership of local Party committees in order to coordinate the diverse social groups and multiple settings involved. It therefore contradicts Western expectations of a shift towards police professionalism and a 'rule of law' by reinforcing, rather than severing, the historic link between the CCP and the Chinese police. This renewed connection is demonstrated by the fact that the manifold interactions between the diverse groups that make up the Chinese police and mass-line organizations, under the leadership of local Party cadres, are now collectively referred to as 'the mass-line in policing', which is defined as the guiding principle and method of Chinese policing, and lauded as a sign of the unique nature of public security work in China (Jiang Bo and Dai Yisheng 1990: 1–9; Yu Hongyuan 1999: 40–2).

Nonetheless, recent attempts to revitalize mass-line methods of security work, and hence the reinforced link between the CCP and the Chinese police, cannot be construed as a straightforward return to Maoist methods of effecting social control. For the cooperation of all the above-mentioned forces has been achieved on the basis of inducements that are central to the reform era, but were anathema to revolutionary Maoism, namely, monetary incentives (Dutton 2000b: 61–105). Raising participant wage rates, for instance, has overcome the declining participation of local residents in neighbourhood street committees. Likewise, instead of depending on local residents to voluntarily inform them of the existence of criminal activities in a given locale, the Chinese police now offer financial rewards for information resulting in a conviction. The increasingly monetarized basis of the once highly politicized mass-line is further evidenced by the fact that police-led crackdowns on phenomena such as crime, corruption, prostitution and pornography, are now accompanied by widespread media publicity concerning the existence of 24-hour report-centres with email and telephone hotlines, and special letterboxes. These report-centres are designed to elicit information from the general public about the activities of 'offenders' by appealing to their sense of civic duty, and offering legal guarantees of personal anonymity and financial rewards ('China opens anti-porn hotlines' 2000; 'Police "hotmail" hot in Beijing' 2001).

Although the complexities of this revitalized strategy of urban crime control warrant substantial research, the most controversial aspect of contemporary Chinese policing (particularly in the eyes of Western commentators) has been the deployment of campaigns against crime. Put simply, campaign-style policing is controversial because it is reminiscent of the campaign-style politics that constituted the now denigrated hallmark of radical Maoism. Whereas the Maoist regime launched wave after wave of campaigns against political deviation, class enemies, and so forth, the Chinese police have implemented an ongoing series of campaigns against certain criminal activities and proscribed behaviours since the early 1980s. The first and most notorious of these campaigns was the 1983 'strike hard' campaign against serious crime, which was launched following a meeting between Deng Xiaoping and leading members of the Ministry of Public Security in July 1983. At this meeting, it was concluded that the escalating crime problem could only be resolved by mobilizing 'the masses', but the nature of that mobilization had to be far more discrete than that which characterized the political movements of the Maoist era (Deng Xiaoping 1994: 44–5). In this way, the Chinese police resurrected the campaign process as a pragmatic technology of policing, while simultaneously dissociating it from its not-so-distant Maoist underpinnings as the key mobilizational, pedagogical, and disciplinary, device of unremitting class struggle.

Since the first 'strike hard' anti-crime campaign of 1983, the strategy of launching an all-out assault against selected types of activities, people, and places, for a delimited period of time, has become a key component of Chinese policing. Campaign-style policing initially found favour among China's public security agencies because it offered a practical solution to the difficulties they faced. It enabled them to respond to government and public demands that they do something about the deteriorating public order situation by directing their limited resources at specified targets and circumscribed goals. It was thus a solution born of a paucity of alternatives if the newfound 'social problems' of the reform era, including growing rates and types of crime and phenomena deemed in need of special attention, such as prostitution, trafficking in women, pornography, and drugs, were to be addressed *and* seen to be redressed.

Nevertheless, the efficacy and long-term viability of campaign-style policing have generated considerable debate within Chinese policing circles. For while the strategy of launching short, sharp strikes against certain targeted activities has enabled China's public security forces to carry out their professional obligations as keepers of law and order, it demands a degree of flexibility that undermines efforts to improve standards of police professionalism and accountability. As metropolitan human rights activists have noted, the implementation of a major campaign is often accompanied by the introduction of harsher legislation designed to facilitate easier arrests, detentions, and sentencing, including the extensive use of capital punishment.[3] Concomitantly, huge numbers of people are detained on the basis of the administrative code and held for arbitrary periods of time in centres where the conditions are frequently appalling (Human Rights in China 1999). Contrary to the implication of metropolitan activists, however, who tend to treat the Chinese public security forces as an unreflexive puppet of the 'despotic' CCP, the abuses associated with campaign-style policing have not only been well documented in Chinese policing circles, they are also viewed as a matter of concern. Indeed, in keeping with the development of any modern police force, innovations in Chinese policing have been characteristically self-scrutinizing and accompanied by a phenomenal growth of research and theorizing about law and policing.

To offer but one example, metropolitan human rights activists contend that the problems associated with administrative detentions have received little attention in China, even though upwards of two million people per year are arbitrarily detained in centres that lack all the requirements of a properly run welfare-orientated facility (Human Rights in China 1999). With regard to the subject of prostitution at least, the corollary implication that the Chinese police have chosen to ignore the existence of such problems is patently polemic. Chinese policing scholars have not only argued that regulations pertaining to the types and periods of detention for participants in the prostitution transaction are imprecise, and therefore encourage arbitrary sentencing practices, they have also acknowledged that centres for the rehabilitation of sellers and buyers of sex are understaffed, underfunded, and overcrowded (Wang Dazhong 1995: 57). As a result, many of these centres are unable to provide the services that constitute the theoretical rationale for their very existence. Most notably, due to the combined effects of overcrowding, limited physical space, and a lack of qualified staff, many of those detained as sellers and buyers of sex can neither be educated according to the law nor engage in productive labour. The failure of such centres to provide these forms of 'training' undermines the basic goal of criminal and administrative reform in China, which is to transform offenders into free and law-abiding citizens by equipping them with certain active subjective capacities. In consequence, many policing scholars conclude that campaign-style policing has placed the administrative reform system on the brink of a crisis, even as it was intended to resolve a more generalized policing crisis (Wang Dazhong 1995: 57).

Unlike metropolitan human rights activists, however, who lay the blame for these problems on the CCP's political disregard for individual rights, or the rights enshrined in idealized conceptions of 'Euramerican' criminal procedure law, the Chinese police relate them to a wider range of practical and professional considerations. A standard argument here is that centres for rehabilitative education suffer from problems of overcrowding and related abuses because the PRC's laws are either not strict enough, or else they are not being enforced in a strict enough manner. According to many Chinese policing scholars, the vast majority of people apprehended as minor prostitution offenders are released with a warning or a fine. Moreover, offenders apprehended for repeated involvement in the prostitution transaction, and even serious offenders such as organizers of prostitution, continue to be sentenced to the lesser administrative sanction of rehabilitative education, rather than being handled on the basis of harsher penalties as prescribed by law (Yang Xiaobing 1991: 23–5). Chinese policing scholars thus conclude that the abuses associated with centres for rehabilitative education can be traced to a general proclivity towards leniency, flowing from the (erroneous) perception that prostitution is a minor misdemeanour, the continued existence of low-level police corruption, and the reluctance of poorly trained public security officials to take difficult cases before the criminal courts.

In the eyes of China's newly professionalizing public security forces, therefore, the practical solution to the problem of overcrowding in centres for rehabilitative education is obvious, especially given their continued obligation to control prostitution businesses and practices. Stricter sentencing procedures are required to relieve the pressure that has been placed on the lowest levels of the administrative reform system. Moreover, strict adherence to the letter of the law is required to 'silence' domestic and international criticisms of China's perceived failure to embrace a modern (read impartial and routinized) 'rule of law'. The evident irony here is that by continuing to attribute the problems of 'Chinese law and order' to communist authoritarianism, instead of acknowledging the practical dilemmas faced by the Chinese police, metropolitan human rights activists may be inadvertently promoting a more punitive approach to law enforcement practices in China.

This may be the case for several reasons. To begin with, although metropolitan human rights activists have quite rightly criticized the Chinese police for profiting from the arbitrary fining of prostitution offenders, they tend to overlook the fact that fining was also viewed as a 'soft' way of handling participants in the prostitution transaction, and that recent efforts to stamp out corrupt and irregular policing practices have generated calls for stricter sentencing practices. In addition, although metropolitan commentators have quite rightly criticized the abuses associated with administrative detention centres, they tend to forget that administrative detention is still legally conceived of as a lenient approach to the reform of minor offenders, one that is supposed to avoid the stigmatization associated with criminal sanctions. By pursuing the antagonistic approach of relating the problems associated with 'fines' and 'detentions' to China's perceived lack of a proper criminal justice system, therefore, metropolitan commentators may well be adding fuel to domestic calls to criminalize the prostitution transaction, and thus have done with the problems that currently surround the use of more flexible administrative sanctions.

Adding to this point, one specified goal of NGOs' lobbying for prostitutes' rights in China, namely, to see rehabilitative education turned into a voluntary as opposed to compulsory practice (Human Rights in China *et al.* 1998), might be better advanced by working within – rather than rejecting – the organizing rationales of 'mainland solutions' to the perceived problems surrounding the PRC's prostitution controls. Arguments in favour of a less punitive approach to the handling of female sellers of sex could be promoted by stressing the historically ameliorative origins of rehabilitative education as a measure that is supposed to 'assist' rather than penalize those who have engaged in what are construed to be 'socially undesirable' but not criminal acts, and thus offering interim support for the domestically generated recommendation that the Chinese government should provide supportive programmes for women in prostitution, while simultaneously relocating the punitive emphasis of China's prostitution controls onto the organizers and buyers of sex. Such support could translate into a recommendation, which Chinese scholars have variously expressed, that revenue generated from the fining of minor prostitution offenders, and the confiscation of monies and property derived from the organization of prostitution, should be administered through a new organizational structure designed to provide welfare programmes specifically for women, rather than being redirected throughout the broader administrative system (Wang Xingjuan, cited in Hershatter 1997: 377).

If acted upon, such a recommendation could lead to the establishment of better 'welfare-orientated facilities' by obliging the relevant authorities in China to reconsider what, if anything, is achieved by the practice of holding minor prostitution offenders in re-education centres that cannot fulfil their allocated tasks. Furthermore, it might enable the limited resources of the Chinese public security forces to be more effectively centred on a major target of all recent campaigns, i.e., governmental corruption, including police complicity in the organization and abetting of prostitution, and the extensive abuse of public monies to finance the demand for prostitution. Given recent indications that the Chinese police are moving towards discouraging those who encourage and demand prostitution practices by utilizing techniques of public shaming ('Police strengthen inspection of recreation places' 1999), it also does not follow that relocating the punitive bias of China's prostitution controls onto the male side of demand will simply result in more men, rather than women, being held in 'unacceptable' detention centres.

Contrary to the popular rendition of the Chinese police as a 'law unto themselves', media condemnation of police complicity in the running of prostitution businesses highlights the feasibility of working within the interstices engendered by domestic solutions to the problems surrounding the PRC's prostitution controls. In July 2000, coterminous with the implementation of a campaign to reinforce the Entertainment Regulations (Zhonghua renmin gongheguo guowuyuan 1999), China Central Television Station (CCTV) aired a prime-time programme that seriously compromised the Chinese police ('Chinese express outrage over Qingdao brothel fiasco' 2000). The programme *Focus* (*jiaodian fangtan*), which covers the more controversial aspects of contemporary Chinese society, publicly embarrassed the Chinese public security forces by exposing their inability to police prostitution businesses and practices *comprehensively*. I stress the term 'comprehensive' here because Chinese policing scholars often celebrate the mass-line in policing on the grounds that it will create an army of people to work in concert for the all-round management of China's current public order problems (Yu Hongyuan 1999: 40–2).

Following a 'tip-off' about an underground 'casino-cum-brothel', CCTV reporters went to the venue in question and taped secret video footage of the activities occurring within it. These activities reputedly included gambling and naked female dancers, amongst other proscribed behaviours. Subsequent to this event, CCTV reporters accompanied a police investigation of the same venue that revealed nothing untoward; apparently even the internal spatial organization of the venue had been altered. Following the airing of this television show, and subsequent accusations of police complicity in providing illicit business operations with advanced warnings of proposed investigations, the late 2000 variant of the 'strike hard' campaign against prostitution and illegality was ultimately declared to be the most successful reform-era campaign of its kind, precisely because the police had been shamed into acting *professionally* ('Chinese police continue crackdown on recreational businesses' 2000; Kwang 2000). The late 2000 'strike hard' campaign was pronounced a particular success because it twinned 'the campaign against illegality and prostitution' to 'the campaign against corruption', and did so in a quite specific way. During the course of this campaign, the Chinese public security forces were obliged as a professional body to simultaneously police both prostitution businesses and practices *and* the policing of such phenomena.

Viewed in this context, the utility of contemporary campaign processes cannot be explained exclusively in terms of their pragmatic utility to the Chinese police or, conversely, in terms of their presumed value to the CCP as a familiar method of effecting social control. For, on the one hand, the symbolic and disciplinary side of police-led campaigns against crime and prostitution, particularly as relayed through the individuating and signifying power of the Chinese media, is clearly intended to ensure public conformity to the law by demonstrating that 'offenders will be caught and punished'. But, on the other hand, it appears that this same disciplinary technology can also be directed at the conduct of those who are responsible for managing the conduct of others, especially if they are deemed to be acting in ways that do not conform with their professional commitments. The tendency of metropolitan commentators to present campaign-style policing as a rigid, coercive expression of the sovereign will of the CCP thus elides the fact that the redeployment of campaign technologies in new domains and for new purposes is both a product and generator of social change.

In sum, I have highlighted some of the complexities surrounding contemporary Chinese policing because it acts as a useful counter to the popular construction of police-led campaigns against prostitution as a straightforward instance of communist repression. The very existence of policing debates on the utility of such strategies indicates that solutions to policing problems in China, like anywhere else, are not simply handed down by some omnipotent and omnipresent supra-elite: rather, they are internally generated from within the ranks of the public security forces. Likewise, the manifold settings and social forces associated with the implementation of campaign strategies suggest that techniques of policing or crime control are not explicable in terms of some over-arching political ideology. Campaign-style policing may bear a surface resemblance to Maoist methods of effecting social control, a similarity that has no doubt helped to authorize the campaign process by reinforcing a sense of continuity with the past. But this resemblance is better understood as a 'repetition with a difference' rather than as a Maoist reprise (Dutton 1995: 418).

Put another way, the campaign process might be more productively read as a sign of governmentality in action. As the aforementioned reference to CCTV would suggest, China's prostitution controls offer more than a straightforward illustration of the deleterious effects of implementing punitive central policies. They are the locus for a new and complex field of forces, wherein questions concerning both the conduct of the governed, *and* the conduct of government, are being negotiated. Metropolitan commentators have tended to ignore the strategic and relational nature of campaign processes, however, as the next section shows.

Changing police: policing prostitution

In keeping with broader criticisms of the PRC's response to crime, metropolitan commentators have roundly condemned China's prostitution controls in the form of police-led campaigns against prostitution businesses and practices. Like campaign-style policing in general, anti-prostitution campaigns have been collectively presented as draconian yet ineffective displays of law and order that retain a cachet with 'hard-line' members of the CCP leadership, even though they have no 'real hold' on the post-Cultural Revolution, campaign-fatigued, Chinese public. This mode of argumentation is usually underscored with reference to statistics indicating that rates and types of prostitution in China continue to proliferate, and by comparing the success of campaigns to eradicate prostitution in the 1950s with the apparent failure of campaign technologies in the present-day. To quote Zha Jianying:

> Campaigns worked in the fifties, and they worked in the sixties and seventies ... In the reformed eighties, however, campaigns became something else ... As people turned their minds more and more to economic matters and daily life, political movements inevitably lost their hold ... It was all turning into a hollow echo of a bygone era.
>
> By the time the Party decided to fight against pornography [and

> prostitution], the crowd appeal and mobilizing power of official campaigns had further dwindled ... people read in their local papers about the arrests of pimps and prostitutes ... Yet none of this had any real effect any more ... [The campaigns] came and went, like thunderstorms in summer ... And everyone knew that it would soon be business as usual.
>
> (Zha Jianying 1995: 144–5)

Further highlighting the perceived moribund nature of contemporary campaigns, Gail Hershatter (1997: 363) argues that government authorities responded to the appearance of prostitution in 1980s' China in two distinct ways. First, they 'turned to the legal system as a "modern" weapon in their fight against prostitution'; and, second, they 'also relied on a more familiar form of social discipline: the campaign (*yundong*)'.[4] Campaigns, she continues, comprise a 'quintessentially Maoist method' of effecting social change, and refer to 'clearly delineated periods of intense public activity', which, in turn, mobilize the populace to achieve varying but particular objectives, 'rather than relying primarily on the daily operations of institutions like the courts and police' (ibid.: 363–4). The problem here, or so Hershatter claims, is that although campaign technologies enjoyed some success during the Maoist period, they have proved to be far less effective in the reform era. This is because the Chinese leadership is divided with regard to the worth of particular campaigns and because the Chinese populace has grown weary and suspicious of mass mobilization in the years following the 'disaster' of the Cultural Revolution. Hence the organizing question behind Hershatter's critique of the PRC's response to prostitution, and one that she implies is also of paramount importance to China's governmental authorities, is whether prostitution should 'be dealt with by strengthening the legal system – a modernizing project of the late twentieth century – or by turning to the familiar but decreasingly effective method of political campaigns?' (ibid.: 358).

Hershatter concludes that the Chinese response to prostitution is predicated on an out-dated 'ideological' construction of prostitution, and that attempts to implement the PRC's prostitution laws have floundered due to the CCP's continued reliance on the equally outmoded campaign formula of the 1950s. To paraphrase her own words, recourse to the law has done little to change the way China's state authorities have dealt with law enforcement – the implementation of periodic crackdowns, followed by the announcement of arrest statistics (and the gradual reappearance of prostitution), and then by sober official statements suggesting that the struggle to eliminate prostitution will be a long one (ibid.: 363). This strategy remains in place even though forms of prostitution continue to proliferate, and even though many people, including law enforcement officials, have '*privately* [my italics] expressed' reservations about the efficacy of such a response, and intimated that the successful 1950s' model is unlikely to be repeated (ibid.: 367). In a similar manner to Zha Jianying, therefore, Hershatter implies that the only reason the PRC's 'anachronistic' prostitution controls remain in place is because the 'hard-line' CCP is unable to think beyond the ideological strictures and organizational practices inherited from the Maoist 1950s.

This continued framing of the Chinese polity in terms of the liberal binary of 'state versus civil society' presents an unsustainable picture of the Chinese government as vegetating in the teeth of time. After all, although Hershatter valorizes a growing number of people for 'daring' to think outside of the rigid official language of Marxism-cum-Maoism, and *privately* expressing doubts about the efficacy of the 1950s' approach for eradicating contemporary prostitution, the Chinese police and hard-line members of the CCP do not appear to have experienced any qualms about making the same reservations public. In 1993, the Police Officer Educational Publishing House in Beijing released a text by Ma Weigang, entitled *Jinchang jindu* (On Strictly Forbidding Prostitution and Drugs), which explicitly states that the example of the 1950s offers 'lessons' but not 'solutions' for the policing of prostitution today. In fact, following an overview of Maoist-era prostitution controls, Ma (1993: 13) concludes that it is not possible simply to look at that period and emulate it, because the conditions that contributed to the eradication of visible prostitution in the 1950s and 1960s no longer exist. Likewise, while making a public announcement in support of the 1996 'strike hard' campaign, Jiang Zemin stated that it was unrealistic to expect that China's social order problems would be resolved by resorting to anti-crime campaigns and 'special campaigns' against phenomena such as prostitution, pornography, gambling, and drugs ('Anti-crime campaign to be continued, deepened' 1996). The implementation of anti-crime and special campaigns, he suggested, should be undertaken in tandem with the more important and long-term task of developing preventive policing and other governmental strategies.

Viewed from this perspective, China's prostitution controls are premised on a more complicated rationale than the derisory construction of police-led campaigns as anachronistic and moribund technologies of social control allows. To begin with, the very suggestion that the Chinese police have resurrected an out-dated 1950s' model belies the fact that there was more than one strategic approach to the control of prostitution even in 'Mao's China'. As Ma Weigang (1993: 8) explains, following the CCP's victory in 1949, local governmental authorities were charged with the task of realizing the CCP's established goal of eliminating the 'ugly' system of prostitution. Given the sheer enormity of this task, and the myriad other social issues that had to be addressed, the relevant authorities adopted a dual policy of immediately eradicating brothel-prostitution in cities where the problem could or had to be dealt with effectively, and adopted a slower approach in areas where the number of people who depended on institutionalized prostitution for a livelihood was too large for the already over-reached resources of China's new governmental authorities to handle. While not exhausting different localized responses, Ma contends that two measures were favoured in the main: the slow approach of first controlling and then prohibiting brothel-prostitution, which was adopted in cities like Shanghai, Tianjin, and Wuhan; and the fast approach of deploying drastic, emergency-style measures, which was adopted in the capital city of Beijing, to provide a national example and demonstrate the political will and capacity of the new regime.

The example of Beijing is the model celebrated in mainland accounts of the PRC's revolutionary history and the model now decried by Anglophone commentators as being unsuited to the policing of prostitution today. To reiterate the broad parameters of this particular revolutionary story, following the liberation of Beijing in late January 1949, the Beijing Municipal Government, in conjunction with the Chinese public security forces and members of the All-China Women's Federation, immediately set about investigating prostitution businesses and activities (Ma 1993: 10–11). The exact location and number of all the brothels in Beijing were identified, as were the identities, familial connections, economic situation and political background of all the people who owned, managed, lived, and worked within them. With this information in hand, a draft resolution concerning the closure of Beijing's brothels was drawn up and subsequently adopted at the second session of the Beijing People's Representatives Congress on 21 November 1949. This resolution defined the institution of prostitution as an insult and harm to women, and referred to brothels as a backward relic from China's old society that served to suppress women ('Duanping jiefang jinü' 1949: 1). In doing so, the resolution stipulated that all the brothels were to be closed; all brothel property was to be confiscated; all brothel-keepers, procurers, and pimps, were to be detained for trial; and prostitutes within the brothels were to be rounded up for rehabilitative education and costly medical treatment, before being reintegrated into the changed social fabric of 'New China'. Following the completion of the above-mentioned meeting, an estimated 2,400 cadres and community police officers set about closing the city's 224 brothels; and, approximately 12 hours later, they announced that this task had been completed. Thus, in the space of just one day, and less than two months after the founding of the PRC, it appeared that China's new government had managed to eradicate the age-old system of prostitution from Beijing (Ma 1993: 10–11).

Not surprisingly, the example of Beijing was (and still is) lauded in mainland accounts of the history of prostitution in China. But this extraordinary feat was not immediately replicated throughout China's other large cities. Most cities adopted the slower measure of first controlling and then prohibiting brothel-prostitution, due to the huge number of people who were dependent on prostitution for a livelihood, and the limited budgets and human resources of local governments (ibid.: 8–9). As with the methods initially used in Beijing, however, the slower model turned on an attempt to control the number of brothels by placing them under a system of governmental administration. The political and family background of every brothel-keeper was placed on file, as were details concerning the internal architectural layout, hygiene facilities and equipment of all the brothels. Every brothel was given a special licence; and prostitutes residing within them were issued licences with photographic identification, and basically prohibited from leaving the brothels to prostitute elsewhere without police permission. Strict limits were also placed on the number of prostitutes within each brothel and brothel-keepers were banned from recruiting new 'workers', advertising the services of their respective establishments, and keeping women under 18 years of age, pregnant women, women with sexually transmissible diseases, and women who had recently given birth. In addition, brothel-keepers were charged with a wide array of tasks such as forbidding gambling and the use of drugs on the premises, keeping the equivalent of an orderly house, and ensuring that the women in their service were not mistreated.

Apart from regulating the internal arrangements, people, and activities, within the brothels, the slower approach to eradicating the system of prostitution also incorporated a number of 'drastic measures' in an attempt to reduce the male demand for prostitution (ibid.: 9). Brothel-keepers were banned from admitting military personnel, public servants, and men less than 20 years of age, and they were obliged to supply the local police with a daily register of all the men who had patronized their establishment the day before, including details of each man's name, age, address, and occupation. At the same time, the police adopted a broader tactic known as 'inconveniencing the whoremongers'. For instance, if the daily register of brothel patrons included men who were public employees or students, then the police would contact the relevant work-units and not only inform the requisite authorities of the activities of the particular men in question, but also advise them of the need to educate and reform the behaviours of their staff and students. Adding to these measures, the police organized nightly patrols of the brothels to check on the identity of patrons within them and any man found in the general vicinity. The combined effect of such measures was to gradually reduce the number of brothels in each city, until that number reached a point where a 'Beijing-style' closure of the remaining brothels was deemed feasible. Hence somewhere between 1954 and 1958 (depending upon one's sources), the Chinese government declared that the system of prostitution no longer existed in socialist China.

If metropolitan commentators initially endorsed and now challenge the CCP's claim to have eradicated prostitution from China during the 1950s, they also have a curious tendency to simultaneously treat this historical feat as fact. By this I mean that the CCP's claim to have eradicated the system of prostitution is generally treated as a claim to have eradicated prostitution per se, when the closing of the brothels only signified the end of institutionalized forms of commercial prostitution. As a result, the more complicated if mundane story of how the new government set about transforming the social organization of China's cities, and thereby removing the spaces and conditions wherein the overwhelming majority of prostitution activities would have occurred, has gone largely unmentioned. In addition, metropolitan commentators frequently transmogrify the CCP's claim to have eradicated the system of prostitution from 1950s' China into a claim that the current leadership is engaged in a futile attempt to abolish prostitution in precisely the same exemplary manner as its predecessors.

On a symbolic level, there can be little doubt that the learned cultural memory of the CCP's past achievements operates as both an inducement and incitement for the Chinese police to take firm action against the resurgence of prostitution in China today. In practice, however, the Chinese police do not view the past as a source of immediate solutions for contemporary policing problems. Rather, they look to the past to learn the lessons of history; and, constrained as they are by the structural legacies of the Maoist period, the lesson the Chinese police derive from an examination of the 1950s is the importance of strategic thinking and careful planning. Put simply, the lesson to be derived from the 1950s for the Chinese police is that the phenomenon of prostitution cannot be successfully contained until all forms of prostitution are identified and turned into manageable objects of corrective intervention. This task necessarily makes the goal of eliminating prostitution a long-term project, given the diversity and constantly changing nature of prostitution business and practices in China today.

Assessed at the level of practice, therefore, the popular construction of the PRC's prostitution controls as moribund and anachronistic fails to acknowledge the heterogeneous rationales and forms of power that underpin the campaign process. Major campaigns against prostitution, such as the 1989 campaign against the 'six evils' arguably constitute a redeployed version of the original 1950s' 'Beijing model' in the sense that they are similarly premised on the use of emergency-style measures, and aim to demonstrate the will and capacity of government. These campaigns turn on the deployment of juridical forms of power in the sense that coded sets of representations are used to establish the certainty of punishment for any involvement in prostitution. Major campaigns against prostitution have been consistently accompanied by the promulgation of new legislation enlarging the range and scope of China's prostitution controls, as well as by widespread media publicity designed to 'frighten' offenders and encourage 'healthy trends' among the general populace, by promoting knowledge of the law and the perceived harm of prostitution.

But campaign-style policing is not solely a means to punish or cow people into acquiescence with the law; it is also a means to knowledge. Campaigns possess a more technical side in that they are concerned with the collection and evaluation of information, and, subsequently, with rendering the social 'visible' and open to remedial intervention. Analyses of prostitution undertaken by the Chinese police, for instance, evince a marked concern not only with establishing a profile of the age, skills, status, and motivations, of the PRC's 'prostitution-offender population', but also with establishing the kinds of venues and situations in which prostitution activities take place, and the ways in which those involved in prostitution practices and businesses have sought to evade detection (Beijing dongcheng . . . 1993: 14–17). Likewise, police evaluations of a given campaign are never concerned strictly with summarizing its perceived achievements; they are equally concerned with identifying its shortcomings and proposing remedial countermeasures (Kong Wen and Meng Qingfeng 2000: 40–2; Qian Changfu 1995: 51; Xu Hu 1993: 42–51). Metropolitan criticisms of campaign strategies as ineffective – because they are characterized by a cyclical series of crackdowns and the gradual revival of prostitution – thus elide a fundamental issue. The very perception of 'failure' functions as a stimulus for the Chinese police to initiate an additional series of campaigns, ones that continually reinvoke the model of the original 'aborted' schema, yet do so in quite discrete ways.

Certainly, the Chinese police have consistently translated the perceived failures of a given campaign into calls for the formulation of yet another campaign and new legal measures designed to ensure its more effective implementation. Consequently, the bifurcation that supposedly informs the Chinese response to prostitution, i.e., the presumed necessity of deciding in favour of one of two methods – the first modern and legal, the other traditional, arbitrary and ineffective – does not exist in practice. Instead, it appears that campaigns are viewed not only as a means of enforcing the law; the problems associated with their effective implementation are construed as being related to weaknesses or gaps in existing laws, which, in turn, require the formulation of new regulatory measures.

Thus, rather than presenting the cyclical nature of campaign-style policing as a sign of China's political putrefaction, we need to acknowledge that the imperative to identify and rectify 'failure' is characteristic of the programmatic nature of all forms of governmentality. Governmentality is programmatic in the sense that it leads to the proliferation of more or less explicit plans for reforming 'reality', such as government reports, legislative rulings, white papers, and academic papers, proposing various schemes for dealing with diverse problems (Miller and Rose 1990: 4). Governmentality is additionally programmatic in the sense that it is marked by an eternal optimism that it is not only possible to transform the social body (that reality is, in a sense, programmable), but also that it is always possible to administer a given domain more effectively. This optimism is arguably more pronounced in the Chinese setting due to the former absence of Western liberal conceptions of the individual subject and the public/private dichotomy, and because mainland scholarship often holds the positivistic view that there is nothing beyond the calculative grasp of scientific Marxism, i.e., ultimately everything can be 'known'.

This genealogical difference helps to explain why the question that appears to vex many Anglophone commentators on prostitution in the PRC – why the retreat of 'the state' in areas of economic management has not been replicated in relation to the more 'private' arena of the sexual, and thus accompanied by a more relaxed approach to such arguably 'personal' issues as prostitution and pornography – does not feature heavily in accounts intended for a Sinophone readership. On the contrary, mainland scholars tend to assume that the relevant authorities will and *should* intervene in such areas; hence, they are not overly concerned with demarcating the legitimate boundaries of 'the state'. Indeed, they are more concerned to establish how a particular intervention can be implemented most effectively and purposefully. In this way, the perceived shortcomings of a given campaign are always linked to attempts to devise 'better' strategies and tactics that promise to achieve the same ends by somewhat altered means. Failure acts, in effect, as an impetus for the propagation of new campaigns and additional programmes of government.

Once we acknowledge that the imperative to evaluate is characteristic of the programmatic nature of governmentality, the typical post-campaign scenario – public announcements of campaign 'successes', followed by a gradual revival of prostitution, and then sober official statements suggesting that the struggle to eliminate prostitution will be a long one – cannot be held up as proof that nothing has changed, or that it is 'back to business as usual'. The issue that needs to be addressed is how the very perception of failure has fed back into the ongoing development of new policy. In other words, rather than dismissing China's current prostitution controls as moribund because they have failed to eradicate prostitution in the exemplary manner of the 1950s, we need to examine the manifold aspects of the social that have been posited as being in need of remedial attention, flowing from the campaign-related problematization of prostitution businesses and practices as phenomena that can be identified and opened to a process of permanent rectification.

Policing prostitution: changing disciplinary technologies

There can be little doubt that knowledge of prostitution in China today is largely a product of investigations conducted by or under the auspices of the Chinese public security forces and other relevant authorities.[5] For in order to manage 'the problem of prostitution', and hence to render prostitution practices and businesses into a form that can be made open to programmes of corrective intervention, the Chinese police have been obliged to conceptualize the field upon which they are expected to intervene. Police-led campaigns have also been accompanied by nationwide 'media blitzes' – blitzes designed to publicize the PRC's laws and the specific objectives of a given campaign, and thereby induce people to become active citizens by disclosing, reporting, and criticizing the existence of proscribed activities. The general public is thus made aware of how China's policing authorities have chosen to conceptualize and categorize 'the problem of prostitution' ('TV programme helps raise awareness of law' 1996: 12–13; Wang Shouzhi 1995: 47; Zhang Zhiping 2000: 28–33).

What has emerged from the ongoing campaign process is a composite picture of the various forms of prostitution practices and businesses that exist in China today. This 'picture' highlights the heterogeneous nature of sellers and buyers of sex in PRC by showing that prostitution practices are characterized by a proliferation of types, venues, prices, and labour migration patterns, which both reflect and exacerbate the kinds of gendered and socio-economic hierarchies that make up contemporary Chinese society. This 'picture' also undermines the liberal construction of prostitution as a 'private and unremarkable transaction' by exposing the links between certain forms of selling sex and governmental corruption. In the process, it points to the practical difficulty of unifying the forms of selling and buying sex that exist in present-day China under the rubric of sex work.

To elaborate, on the basis of campaigns conducted during the late 1980s and early 1990s, by the mid-1990s the Chinese police had apparently determined that prostitution practices in reform-era China could be categorized according to a descending hierarchy of seven tiers ('China makes headway in fight against prostitution, gambling' 1999; O'Neill 1999). The first level known as *waishi* or *baoernai* refers to women who act as the 'second wives' or long-term 'mistresses' of men with money and influential positions, including government officials and bureaucratic entrepreneurs from the mainland, and businessmen from Hong Kong, Taiwan, Japan, and South Korea. This practice is defined as prostitution, not a genuine love relationship, on the grounds that the women in question actively solicit men with money and rank, i.e., men who can provide them with fixed-term accommodation and a regular allowance. The second tier, *baopo*, a 'hired or packaged wife', refers to women who also solicit men with money and rank, but rather than living in flats provided by male buyers of sex accompany their 'clients' for a fixed duration of time, for example, during the course of a business trip, and receive a set payment for doing so (Liu Fanqui 1993: 24–6; Zhang Yanshang 1993: 12–19).

The third tier, *santing*, or the 'three halls', refers to women who 'accompany' men in recreational business enterprises such as karaoke/dance venues, bars, restaurants, and teahouses, and who receive financial recompense in the form of 'tips' from the individual men they accompany, as well as from a share of the profits generated by informal service charges on the use of facilities and the consumption of food and beverages. Although governmental authorities in China do not equate 'hostessing' with prostitution per se, 'hostessing' is nonetheless viewed as an activity that promotes prostitution and evades policing controls, by abetting the practice of 'accompanying first and engaging in prostitutional sex later'. The fourth tier refers to women who are colloquially referred to as 'door-bell girls' (*dingdong xiaojie*), that is, women who solicit potential buyers of sex by telephoning all the rooms in a given hotel, and subsequently announce their arrival at the room of prospective 'clients' by knocking on the door or ringing the doorbell. The fifth tier, *falangmei*, refers to women who work in places that offer commercial sexual services under the guise of massage treatments, for instance, in health and fitness centres, beauty parlours, hairdressing salons, barber shops, bath-houses and saunas ('Jingcheng . . .' 1996: 4–7; Li Juqing 1993: 40–1; Wang Huanju 1995: 44–9; Xin Ran 1996: 14–20).

Chinese commentators usually differentiate the two lowest tiers of prostitution practices from the aforementioned upper five tiers on the grounds that they are characterized by the more straightforward exchange of sex for financial or material recompense. In other words, they refer to prostitution practices that are neither explicitly linked to governmental corruption, nor directly mediated through China's new commercial recreational business sector. The sixth tier, *jienu*, refers to women who solicit male buyers of sex on the streets, or outside of public places of recreation and entertainment, for example, at the entrances to hotels and cinemas, and in busy public spaces such as railway stations and parks. The seventh and lowest tier, *xiagongpeng* or *zhugongpeng*, refers to women who sell sex to China's new transient labour force of male workers from the rural countryside. That is, women who sell sex predominantly to men (read peasants) from the rural hinterland who have migrated to urban centres in order to work on the construction of primary infrastructure, such as roads and buildings, and who live in temporary work camps or accommodations. Unlike women who sell sex in the first five tiers, the Chinese police maintain that women who sell sex in the lowest two tiers usually do so in return for small sums of money, and women in the lowest tier often do so in exchange for food and shelter.

Although this typology predominantly classifies urban modes of prostitution, and does not exhaust the forms of prostitution businesses and practices that exist in the PRC today, it demonstrates that the campaign process, while apparently 'failing', has not exactly missed its target. On the contrary, the campaign process has functioned to identify and isolate specific types of prostitution-related activities as referring to a complicated but nonetheless potentially penetrable social milieu. In doing so, it highlights the complexity of the issues that the Chinese police have both identified and subsequently been enjoined to address.

For example, two of the most controversial modes of selling and buying sex in present-day China are the practices of keeping a 'second wife' and 'hiring a wife'. These practices have become the focus of heated public debate because they are explicitly linked to government corruption, or the embezzlement of public funds and the appropriation of public resources to finance a 'second home' or to support a 'short-term mistress' (Hu Qihua 2000: 2). In consequence, scholars such as Pan Suiming (1996b: 52–7) contend that these practices should be made the first and foremost subject of China's prostitution controls because they constitute a concrete expression of 'bourgeois right'. That is to say, the continued existence and hence the allegedly diffident policing of such practices demonstrates that government officials both conceive of themselves and are treated as a privileged class that is somehow 'above the law', whereas ordinary citizens are subjected to the full (moral and penal) brunt of China's prostitution controls.

Members of the All-China Women's Federation similarly maintain that the practices of 'keeping a second wife' and 'hiring a short-term mistress' should be made an explicit target of governmental controls, albeit for somewhat different reasons. While concurring that the continued existence of such practices undermines the credibility of the CCP as an exemplary 'vanguard party', the ACWF were actively involved in efforts to see 'concubinage' and 'mistress-related corruption' banned according to the PRC's new Marriage Law of 2001 as practices that violate the emotional and economic surety of the marriage contract. I stress the notion of economic surety here because foreign newspaper correspondents tended to portray the ACWF's efforts as a sign that China is peculiarly anti-sex, or opposed to sex in any form other than monogamous marital sex. However, the underlying logic of the revisions put forward by the ACWF is not so easily dismissed, even though those revisions reinforce the institution of the family. According to members of the ACWF, many divorces stem from infidelity on the part of men, and the PRC's lack of comprehensive legislation regarding the provision of maintenance places women in the undesirable position of having to accept marital infidelity or face economic hardship (Liu Yinglang 1997: 4). Put crudely, therefore, the ACWF's condemnation of practices such as keeping a 'second wife' and 'hiring a short-term mistresses' is premised on the understanding that if men want to 'have their cake and eat it', then they will have to pay for the consequences of doing so.

Adding to such pressure, women's groups in Hong Kong and Taiwan also called on the Chinese government to ban such practices, on the grounds that businessmen from Hong Kong and Taiwan who work in the PRC often maintain a 'second wife' or a series of 'mistresses' on the mainland (Kuo 1999; Lander 2000: 4; McGivering 1998: 8). These concerns not only fuelled the controversy surrounding the promulgation of the PRC's 2001 Marriage Law, they have also resulted in the formulation of various other legal stipulations designed to address the practices of keeping or hiring a 'second wife'. The 'Communist Party discipline regulations' (1997), for instance, contain specific provisions to the effect that Party members will be stripped of their posts for using their positions and/or public funds to keep a 'second wife', a 'hired wife', and to buy sexual services. Nonetheless, the Chinese police have been consistently accused of refusing to actively police such phenomena, with commentators claiming that they endorse and partake of the privileges that accrue to China's governmental and entrepreneurial elite, or China's nouveau riche (Pan Suiming 1996b: 52–7).

But, if China's public security forces have proved unable to police prostitution practices in the form of keeping a 'second wife' or hiring a 'short-term mistress', it is equally clear that the changes engendered by the process of economic reform have effectively robbed them of the capacity to do so. Despite trenchant condemnation of 'concubinage' and 'mistress-related corruption', the growing public acceptance of pre-marital and extra-marital affairs has meant that the Chinese police are now professionally constrained not to intrude on people's personal relationships in an overt or coercive manner. As a result, they are more or less obliged to *know* that the particular relationship in question is bigamous or 'prostitution-like' before they can take appropriate action (Jiang Rongsheng 1992: 34). Previously such knowledge often came from an aggrieved spouse on the understanding that it would result in the 'other woman' being detained by police authorities, whereas no serious action would be taken against the man in question. However, given that government employees convicted of engaging in such practices now stand to lose their livelihood and public standing (i.e., the legal weight of such sanctions is now also located on the male side of demand), this particular source of information is presumably not so forthcoming.

Similarly, the ability of the Chinese police to control 'mistress-related corruption', particularly in the form of hiring a female seller of sex for the duration of a business trip, is limited by the fact that such women are usually presented to hotel personnel as personal secretaries, public relations officers, or lovers. Consequently, the capacity of local security organizations to police this form of prostitution is reduced to the tactic of enforcing laws forbidding the hiring of hotel rooms to members of the opposite sex who cannot produce a valid marriage certificate and, subsequently, by raiding rooms where relevant personnel have informed them that members of the opposite sex are 'keeping company after normal hours'. Not surprisingly, this tactic has proved to be extremely unpopular with the general public and overseas tourists alike. Moreover, it has simply encouraged women who sell sex in hotels to ply their 'trade' during the day instead of during the evening. In fact, although the practice of selling sex by telephoning hotel rooms is now banned as comprising a form of sexual harassment, presumably due to complaints by affronted (male) hotel guests (Pan Suiming 1992b: 39), the Chinese public security forces are still obliged to rely on hotel security personnel to apprise them of the existence of suspected prostitution offenders. And, for a wide variety of reasons – including indifference on the part of hotel personnel, the fact that hotel staff may be receiving 'kickbacks' from sellers and buyers of sex, and a general unwillingness on the part of those in charge to tarnish the 'clean' record of a given venue and thereby bring themselves to the attention of the police – this information is often not forthcoming.

Likewise, apart from conducting regular patrols of public spaces, and hence attempting to use a strong (and costly) police presence as a deterrence, the ability of the Chinese police to apprehend sellers and buyers of sex in the two lowest tiers of China's prostitution hierarchy is heavily dependent on the 'eyes and ears' of members of auxiliary mass-line organizations. In consequence, sellers and buyers of sex who meet on the streets have adopted a wide range of tactics designed to avoid apprehension, such as buying a valid train ticket that can be subsequently (re)sold, and therefore having a legitimate reason for 'hanging around' a busy train station and engaging in 'idle conversation' with various people. Concomitantly, prospective sellers and buyers of sex may simply establish, often via a 'go-between', that they have a mutual interest in participating in the prostitution transaction, and then arrange to meet at a later hour or day, and in a different place, in order to reduce the initial negotiation time, and avoid attracting unwanted attention by leaving together. Indeed, Chinese policing scholars often aver that the spatial mobility which is afforded to the 'prostitution-offender population' by virtue of modern communications systems, such as mobile phones and electronic pagers, and by modern forms of transportation, such as taxis and private cars, has severely reduced their ability to determine exactly who is engaged in acts of solicitation and who constitutes a legitimate suspect (Ouyang Tao 1994: 15–18).

Unlike street sellers of sex, who utilize spatial tactics to evade the 'eyes and ears' of localized mass-line security organizations, women who sell sex to migrant workers feature in apprehension statistics precisely because of the 'floating' nature of the transient population. Women in the lowest tier of China's 'prostitution hierarchy' are far more likely to be apprehended as an indirect result of the system of establishing checks over the transient labour force and migrant-related accommodations than as a direct consequence of the implementation of 'draconian' anti-prostitution campaigns. For although such women feature in the above-mentioned hierarchy of prostitution practices, they feature less heavily in campaign-related evaluations than women who sell sex in recreational business enterprises (Beijing dongcheng . . . 1993: 14–17).

This latter consideration brings into question the standard feminist criticism that the PRC's prostitution controls, as with prohibitory approaches everywhere, are targeted primarily at the lowest levels of the prostitution hierarchy. Women who sell sex to migrant workers are indubitably vulnerable to police apprehension by virtue of their low socio-economic position and due to the problematic nature of existing controls over the transient labour force. But this vulnerability is not the result of a deliberate attempt on the part of the Chinese public security forces to target the most downtrodden of female prostitutes. It is a side-effect of various mass-line policing efforts – often conducted under the auspices of non-professional, localized crime prevention teams – to ensure that male members of the 'floating population', in particular, possess appropriate work-cards and temporary residency permits, so as to contain the perceived high levels of criminality associated with this new sector of China's urban population (Zhao Shukai 2000: 101–10).

The primary target of the PRC's prostitution controls in practice, therefore, is China's burgeoning hospitality and entertainment industry. Recreational venues were made an increasing focus of new regulatory measures and policing campaigns throughout the 1990s, culminating in the 'strike hard' campaigns of late 1999 and 2000 to enforce the Entertainment Regulations. This sector of the economy has become an explicit target of combined campaigns against illegality, prostitution, and corruption, because campaigns conducted during the late 1980s and early 1990s, particularly in southern China's new Special Economic Zones or open coastal cities, demonstrated that recreational business enterprises frequently operate as 'fronts' for the crime of organizing prostitution, and what is now described as the crime of hiring or keeping women to engage in obscene activities with other people. These preliminary investigations also revealed that recreational business operations are directly linked to governmental corruption, in the form of local government involvement or collusion in the running of such enterprises, and in the more indirect form of the widespread abuse of public funds to finance consumption within such venues.

In the early 1990s, for instance, the National Bureau of Statistics estimated that between 60–70 per cent of the income accruing to high grade hotels, guesthouses, restaurants, and karaoke/dance venues came from consumers spending public funds, at an estimated annual cost to the public of around 800 billion *yuan* (Wang Tie 1993: 35; Zhang Ping 1993: 25; Zhao Jianmei 1994: 35). Given that these consumers are predominantly (male) government employees, it is generally accepted that their conduct has to be corrected. Thus, practices such as spending public funds within commercial recreational venues, using public funds to hire the company of 'short-term mistresses/hostesses', and local government complicity in the running of illicit businesses, were constructed as problems in need of urgent remedial attention. During the mid to late 1990s, therefore, China's relevant authorities introduced a whole host of regulations designed to ban members of the public security forces, and other kinds of government employees, both from running recreational and entertainment venues and from protecting illegal business operations in this connection. Concomitantly, numerous regulations were introduced to curb the spending of public funds within such venues ('Army banned from business' 1998; 'China bans public-funded police entertainment' 1995). These measures are now being policed, not strictly on the basis of police-led campaigns and information derived from public informants, but also on the basis of disciplinary procedures that are both new and integral to the reform era itself, namely, via the practice established in 1998 of auditing government officials, and thereby combining the resources of the CCP's disciplinary committees with those of the State Auditing Administration (Bruel and Wu 2000).

However, if campaigns conducted during the late 1980s and early 1990s helped to expose the complex links between governmental corruption and commercial sexual activities, the process of economic development itself has effectively ensured that the task of 'cleaning up' China's burgeoning hospitality and recreational business sector, now collectively referred to as 'the cultural market', has only recently been presented as a task for *national* government. To offer one example, reports by the public security forces in Beijing suggest that they were not aware of any commercial enterprises offering recreational, as opposed, to medical massage services in the capital until late 1992. By the end of 1993, however, the Beijing police had either registered, or were aware of, 21 such businesses. This number expanded to 77 in 1994, and to more than 300 by the end of 1995. Accordingly, at the start of 1996, Chinese policing authorities estimated that the city of Beijing alone contained 142 business enterprises offering massage-related services within the confines of high grade hotels, and therefore operating on the basis of high capital overheads, and 180 businesses offering massage-related services within more localized venues such as health centres, hairdressing salons, and beauty parlours, and therefore operating on the basis of a lower capital outlay ('Jingcheng . . .' 1996: 4; Xin Ran 1996: 14–20).

Following the strategy used to regulate the capital's burgeoning number of karaoke/dance venues in 1993–4, the public security forces in Beijing subsequently conducted an 'open investigation' of all business enterprises within the metropolis that offered massage-related services. Owners and managers of such ventures were informed that the local police intended to conduct an investigation into the nature of their business operations. Following this investigation, it was concluded that the city of Beijing alone contained 2,100 rooms for the purposes of offering massage services, 4,431 massage tables, and 4,708 people providing various forms of massage. Of the total number of people providing massage services, 3,179 were women, with the overwhelming majority being migrants from the rural hinterland, most of whom served an almost exclusively male clientele and possessed no formal training in massage ('Jingcheng . . .' 1996: 4–6; Wang Huanju 1995: 44–9; Xin Ran 1996 14–20). Despite the virtual absence of trained staff, however, many of these venues were charging up to ten times the cost of a professional massage. Hence, as with informal consumption taxes in karaoke/dance venues, they were deemed to be operating by exceeding notions of consumer fair-pricing. It was also revealed that many of the 'masseuses' within such venues were not formally employed; but rather, like 'hostesses' in karaoke/dance venues, they depended on 'tips' from clients for their livelihood, and even had to pay various 'management fees' for the use of facilities. Not surprisingly, the Beijing police concluded that most of these venues were profiting from the expropriation of public funds and from the provision of illicit sexual services ('Jingcheng ...' 1996: 4–7). Thus they determined that venues offering massage-related services had to be made open to stricter processes of professional standardization and governmental administration.

Adopting regulatory measures formulated in Shanghai, on 5 July 1996, the Ministry of Public Security and the Bureau of Industry and Commerce issued the 'Notice concerning the rectification of the massage industry in Beijing (hereafter the Notice) ('Jingcheng ...' 1996: 7). This Notice stipulated that all business enterprises offering massage-related services had to register with the relevant authorities before the end of the month, in order to obtain the requisite operating licences. The Notice also explicitly forbade the provision of body massages to members of the opposite sex, unless such massages were provided by professionally trained personnel in centres regulated by the Department of Health and Hygiene, and unless such services were restricted to the provision of head and foot massages in venues that conformed to detailed specifications. As with measures designed to regulate the internal spatial organization of karaoke/dance venues, these restrictions included stipulations to the effect that the total size of venues offering massage services must be no smaller than 80 square metres, and that small rooms within such venues, in which private massages take place, must be no smaller than 10 square metres (Wang Huanju 1995: 49). Also in keeping with attempts to govern the activities within karaoke/dance venues, the Notice further stipulated that all people providing massage services must be formally trained and legitimately employed, and therefore must possess relevant qualifications, as well as the requisite identity cards, work permits, and residency permits. Last but not least, in keeping with efforts to regulate the cultural market in general, the Notice intimated that all personnel within such enterprises should receive legal education so as to encourage legitimate business practices.

These newly designed measures to standardize the 'massage industry' were sporadically enforced during the course of localized versions of the 1996–7 'strike hard' campaign against illegality and prostitution. Between December 1998 and May 1999, however, business enterprises offering massage-related services of a 'non-professional/non-medical' nature were made an explicit focus of a nationwide campaign. The Chinese public security forces subsequently investigated an alleged 152,000 massage-related business operations throughout China, and penalized 33,000 businesses, or approximately one-fifth of the total, for providing commercial sexual services ('Police say one-fifth of inspected massage parlours involved in vice' 1999). In Beijing alone, they reputedly investigated 10,000 massage-related businesses, and penalized 6,162 for being involved in illegal activities of non-specified forms ('Chinese police trying to improve situation at massage parlours' 1999). I say 'reputedly' because the figure provided for Beijing, which constitutes a dramatic increase over the 322 venues that were known to exist in 1996, presumably refers to the total number of recreational business enterprises of all forms that were investigated during the course of this particular campaign. The non-specific nature of the penalties involved indicates that some business ventures would have been penalized for providing commercial sexual services, whereas the vast majority were probably penalized for operating without appropriate business licences or for contravening regulations. I therefore also qualify the above-mentioned national statistics with the term 'alleged' because they presumably refer to the aggregate number of diverse forms of recreational business enterprises that were investigated during this period, not strictly to 'massage parlours' per se.

In any event, until the promulgation of the Entertainment Regulations in July 1999, the Chinese public security forces would have experienced the same difficulties in policing the existence of 'accompaniment' or 'hostess-style' services within massage-related business enterprises as those they had encountered while attempting to regulate the activities within karaoke/dance venues. Their ability to ascertain whether or not a business operation was providing or promoting illicit sexual activities would have been largely reduced to the tactic of determining which individual female subjects within such venues constituted neither legitimate patrons nor legitimate employees. This tactic is undeniably gendered and discriminates against female migrants from the rural hinterland, in particular. Furthermore, it is a tactic that is unlikely to be superseded by the introduction of the Entertainment Regulations, even though they place a greater onus on the owners and managers of recreational venues to conduct business, and employ personnel, in a legitimate manner.

Nonetheless, the nature and effects of recent tactics designed to curb the spread of 'hostessing' and prostitution-related activities within China's burgeoning leisure and entertainment sector cannot be adequately explained by alluding to the inherently patriarchal and repressive nature of the PRC's prostitution controls. What we need to examine is the nexus between the historically enforced reliance of China's governmental authorities on the practice of 'registration' – i.e., making the population 'visible' by obliging individuals to possess appropriate work, residency and business permits, thereby tying groups of individuals to their place of work as a self-regulating and 'policeable' unit – and the complex system of social relations that underpins the establishment and patronage of China's new recreational business sector. Likewise, we need to examine the complex governmental landscape in which sexual-political subjects such as sellers and buyers of sex have been both created and positioned in China, and the accompanying changes that have taken place within the field in which the policing of prostitution occurs. As the conclusion to this text suggests, an analysis of the campaign process as a practice of governmentality calls into question the recent feminist insistence that the international community should oblige national governments to legally recognize the 'sex sector' and hence 'sex workers'.

7 Conclusion

China, sex and prostitution reconsidered

China's response to prostitution reconsidered

By the start of the new millennium, a whole host of disparate concerns had converged to ensure that China's burgeoning hospitality and service industry was posited as a necessary target of 'macro political' intervention. I say 'necessary' in the sense that, if the late 1999 'strike hard' campaign to enforce the Entertainment Regulations was designed to control illicit business operations and the activities of 'hostesses-cum-sexual service providers', the follow-up campaign of 2000 further aimed to address public and governmental concerns over the continued link between the provision of commercial sexual services and governmental corruption. As a result, the Ministry of Public Security and the Ministry of Culture were urged by the National People's Congress to organize a major crackdown on 'accompaniment-style services' within China's recreational venues, irrespective of the cost to relevant departments, and irrespective of local government fears concerning the potentially deleterious short-term economic effects of doing so. The response was a nationwide campaign to drastically reduce the number of recreational business operations in the PRC, in order to control the heavy competition amongst them (which is deemed to encourage prostitution and illegality) and to curb the excessive establishment of luxury nightclubs and 'private' or 'covert' venues, i.e., business enterprises that are not patronized routinely or openly by the general public, and thus may be profiting from the abuse of public funds, the provision of proscribed activities, and on the basis of local government and police protection (Zhang Zhiping 2000: 33).

During the latter half of 2000, therefore, the Chinese police, in conjunction with numerous other government departments, closed down nearly one million recreational business operations of miscellaneous forms, including hotels, karaoke/dance venues, bars, 'massage parlours', saunas, bath-houses, health and fitness centres, beauty salons, hairdressing salons, teahouses, video arcades, and Internet cafés, the overwhelming majority of which were closed for not possessing relevant business licences and standard fire and safety equipment ('Million bars closed' 2001: 22). The tactics used to achieve the temporary and possibly permanent closure of such business operations merit attention, not because they underscore the 'arbitrary powers' of the Chinese police, but rather because they reveal an underlying desire to bring all commercial enterprises into the domain of governmental administration, by obliging them to 're-register' with the relevant authorities and thereby obliging them to further comply with existing regulations, including commerce and labour laws. Likewise, the very diversity of venues that were closed down by the Chinese police demonstrates that this campaign did not target prostitution alone. It targeted a whole host of 'ungoverned', as in illicit, irregular, or unlicensed, business operations.

The very diversity of venues and people that were targeted by this campaign undermines recent claims by foreign correspondents to the effect that it was strictly a moral campaign against prostitution, one that inadvertently exposed the entrenched size and economic significance of the 'sex industry' in China, and hence the political futility of attempting to ban it. According to one business report, for instance, bank deposits in Guangdong Province alone dropped by 36 million *yuan* as a result of the decision to launch this campaign, with prostitutes withdrawing their savings and returning to their native places of origin until the campaign was over, after which it would be 'back to business as usual' ('Banking, the oldest profession' 2000: 11). In a similar vein, another report maintains that China's 'new left' economist, Yang Fan, estimates that, following the implementation of the 1999 Entertainment Regulations, the Chinese Gross Domestic Product (GDP) slumped by 1 per cent, due to the lack of consumption on the part of female prostitutes (Zhong Wei 2000).[1] As this latter report concludes, it is thus not 'moonshine to talk about the economic importance of the "sex industry"', since it may well move the Chinese economy along 'with an annual level of consumption of 1 trillion RMB' (ibid.).

What these economistic arguments elide, even as they offer implicit support for liberal arguments concerning the need to legally recognize the 'sex sector', is that their estimated figures with regard to bank deposits and the Chinese GDP are not indicative of the supposedly high earnings of female prostitutes. These estimated figures refer to the 'untaxable' profit derived from a whole host of 'ungoverned' business operations and to a related rate of consumption that is fuelled in no small part by bribery and corruption. Given that the monies derived from unlicensed and illicit business operations are subject to fines and even confiscation by the Chinese government, the aforementioned 36 million *yuan* points less to the lucrative nature of prostitution for female sellers of sex and more to the profits to be gained by those who run illicit or unlicensed business enterprises with low capital overheads for a delimited period of time, namely, in the less risky 'non-campaign' period.

At first glance, this latter consideration would appear to support the popular construction of campaigns as punitive crackdowns that, once concluded, are promptly followed by the restoration of 'business as usual'. However, this conclusion can only be forwarded by claiming that the combined efforts of China's governmental authorities to standardize and regulate the commercial hospitality and service industry have been to no avail. Such a conclusion is flatly countered by recent reports to the effect that prostitution activities have been severely curtailed in site-specific business operations such as karaoke/dance venues and hairdressing salons, even as new and non-site-specific forms of commercial sex, such as 'telephone sex', have begun to emerge in China (Kwang 2000).

In short, campaigns against prostitution businesses and practices may have failed to eradicate prostitution *in toto*, but the conclusion of each and every campaign has not exactly been accompanied by a return to the status quo. On the contrary, the productive nature of regulatory measures to turn China's recreational venues into 'amenable public spaces' is demonstrated by the fact that, even though campaign-related investigations have resulted in expanded legal definitions of what counts as a prostitution-related offence, they have simultaneously helped to create a legitimate female service worker with the right to refuse to engage in practices that do not conform with the 'valid labour contract', as well as the right to be free from sexual harassment in the work-place. Furthermore, such measures have not only demonstrated that 'sex sellers' do not form a homogeneous group of wage labourers; they have also done much to draw attention to the varied nature of what, in the absence of any agreed upon terminology, might be loosely called 'sex-sector consumers' and 'sex-sector capitalists'. Indeed, the productive nature of such measures is demonstrated by the fact that the practice of top-ranking officials accepting bribes in the form of female sexual service providers is now a focus of considerable controversy in China (Wu Yaonong 2000).

Transnational prostitution debates reconsidered

A critical appraisal of the Chinese case brings into sharp relief the unproductive nature of recent debates concerning the optimal transnational response to prostitution, and hints at the insights a reconfigured form of China studies could bring to these and other critical debates within the new humanities. Most notably, the ongoing struggle of China's governmental authorities to turn the commercial hospitality and service industry into a standardized and regulated sector of the economy calls into question the recent feminist insistence that the international community should oblige national governments worldwide to legally recognize the 'sex sector' and hence 'sex workers'. While not disputing the validity of concerns about prostitutes' rights, a consideration of the Chinese case suggests that such concerns are not only underpinned by liberal conceptions of the sexual-political subject, but also presume that the organization of modern societies is to all intents and purposes identical. To put the matter bluntly, arguments concerning the perceived benefits that will accrue to women in prostitution, flowing from a legal recognition of the 'sex sector', effectively assume that all nations possess an established commercial business sector, with equitable and enforceable labour laws, into which the 'prostitute-as-(rightful)-worker' can somehow be slotted. This is demonstrably not the case in present-day China.

An examination of the Chinese case further questions the tendency of pro-sex work activists to homogenize all female sellers of sex as 'sex workers' and to treat male buyers of sex as 'private consumers'. Given the controversy that currently surrounds the first two tiers of China's 'prostitution hierarchy' (namely, the practices of 'keeping a second wife' and 'hiring a short-term mistress'), the act of legally recognizing prostitution, if such an option were socially acceptable and politically feasible in the PRC, would oblige the Chinese government to determine which particular forms of 'selling sex' could be legitimately defined as 'work' and which could not. Likewise, the tendency of the pro-sex work lobby to elide the male side of demand, on the grounds that male buyers of sex are individual citizens participating in an unremarkable 'private' transaction, is seriously challenged in the context of China by the demonstrated link between the demand for prostitution and the expropriation of public funds.

An examination of the Chinese case thus brings into focus the constant reliance of pro-sex work activists upon a meta-discourse bounded by Western liberal conceptions of 'the individual', 'the state', 'the law', and ultimately 'the UN', to resolve a series of historically and culturally specific problems with moral dimensions. For all of the aforementioned reasons, we need to resist the popular association of the concept of sex work with theoretical and political 'correctness'. Even more importantly, we have to question the tendency of metropolitan commentators to mobilize the concept of sex work as a means to demonstrate the assumed (i.e., 'already known') inadequacy of the PRC's response to prostitution. Exponents of this approach claim all the kudos that accrues to those who speak with moral indignity against the Chinese government, and on behalf of the 'downtrodden subaltern', without the accompanying ethical burden of investigating whether the strategy they want adopted can be operationalized in different cultural contexts in a way that is unambiguously better than the strategy which they want replaced.

As a corollary, therefore, we need to be wary of dismissing the platform of the feminist anti-prostitution lobby out of hand. Radical feminist theorizations of sexuality may be institutionally outmoded, but this does not mean that the strategy advocated by the feminist anti-prostitution lobby possesses no practical utility. There can be little doubt that the 'learned' cultural memory of the CCP's successful eradication of brothel-prostitution in the 1950s, combined with growing international concerns over transnational crime and women's human rights, has meant that the PRC's prostitution laws bear a *surface* resemblance to the strategy advocated by the feminist anti-prostitution lobby. This commonality could offer feminist activists on both sides of the 'prostitution/sex work divide' a means to agitate for improvements in the PRC's prostitution controls, not by demanding the socially and politically 'unthinkable', but rather by following the ACWF's tactic of exploiting the interstices created by the historical and legal indeterminacy of the prostitution transaction in China as neither a crime nor an accepted social practice, and by encouraging the recent shift of China's governmental authorities towards problematizing the male side of demand. Concomitantly, an examination of the diverse ways in which China's governmental authorities have sought to transform the ethical milieux of recreational business ventures could open the theoretical space for inventing other possible practicable alternatives to the governance of prostitution. Both tactics would be possible if 'China' were not always already precluded from being treated as a subject rather than an object of theorization by the statist bias of extant China studies scholarship and by the general conviction that Marxism is gender-blind and radical feminism is anti-sex, which means that both are assumed to have passed their political use-by-date.

In this respect, the antipathy with which we are disposed to assess the PRC's response to prostitution, a disdain born of the nation-translating convention of presenting campaign-style policing as a self-evident instance of communist repression, has functioned as little more than an occluding disciplinary device. Recourse to the concept of governmentality decentres this mode of criticism by highlighting the complexity of the issues that surround the problematization of prostitution as an object of government in China today. In doing so, it underscores the limitations of continuing to posit 'the Chinese Party police state' as an apparatus or instance that is separate from the social body. The manner in which the Chinese public security forces have chosen to classify reform-era prostitution businesses and practices can no doubt be called into question. But rather than deconstructing China's 'prostitution hierarchy' as a means to further underscore the ideological irrationality of 'the Chinese state', a far more important focus for analysis is the kinds of transformations that the very process of identifying this 'hierarchy' has engendered within the field in which the policing of prostitution takes place.

These transformations have involved the elaboration of campaign technologies in a distinctively 'modern' governmental way. They include: the introduction of a heterogeneous body of prostitution-related legislation; the emergence of conflicting interests within governmental and other bodies regarding the appropriate management of prostitution businesses and practices; the dispersal of China's public security forces via mass-line auxiliary organizations; the deployment of a wide array of individuating techniques designed to garner public support for policy objectives; the practise of auditing governmental officials, and thereby opening their activities to a process of public and individual scrutiny; and the development of diverse regulatory measures designed to transform the new kinds of social spaces and recreational habits that have accompanied the reform programme. Viewed from this perspective, we have not even begun to consider the complexity of the questions involved in the political evaluation of policing as an object and practice of government in China. We have also barely begun to examine the nexus between 'sex' and 'power' in the PRC today.

However, if the objective of practising criticism is to acknowledge that what has been accepted as self-evident is not necessarily so, then this text usefully admits two unwelcome 'home truths'. First, the problems surrounding the PRC's response to prostitution are neither reducible to the nature of 'the Chinese Party police state', nor are they amenable to resolution via the imposition of some idealized, transnational feminist response. The very diversity of prostitution businesses and practices that exist in present-day China demonstrates that it is not possible to characterize 'sex work' as a unified target of governmental intervention either in China or more generally. Until this simple fact is acknowledged, there will be no end to the feminist 'sex wars' and the current 'prostitution war'. Instead of working towards disaggregating prostitution practices and specifying the nature of their organization and regulation in different cultural and temporal contexts, we will continue to fight unproductively over what constitutes the best transnational response. In the process, the question of whose interests – apart from the assumed interests of women in prostitution – are best served by doing so will also continue to be elided.

Second, and in consequence, the professed aim of contemporary sinological studies, namely, to 'enter into China' and thereby offer a more vital cross-cultural perspective to critical studies 'at home', might be better advanced by abandoning the practice of nation-translating and viewing the exercise of government in China more productively. With regard to the subject of prostitution, the adoption of such a reading tactic would allow for different kinds of questions to be asked and different local responses to the governance of prostitution businesses and practices to be envisioned. It would enable us to analyse and politically engage with the operation of government in present-day China without assuming that sexual-political, legal categories such as 'sex worker' refer to universal 'givens' and subsequently resorting to the prescriptive dead ends of morally impelled criticism.

Notes

Introduction: telling tales

1 I place the term 'hostess' in citation to mark its imprecise nature as a translation for the Chinese term *sanpei xiaojie*. In Chinese-language writings, the term *sanpei xiaojie* refers to a woman who acts as a paid companion for a man in three main ways, and whose defining activities primarily occur in public entertainment and leisure venues. However, the 'three activities' that comprise *sanpei* have been variously defined. Discussed in relation to the kinds of activities that occur within karaoke/dance venues, the term refers to the notion that some women will talk, sing, and dance with a man in return for material gifts or financial compensation. At other times it is taken to mean that such women will talk, smoke, and drink with a man in return for financial recompense. In other contexts, it refers to women who offer their services in health, hairdressing, and beauty centres, and women who accompany men to eat at restaurants, to watch a film at the cinema, or to swim at the beach, in return for material or financial compensation. By other definitions, however, *sanpei* activities invariably involve sexual services of some form. This understanding of *sanpei* is sometimes dubbed *duopei* (accompanying in many ways) and refers to a woman who offers a man 'extra' (read sexual) services in return for material gifts or financial recompense (Fan Benji 1994: 82–6; Song Zhenyong 1996: 69–70).

2 The term *gewuting* can be literally translated as a 'song and dance hall', but refers to a highly diverse range of entertainment venues in terms of quality, size, and function. For example, while many of these venues now offer singing in the form of karaoke entertainment, dancing activities may centre on such different dance forms as modern ballroom dancing and disco. Although many of these venues are organized in such a way that they could be referred to as bars, discos or nightclubs (and are often advertised as such), other venues are not marked by the kinds of spatial organization, clientele or activities, that the use of such terms may connote in a Western context. I use the term 'karaoke/dance venue', therefore, not only to highlight the diversity and cultural specificity of entertainment venues in present-day China, but also to distinguish such venues from the kinds of 'song and dance halls' that existed in China prior to 1949. This is because the existence of privately operated, commercial entertainment venues in the PRC is a relatively new phenomenon, flowing from the introduction of the economic reform and the Open Door policy in December 1978.

3 In 1994, the standard salary for legal female service workers or waitresses in a middle- to high-grade karaoke/dance venue in Beijing was around 300 to 500 *yuan* a month. In return, these women were expected to work from 8 p.m.

until the venue closed (usually around 2 a.m.) and were entitled to two evenings off per month (subject to negotiation with the management). In her capacity as a 'hostess', however, X expected to receive a tip of at least 50 to 100 *yuan* for sitting with and talking to a group of men, and a tip of at least 100 to 200 *yuan* if she sang and danced, or spent an extended period of time, with them. Depending on the amount of time she was willing to spend in such venues (combined with variable factors such as the spending capacity and whimsy of the patrons she accompanied, as well as the actual number of patrons she encountered) X could earn several thousand *yuan* per month. By way of further comparison, 'hostesses' who were willing to be more overtly flirtatious apparently expected to receive a tip of around 200 to 400 *yuan*, and, 'hostesses' who were willing to enter into sexual activities of some kind demanded between 400 to 1,000 *yuan* per evening (Personal conversations with 'hostesses', Beijing 1994).

4 The cost of visiting a karaoke/dance venue varies according to the particular location, quality, and size of a given venue, and the kinds of services one wishes to purchase. In 1994, however, the cost of hiring a small room for a group of people to sing along with karaoke videos and relax in private ranged from between 800 to 2,000 *yuan* per evening (Personal conversations with 'hostesses', Beijing 1994).

5 In middle-grade to higher-grade karaoke venues in Beijing during 1994, it was not standard practice for 'hostesses' to actively solicit the custom of male patrons. Instead, the owners and/or managers of a given venue usually introduced two or more 'hostesses' to a group of prospective 'clients'. When custom was slack, this practice meant that 'preferred hostesses' were the first to be notified of the arrival of a group of male patrons; hence they were afforded greater income earning opportunities. Experienced 'hostesses' also usually negotiated a percentage of the profits generated from the consumption of food, beverages, and services, on the part of each particular group of patrons they accompanied (Personal conversations with 'hostesses', Beijing 1994).

6 The Chinese police would have viewed X's presence in such a venue as suspicious because karaoke/dance venues were highly gendered and socially stratified spaces. The clientele were predominantly male (usually aged between 30 and 60 years), whereas the service personnel were primarily female (usually under 26 years of age), and an estimated 80 per cent of the money spent in middle- and higher-grade karaoke venues allegedly came from public funds, with government officials (primarily men) using public monies for the purposes of business-cum-entertainment (Wang Tie 1993: 35; Zhang Ping 1993: 25; Zhao Jianmei 1994: 35). Consequently, the presence of a young, unaccompanied woman in such a venue, especially one who was not wearing a staff uniform, would have been viewed as just cause for suspicion by investigating police (Personal conversations with 'hostesses', Beijing 1994).

7 Prostitution and *sanpei* activities constitute a new and controversial phenomenon in present-day China due to the unique history of the PRC. Following the Chinese Communist Party's accession to political power in 1949, the Maoist regime implemented a series of campaigns, which allegedly eradicated prostitution from mainland China by the mid to late 1950s. Since the early 1980s, however, governmental authorities in the PRC have acknowledged that prostitution has not only reappeared on the mainland, it also constitutes a widespread and growing problem. For examples of English-language literature on the subject of prostitution in the PRC, see Gil 1994; Gil and Anderson 1998; Gil *et al.* 1994, 1996; Hershatter 1996a, 1997; Jeffreys, E. 1997a, 1997b; Ruan 1991; Xin Ren 1993, 1999.

8 The term 'Anglophone' refers to an English-speaking person. However, to

make an often necessary distinction between English-language scholarship about China and mainland Chinese scholarship about China, I will use this term to refer to English-language writings about China that are produced for consumption predominantly by an Anglophone readership, including writings that are produced by non-native English (Sinophone) speakers for an Anglophone readership. Conversely, I will use the term 'Sinophone' to refer to Chinese-language writings about China that are produced for consumption by a mainland Chinese audience, including writings that are produced by native Chinese speakers who reside outside of China's territorial boundaries for consumption primarily by an expatriate Sinophone audience.

9 Hershatter (1996a: 200, 201, 212, 215, 218, 219, 220, 223) insists that she is not suggesting that prostitution is 'really' labour, but she consistently endorses the notion of sex work and castigates Chinese commentators for having failed to recognize that prostitution constitutes a form of labour.

10 The term 'voluntary' prostitution is used by various prostitutes' rights activists as a means to distinguish prostitution that is freely chosen as a means of livelihood from 'forced' prostitution (understood as lacking the element of conscious choice, or being forced into prostitution due to dire economic hardship, or as a result of physical and/or psychological coercion).

11 Although Hershatter (1996a: 203–4) refers to the women whom she observed in a Shanghai Hotel as prostitutes, this may not be the case. As she notes, a woman could converse with male patrons for financial recompense, and therefore make a substantial sum of money without ever leaving the hotel's disco or agreeing to an act of sexual intercourse. This suggests to me that many of these women may have conceived of themselves as 'hostesses', not 'sex sellers'.

12 The persuasiveness of Hershatter's argument rests, in no small part, on the fact that the term 'work' concludes both this joke and her text. The Chinese original, however, does not necessarily refer to prostitution as 'work', since the daughter replies: 'Na wo haishi gan zhege geng hao'. The Chinese term 'gan' is a verb meaning 'to do' and can refer to the act of working. But, given the cumulative nature of the joke, the daughter's response is more like: 'if that's the case, it would be better if I did it' (Pan Suiming 1992: 26). It also bears noting that the objective of this particular article by Pan Suiming is to counter the popular conception that women in prostitution enjoy the sex in their 'work' and earn substantial sums of money.

13 Chakrabarty (1992: 1–2, 18–19) defines 'Europe' as a hyperreal term in the sense that it refers to a certain figure of imagination whose geographical referents are somewhat indeterminate. While noting that it is impossible to conceive of 'Europe' as a homogeneous and uncontested ideal, Chakrabarty points out that a certain version of Europe, 'reified and celebrated in the phenomenal world of everyday relationships of power as the scene of the birth of the modern', continues to dominate the institutional field of history. Thus, so far as the academic discourse of history is concerned – that is, 'history' as a discourse produced at the institutional site of the university – '"Europe" remains the sovereign, theoretical subject of all histories, including the ones we call "Indian", "Chinese", "Kenyan", and so on'.

1 Changing China: changing China studies

1 The terms 'sinological studies' and/or 'sinology' with a small 's' are often deployed within recent publications produced within the Western academic field of China studies. Although I have yet to see a sustained discussion of what these terms actually signify, it is clear that certain China scholars use these terms as a means to differentiate their more theoretically informed work from the negative

connotations that accrue to the positivistic area field of Sinology, and/or as a means to tie the study of China to the more theoretically-informed academic enterprises of cultural studies and postcolonial studies. Accordingly, I will use these terms throughout this text either to indicate how certain scholars have chosen to describe their own work, or else to highlight the kinds of divisions that structure China studies as a field of knowledge production/reception.

2 Jankowiak (1999: 31–7), for instance, dismisses poststructuralist-feminist accounts of gender and sexuality in China on the grounds that they are too theoretical and have therefore missed the obvious empirical details. Harold Tanner (1995: 289) similarly dismisses Michael Dutton's (1992) *Policing and Punishment in China* on the grounds that Dutton's use of Foucauldian jargon makes the text virtually unreadable for any but the most dedicated scholar. While theoretical discourse is often dense and technically difficult, such criticisms turn on the problematic assumption that language is given and transparent, that we already have the words to express everything that can be said.

2 Changing institutional categories and academic legitimacy

1 This is not to deny that scholars such as Foucault and Derrida have noted the impossibility of going beyond the endless discourses made possible by Marxism, nor that many postcolonial scholars retain a marked interest in Marxist categories of analysis. It is to highlight the popular perception that Marxism–socialism is a 'spent force', as indicated by the rapid expansion of what might be loosely called 'post-communist studies'.

2 As Foucault (1978: 36–49) explains, the popular history of Western sexuality is routinely framed in terms of two historical ruptures. A slowly intensifying curve of repression is said to have started in the beginning of the seventeenth century, to have reached a peak in the puritanical Victorian era, and then to have declined in the twentieth century with the development of more liberal and permissive attitudes to sex. Foucault proceeds to undermine this account by showing how the modern discourse of repressed sexuality emerged from a particular conjunction of historical forces. In doing so, he demonstrates that there is no such thing as a single or unitary discourse on the subject of sexuality. Instead, there are multiple and heterogeneous discourses produced by a whole series of mechanisms operating in diverse institutions. Insisting that the history of sexuality is comprised primarily of various and repeated attempts to reduce 'sex' to its reproductive function, namely, its marital, heterosexual, and adult form, thus fails to take into consideration the manifold objectives, and also the diverse array of means, that have characterized attempts to regulate the relations between and among the two sexes.

3 In fact, there are no laws against homosexuality in China. Although homosexuals in China may be subjected to police harassment, and even detained for varying periods on the basis of administrative regulations, homosexuality is increasingly represented in Chinese discourses as a legitimate subculture rather than in terms of abnormality or psychological illness. The classic text in this regard is Li Yinhe and Wang Xiaobo's (1992) *Tamen de shijie: Zhongguo nan tongxinglian qunluo toushi* [Their World: A Perspective on China's Male Homosexual Community].

3 Feminist prostitution debates and responses

1 Of course, these two positions are not quite so clear-cut. There are significant internal differences within the community of scholars who claim allegiance to the radical feminist camp, and scholars who reject radical feminist theorisations

of the nature of sexuality and commercial sexual practices draw on a wide array of theoretical perspectives. Nevertheless, the rhetorical persuasiveness of much feminist literature on prostitution stems from the use of homogenizing conceptions of 'us' versus 'them'. I have thus replicated this general move in order to highlight the common construction of feminist prostitution debates in terms of those who utilize the insights made available by the discourse of theory and those who do not (i.e., radical feminists).

4 Prostitution debates and a changing China

1 Although the 1991 Decision is usually translated in abbreviated form as the Decision Concerning the Prohibition of Prostitution, I have chosen to translate it as the Decision on Strictly Forbidding the Selling and Buying of Sex for two reasons. First, I have translated the Chinese term *yanjin* as meaning to strictly forbid, rather than to prohibit, in order to make a distinction between the feminist understanding of prohibition as involving the criminalization of *all* participants in prostitution activities and the Chinese practice of criminalizing third-party involvement in prostitution (i.e., the activities of brothel keepers, pimps, panderers, and procurers), while handling the activities of participants in the prostitution transaction on the theoretically more lenient basis of the Chinese system of administrative measures and sanctions. Second, the particular combination of Chinese characters used to denote prostitution, namely, *maiyin piaochang*, highlights the fact that the prostitution transaction involves at least two parties, since *maiyin* refers to the practice of selling sex and *piaochang* refers to the practice of frequenting prostitutes. Acknowledging the relational configuration of prostitution in the Chinese language acts as an important counter to the common assumption that the problem of prostitution relates more to those who provide such services (usually women) than those who demand them (usually men). The importance of highlighting this relational aspect is underscored by the fact that many Western commentators wrongly assume that Chinese prostitution statistics refer to the number of women apprehended as prostitutes, when such statistics usually offer an aggregate figure of men and women apprehended for prostitution-related offences, including those apprehended as organizers and promoters of prostitution, and those apprehended as sellers and buyers of sex.

2 In 1998, for instance, the story of Tang Shengli, a 23-year-old waitress who broke her spine when she jumped from a 6-metre-high window to escape from being forced into prostitution by the owner of a nightclub she worked in, attracted widespread publicity (see Jiang Jingen 1998; 'Ju dang sanpei tiaolou zhitan de chuanmeizi hanlei hujiao "saohuang" qianwan buneng shouruan' 1998; 'Ju "sanpei" you you san nü tiaolou' 1998).

3 The term 'bureaucratic entrepreneur' is used by Lance Gore (1999: 30) to refer to those 'party-state officials who are directly engaged in business activities and other activities aimed at promoting economic expansion'. Unlike cadres under the pre-reform command economy, who were primarily implementors of the state plan and other Party directives, bureaucratic entrepreneurs are expected to perform their political duties and take initiatives in the marketplace.

4 The 1991 Decision gave China's public security organs the authority to compel participants in the prostitution transaction to receive legal and moral education, and engage in productive labour for a designated time period of between six months and two years; to undergo a compulsory medical examination in order to check for sexually transmittible diseases; and to receive compulsory curative medical attention if necessary. The 'Decision' also stipulates that those who have been handled by the Chinese public security forces for involvement in

prostitution activities, and who are apprehended for a second time, should be subjected to the more severe administrative penalty of reform through labour and fined up to 5,000 *yuan*. In practice, however, it appears that repeat offenders are still sentenced to the more lenient sanction of rehabilitative education (Wang Dazhong 1995: 57).

5 While Ruan intimates that the lack of nationwide statistics is indicative of the CCP's historical and repressive approach to sexuality, this absence could be read as a sign that that sexuality has only recently been constructed as a problem for government in China (Li Yinhe 1997).

6 As Foucault (1978: 3–13), explains, once the relationship between sexuality and power is defined purely in terms of repression, it declares that the freedom to speak of sex and sexuality is something that cannot be easily achieved – it must be fought for. Hence the demand for sexual freedom, that is, both the knowledge to be gained from sex and also the 'right' to speak of it, has been accorded a status something akin to that of a legitimate political cause. Speaking about sex has gained in significance as an act of defiance against established rules. It is generally perceived as an act that not only promises to reveal previously suppressed 'truths', but also purports to herald the dawn of a new and brighter future.

7 The reference to a more humanitarian and normal sex life comes from Xin Ren (1993: 100), who thereby replicates the broad parameters of Ruan's arguments. In a more recent article on reform-era prostitution, Gil and Anderson (1998: 139) similarly contend that the relationship between 'sex' and 'government' in China is one of repression. To use their own words, 'the "Strike Hard" response [a 1996 campaign against illegality, prostitution and pornography] has been one of forcefully repressing wide-spread promiscuity while also attempting to suppress people's desires for a humanitarian and normal sex life'.

8 This line of argument is flatly contradicted by investigations conducted by the Chinese police. For example, of the 260 men and women detained by the Dongcheng police department in 1992 for involvement in prostitution, 45.2 per cent were apprehended in high-class entertainment venues (Beijing dongcheng . . . 1993: 14–17).

9 Given the high social status that accrues to a good education in China, it is standard practice for people of both sexes to claim a university education if such a claim may work to their advantage. Thus women who work in karaoke/dance venues, whether as service workers, 'hostesses', or sellers of sex, frequently state that they are tertiary students either to demonstrate that their current form of employment is temporary (hence they are potential 'girl-friend material'), or as a means to increase their 'negotiable' perceived value. The utility of this tactic is borne out by conversations with a number of Australian businessmen and male academics who, upon discovering the nature of my research interests, informed me that they were accosted by female prostitutes at select venues in China, and, while denying any involvement in the prostitution transaction per se, they all claim to have spent considerable time conversing with the women in question, and ultimately paying for their meals, drinks, and entertainment, on the grounds that the women were university students not professional sex workers.

5 Re-situating the Chinese response to prostitution

1 Article 6 of CEDAW (United Nations 1979) calls upon State parties to 'take all appropriate measures, including legislation, to suppress all forms of traffic in women and exploitation of prostitution of women'. Supporters of feminist anti-prostitution contend that this Article refers to all forms of prostitution. However, supporters of the pro-sex work lobby have drawn on other UN legis-

lation, including the Beijing Platform's acknowledgement of women's rights to sexual self-determination, to insist that it refers solely to 'forced prostitution'.

2 This is not to deny the existence of prostitute collectives and organizations. It is to point out that, unlike trade unions, these organizations are not based on a group of workers – identified and unified by a shared or similar form of occupation – who collectively agitate within their workplaces, and with union members from other workplaces, to improve their conditions of employment. In fact, attempts to unionize sex workers in Australia have proved unsuccessful to date, largely because the majority of women who work in the 'sex sector' do not want to be formally identified and thereby represented as *sex workers*.

3 The term *maiyin funü* (a woman who sells sex) is an invention of the economic reform period. This term is used in preference to pre-liberation terms like *changji* and *jinü* (female prostitute), and *anchang* (unlicensed female prostitute, i.e., a prostitute who was not registered with governmental authorities in the Republican period and early 1950s), because it is less pejorative and refers to a temporary action, rather than an occupation or permanent identity. The Chinese terms for men who demand the services of women in prostitution, *piaochang* and *piaoke*, at least in their contemporary usage, are probably closer to the now uncommon English term, 'whoremonger', or frequenter of prostitutes. As with English language literature on prostitution, however, Chinese literature on prostitution is replete with discussions regarding appropriate terminology, and terms such as 'sex worker' (*xing gongzuozhe* or *xing fuwuzhe*), 'sex industry' (*xing gongye* or *xing fuwu hangye*), and 'client' (*guke*) have emerged in the recent academic literature.

4 Although China's public security forces and the ACWF are often dismissed as the puppets or mouthpieces of the CCP leadership, this tactic elides the fact that they possess their own internal objectives and agendas, which may neither reflect nor coincide with central government initiatives.

5 The task of building socialist spiritual civilization is variously yet broadly defined as fostering new and healthy tendencies and trends in society, including fostering 'new' people with a set of personal capacities known as the 'four haves' – high ideals, high moral standards, education, and discipline ('Party official maps out "spiritual civilization" work for 2000' 1999).

6 Policing change: changing disciplinary technologies

1 This is not to deny that there is little scholarship that can be construed as representing the 'voice' of the Chinese prostitute subject. It is simply to point out that metropolitan commentaries on the PRC's response to prostitution are marked by diverse attempts to speak for, or in the place of, the subaltern prostitute subject, and they are highly critical of China's prostitution controls. Yet this same body of literature makes scant reference to the work of mainland police on the subject of prostitution.

2 Issues relating to contemporary Chinese policing practices have attracted 'empirical' interest in the areas of criminology and policing studies. However, there is only a small body of literature on the nature of Chinese policing produced within the disciplinary space of the Anglophone humanities. Moreover, with the notable exception of Michael Dutton's work, this body of literature is couched in terms of conventional statist-based analyses (Dutton 1992, 1995; Dutton and Lee 1993; Seymour and Anderson 1998; Tanner, H. 1999; Tanner, M. 1999, 2000). There is an even smaller body of literature that deals with issues of Chinese law and policing from what might loosely be termed a feminist perspective (Biddulph and Cook 1999; Xin Ren 1999).

3 It bears noting that the template for this standard criticism is the 'strike hard'

campaign of 1983–6, namely, a campaign that took place before many of the PRC's current laws were put in place.

4 Although Hershatter uses the conventional term *yundong* to denote campaigns, the Chinese police do not refer to reform-era campaigns as *yundong* (mass political movements), but rather as *jizhong tongyi xingdong*, that is, concentrated, unified actions or activities undertaken by the Chinese police in conjunction with other relevant departments, under the leadership of the CCP, and with the help of the masses. With reference to the 1983–6 'strike hard' campaign, Murray Scot Tanner (2000: 107) suggests that this is simply a way of calling a campaign by another name. But anti-crime campaigns can be differentiated from the political campaigns of the Maoist era in that they aim to rectify a particular state of affairs (*zheng dun*) rather than transform the 'political consciousness' of those designated as 'enemies of the people'.

5 Even the work of China's 'new social scientists' on prostitution is often conducted in conjunction with the Chinese police, the ACWF, or local health authorities; and, popular Chinese-language texts on prostitution generally consist of a sensationalized reworkings of cases investigated by the public security forces.

7 Conclusion: China, sex and prostitution reconsidered

1 Quite apart from the notorious problems economists face in assessing the accuracy of China's official statistics, any such 'precise' claim has to be viewed with considerable caution, given the inherent difficulties involved in quantifying the share of GDP constituted by the consumption of participants in a black market sector of the economy, on the one hand, and the problem of isolating factors determining the marginal propensity to consume of so variegated population as 'female sellers of sex', on the other.

Bibliography

1997 Criminal Code of the People's Republic of China (1998) trans. Wei Luo, Buffalo, New York: W.S. Hein & Co.

'1998 nian quanguo gongan jiguan li'an de xingshi anjian fenlei tongji biao' [A table of statistics concerning criminal cases placed on file for investigation and prosecution by the public security organs in 1998] (1999) *Gongan yanjiu*, 3: 95.

'1999 nian quanguo gongan jiguan li'an de xingshi anjian fenlei tongji biao' [A table of statistics concerning criminal cases placed on file for investigation and prosecution by the public security organs in 1999] (2000) *Gongan yanjiu*, 5: 95.

'A taxing question of hostess earnings' (1998) *South China Morning Post*, 5 September.

Acton, W. ([1857] 1968) *Prostitution*, London: Macgibbon & Kee.

Alexander, P. (1997) 'Feminism, sex workers, and human rights', in J. Nagle (ed.) *Whores and Other Feminists*, New York; London: Routledge, 83–97.

'Anti-crime campaign to be continued, deepened' (1996) Xinhua News Agency, Beijing, 22 August, in *Selected World Broadcasts – China*, 24 August, FE/2699, G/8–9.

Apter, D.E. and Saich, T. (1994) *Revolutionary Discourse in Mao's Republic*, Cambridge, MA: Harvard University Press.

'Army banned from business', *Beijing Review*, <http://202.96.63.1/bjreview/98Aug/bj98-33-4.html> (21 September 1998).

Bakken, B. (1993) 'Crime, juvenile delinquency and deterrence policy in China', *Australian Journal of Chinese Affairs*, 30: 29–58.

'Banking, the oldest profession' (2000) *ABIX – Australasian Business Intelligence Asiaweek (abstracts)*, 6 October: 11.

'Barbara' (1993) 'It's a pleasure doing business with you', *Social Text*, 37: 11–22.

Barrett, M. (1992) 'Words and things: materialism and method in contemporary feminist analysis', in M. Barrett and A. Phillips (eds), *Destabilizing Theory: Contemporary Feminist Debates*, Cambridge: Polity Press.

Barry, K. (1995) *The Prostitution of Sexuality*, New York: New York University Press.

Beijing dongcheng gongan fenju [Dongcheng district division of the Public Security Bureaux in Beijing] (1993) 'Dui erbailiushi ge maiyin piaochang renyuan de fenxi' [An analysis of 260 participants in the prostitution transaction], *Fanzui yu gaizao yanjiu*, 10: 14–17.

Bell, D. and Klein, R. (eds) (1996) *Radically Speaking: Feminism Reclaimed*, Melbourne: Spinifex.

Bell, S. (1994) *Reading, Writing and Rewriting the Prostitute Body*, Bloomington, IN: Indiana University Press.

Benjamin, H. and Masters, R.E.L. (1965) *Prostitution and Sexual Morality*, London: Souvenir Press.

Biddulph, S. and Cook, S. (1999) 'Kidnapping and selling women and children: the state's construction and response', *Violence Against Women*, 5: 1437–68.

Blecher, M. (1986) *China: Politics, Economics and Society (Iconoclasm and Innovation in a Revolutionary Socialist Country)*, London: Francis Pinter.

Bo Xu (1994) 'Qingchu "jingshen yapian" keburonghuan – quanguo fulian fuzhuxi Huang Qicao tan "saohuang dafei"' [The elimination of 'spiritual opium' demands immediate attention: the National Women's Federation Chairperson, Huang Qicao, talks about the campaigns to 'clear away pornography and fight illegality'], *Renmin ribao*, 18 November: 4.

Borrack, M. and Davies, B. (1998) 'Call for brothel crackdown', *Northcote Leader* (Victoria, Australia), 21 January: 3.

Bourdieu, P. (1987) 'The biographical illusion', in *Working Papers and Proceedings of the Centre for Psychosocial Studies*, Chicago: University of Chicago Press, 14: 1–7.

Bray, D. (1999) 'The Chinese danwei: a genealogy of space and power', unpublished thesis, University of Melbourne.

Broyelle, C. (1977) *Women's Liberation in China*, Hassocks: Harvester Press.

Bruel, S. and Wu Yiyi (2000) 'Misuse of over 96 billion yuan since 1998: auditors', *China News Digest* (Global News, No. GL00–133), 30 October: 36.

Bulbeck, C. (1994) 'Sexual dangers: Chinese women's experiences in three cultures – Beijing, Taipei and Hong Kong', *Women's Studies International Forum*, 17, 1: 95–103.

Burchell, G. (1993) 'Liberal government and techniques of the self', *Economy and Society*, 22: 267–82.

Burchell, G., Gordon, C. and Miller, P. (eds) (1991) *The Foucault Effect: Studies in Governmentality*, London: Harvester Wheatsheaf.

Burton, S. (1988) 'The sexual revolution hits China', *Time*, 12 September: 65.

Butler, J. (1990) *Gender Trouble: Feminism and the Subversion of Identity*, New York: Routledge.

Butler, J. (1993) *Bodies that Matter: On the Discursive Limits of "Sex"*, New York: Routledge.

Butler, J.E. (1896) *Personal Reminiscences of a Great Crusade*, London: Horace Marshall & Son.

Califia, P. (1988) *The Lesbian S/M Safety Manual*, Boston: Lace Publications.

Califia, P. (1994) *Public Sex: The Culture of Radical Sex*, Pittsburgh, PA: Cleis Press.

'Campaign against prostitution: motion for a recommendation' (1997) <http://stars.coe.fr/doc/doc97/EDOC7868.HTM#Footref1> (accessed 9 November 1998).

Chakrabarty, D. (1992) 'Postcoloniality and the artifice of history: who speaks for "Indian" pasts?' *Representations*, 37: 1–26.

Chan, A. (1994) 'In defence of Asian studies', *Australian*, 20 April: 21.

Chan, S. (1999) 'Introduction: more problems and more -isms', *Postcolonial Studies*, 2: 173–83.

Chancer, L.S. (1993) 'Prostitution, feminist theory, and ambivalence: notes from the sociological underground', *Social Text*, 37: 143–71.

Chang Xumin (1994) 'Zhide shensi de san ge baifen zhi bashi' [Three 80 per cents worth thinking about], *Renmin ribao*, 13 December: 1.

Chapkis, W. (1997) *Live Sex Acts: Women Performing Erotic Labour*, New York: Routledge.

Charlesworth, H. (1995) 'Human rights as men's rights', in J. Peters and A. Wolper (eds) *Women's Rights, Human Rights: International Feminist Perspectives*, New York: Routledge, 103–13.

Cheah, P., Fraser, D. and Grbich, J. (eds) (1996) *Thinking Through the Body of the Law*, St. Leonards, NSW: Allen & Unwin.

'Cheats pay for fun with company cash' (1994) *China Daily*, 25 November: 3.

Chen, A.H.Y. (1996) 'The developing theory of law and market economy in contemporary China', in Wang Guiguo and Wei Zhenying (eds) *Legal Developments in China: Market Economy and Law*, Hong Kong: Sweet & Maxwell Asia, 3–20.

Chen Siyi (1995) 'Bushi xiaren' [Is anyone concerned?], *Fazhi ribao*, 21 February: 2.

Chen Yanni (1996) 'Progress in battle against abduction', *China Daily*, 5 September: 2.

'China abhors calls for legal prostitution' (1994) *Reuters News Service*, Beijing, 19 July © Reuters.

'China among Asian countries most seriously plagued by AIDS' (1999) Xinhua News Agency, Beijing, 1 December, in *Selected World Broadcasts – China*, 3 December, FE/3708, G/8–9.

'China bans public-funded police entertainment' (1995) *Reuters News Service*, Beijing, 15 March © Reuters.

'China makes headway in fight against prostitution, gambling' (1999) *Xinhua News Agency Bulletin*, 12 October © Xinhua News Agency.

'China opens anti-porn hotlines' (2000) Xinhua News Agency, Beijing, in *Selected World Broadcasts – China*, 4 February, FE/3755, G/5.

'China rediscovers the joy of sex' (1997) *The Economist*, UK, 4 October.

'China's crusade against prostitution, gambling successful' (1999) *Xinhua News Agency News Bulletin*, 10 September © Xinhua News Agency.

'Chinese express outrage over Qingdao brothel raid fiasco' (2000) Hong Kong iMail website, Hong Kong, 13 July, in *BBC Worldwide Monitoring Service: Asia Pacific*, 14 July © BBC.

'Chinese police continue crackdown on recreational businesses' (2000) Xinhua News Agency, Beijing, 13 September, *BBC Worldwide Monitoring Service: Asia Pacific* © BBC.

'Chinese police trying to improve situation at massage parlours' (1999) *Xinhua News Agency Bulletin*, 9 June © Reuters.

Chow, R. (1994) 'Where have all the natives gone?', in A. Bammer (ed.), *Displacements: Cultural Identities in Question*, Bloomington, IN: Indiana University Press, 124–51.

Chow, R. (1998) *Ethics After Idealism: Theory, Culture, Ethnicity, Reading*, Bloomington, IN: Indiana University Press.

Clifford, J. (1992) 'Travelling cultures', in L. Grossberg, C. Nelson and P.A. Treichler (eds) *Cultural Studies*, New York: Routledge, 96–116.

Coalition Against Trafficking in Women (1995) 'Proposed United Nations convention against sexual exploitation', <http://www.catwinternational.org/about/UNconv.html> (accessed 1 February 2003).

Cohen, P.A. (1984) *Discovering History in China: American Historical Writing on the Recent Chinese Past*, New York: Columbia University Press.

'Communist Party discipline regulations' (1997) Xinhua News Agency, Beijing, 10 April, trans. *Selected World Broadcasts – China*, 14 April, FE/2892 S2/1–18.

'Consensus and recommendations on HIV and prostitution' (1996) in *Aizibing: shehui, lunli he falü wenti zhuanjia yantaohui* [Report of the Expert Workshop on HIV and Prostitution: social, ethical and legal issues], Beijing: Chinese Academy of Social Sciences, 29–31 October, 29–31 October: 104–6.

Cook, R.J. (ed.) (1994) *Human Rights of Women: National and International Perspectives*, Philadelphia, PA: University of Pennsylvania Press.

Coomaraswamy, R. (1996) 'Reinventing international law: women's rights as human rights in the international community', *Bulletin of Concerned Asian Scholars*, 28: 16–26.

Criminal Law and the Criminal Procedure Law of the People's Republic of China (1984) Beijing: Foreign Languages Press.

Croll, E. (1978) *Feminism and Socialism in China*, London: Routledge & Kegan Paul.

'Cruel trade hard to end' (1995) *China Daily*, 30 March: 7.

Davidson, A.I. (1987) 'Sex and the emergence of sexuality', *Critical Inquiry*, 14: 16–48.

Davies, G. (1992) 'Chinese literary studies and post-structuralist positions: what next?' *Australian Journal of Chinese Affairs*, 28: 67–86.

Davies, G. (1998) 'Professing postcoloniality: the perils of cultural legitimation', *Postcolonial Studies*, 1: 171–82.

Davies, G. (2000) 'Theory, professionalism and Chinese studies', *Modern Chinese Literature and Culture*, 12, 1: 1–42.

Davies, G. (2001a) 'Introduction', in G. Davies (ed.), *Voicing Concerns: Contemporary Chinese Critical Inquiry*, Lanham, MD: Rowman & Littlefield, 1–16.

Davies, G. (2001b) 'The self-made maps of Chinese intellectuality', in G. Davies (ed.), *Voicing Concerns: Contemporary Chinese Critical Inquiry*, Lanham, MD: Rowman & Littlefield, 17–46.

Davin, D. (1976) *Woman-Work: Women and the Party in Revolutionary China*, Oxford: Clarendon Press.

de Certeau, M. (1984) *The Practice of Everyday Life*, trans. S.F. Rendall, Berkeley, CA: University of California Press.

Delacoste, F. and Alexander, P. (eds) (1987) *Sex Work: Writings by Women in the Sex Industry*, San Francisco: Cleis Press.

Deng Xiaoping (1994) 'Crack down on crime', *Selected Works of Deng Xiaoping*, Vol. 3, Beijing: Foreign Languages Press, 44–5.

Diamond, I. and Quinby, L. (eds) (1988) *Feminism and Foucault: Reflections on Resistance*, Boston: Northeastern University Press.

Dikötter, F. (1995) *Sex, Culture and Modernity in China: Medical Science and the Construction of Sexual Identities in the Early Republican Period*, London: Hurst & Co.

Ding Juan (1996) 'Guanyu jinü, xing boxue, baoli de gean yanjiu' [A case study on female prostitutes, sexual exploitation and violence], in *Aizibing: shehui, lunli he falü wenti zhuanjia yantaohui* [Report of the Expert Workshop on HIV and Prostitution: Social, Ethical and Legal Issues], Beijing: Chinese Academy of Social Sciences, 29–31 October: 9–10.

Dong Yunhu and Zhang Shiping (eds) (1995) *Zhongguo de funü renquan* [Women's Human Rights in China], Sichuan: Renmin chubanshe.

'Duanping jiefang jinü' [A brief commentary on the liberation of female prostitutes] (1949) *Renmin ribao*, 22 November: 1.

Dutton, M. (1992) *Policing and Punishment in China: From Patriarchy to "the People"*, Cambridge: Cambridge University Press.

Dutton, M. (1995) 'Dreaming of better times: "repetition with a difference" and community policing in China', *positions: East Asia cultures critique*, 3: 415–47.

Dutton, M. (1996) 'Inventing a revolutionary tradition' (a review of *Revolutionary Discourse in Mao's Republic* by D.E. Apter and T. Saich), *Review of Politics*, 58: 172–6.

Dutton, M. (2000a) 'Orient-ing postcolonialism, translating theory', paper presented to the American Asian Studies Conference, San Diego, USA, March: 3–33.

Dutton, M. (2000b) 'The end of the (mass) line? Chinese policing in the era of the contract', *Social Justice: Criminal Justice and Globalization at the New Millennium*, 27: 61–105.

Dutton, M. (2002) 'Lead us not into translation: notes towards a theoretical foundation for Asian studies', *Nepantia: Views from the South*, 3, 3: 495–538.

Dutton, M. (forthcoming) *Policing the Chinese Political.*

Dutton, M. and Lee, T. (1993) 'Missing the target? Policing strategies in the period of economic reform', *Crime and Delinquency*, 39: 316–36.

'Eastern Chinese city giving ID cards to karaoke girls' (1998) *Xinhua News Agency Bulletin*, 1 December © Reuters.

Edwards, S. (1997) 'The legal regulation of prostitution: a human rights issue', in G. Scambler and A. Scambler (eds) *Rethinking Prostitution: Purchasing Sex in the 1990s*, London: Routledge, 57–82.

Edwards, S. and Armstrong, G. (1988) 'Policing street prostitution: the street offences squad in London', *Police Journal*, July: 209–19.

Eisenstein, Z.R. (1990) 'Specifying U.S. feminism in the 1990s: the problem of naming', *Socialist Review*, 20: 45–56.

Engels, F. ([1884] 1972) *The Origin of the Family, Private Property and the State*, New York: International Publishers.

Evans, H. (1995) 'Defining difference: the "scientific" contruction of sexuality and gender in the People's Republic of China'. *Signs: Journal of Women in Culture and Society*, 20, 2: 357–94.

Evans, H. (1997) *Women and Sexuality in China: Dominant Discourses of Female Sexuality and Gender since 1949*, New York: Continuum.

Fan Benji, (1994) 'Zai "sanpei" xianxiang de beihou' [Behind the phenomenon of 'sanpei'] transcript of a programme, *Focus* (*Jiaodian fangtan*), inquiring into the nature of sanpei activities, broadcast by China Central Television Station on 24 May 1994: 82–6.

Firestone, S. (1970) *The Dialectics of Sex: The Case for Feminist Revolution*, New York: Morrow.

Fisher, T. (1996) 'Josephine Butler: feminism's neglected pioneer', *History Today*, 46: 32–8.

Flowers, R.B. (1987) *Women and Criminality: The Woman as Victim, Offender, and Practitioner*, New York: Greenwood Press.

Foucault, M. (1978) *The History of Sexuality: An Introduction*, trans. R. Hurley, Harmondsworth: Penguin Books.

Foucault, M. (1979) 'On governmentality', *Ideology and Consciousness*, 6: 5–19.

Foucault, M. (1981) 'The order of discourse', in R. Young (ed.) *Untying the Text: A Post-Structuralist Reader*, Boston: Routledge & Kegan Paul, 51–77.

Foucault, M. (1982) 'The subject and power', *Critical Inquiry*, 8: 777–95.

Foucault, M. (1988a) *Politics, Philosophy Culture: Interviews and Other Writings 1977–1984*, trans. A. Sheridan, New York: Routledge.

Foucault, M. (1988b) 'Truth, power, self: an interview with Michel Foucault by Rex Martin', in L.H. Martin, H. Gutman and P.H. Hutton (eds) *Technologies of the Self: A Seminar with Michel Foucault*, Amherst, MA: University of Massachusetts Press, 9–15.

Foucault, M. (1988c) 'Technologies of the self', in L.H. Martin, H. Gutman and P.H. Hutton (eds) *Technologies of the Self: A Seminar with Michel Foucault*, Amherst, MA: University of Massachusetts Press, 16–49.

Gargan, E.A. (1988) 'Newest economics revives the oldest profession', *New York Times*, 17 September: 4.

Gil, V.E. (1994) 'Sinic conundrum: a history of HIV/AIDS in the People's Republic of China', *Journal of Sex Research*, 31: 211–17.

Gil, V.E. and Anderson, A.F. (1998) 'State-sanctioned aggression and the control of prostitution in the People's Republic of China: a review', *Aggression and Violent Behaviour*, 3: 129–42.

Gil, V.E., Wang, M.S., Anderson, A.F. and Guao (sic), M.L. (1994) 'Plum blossoms and pheasants: prostitutes, prostitution, and social control measures in contemporary China', *International Journal of Offender Therapy and Comparative Criminology*, 38: 319–37.

Gil, V.E., Wang, M.S., Anderson, A.F., Guo, M.L. and Wu, Z.O. (1996) 'Prostitutes, prostitution and STD/HIV transmission in mainland China', *Social Science and Medicine*, 42: 141–52.

Gilmartin, C.K., Hershatter, G., Rofel, L. and White, T. (eds) (1994) *Engendering China: Women, Culture and the State*, Cambridge, MA: Harvard University Press.

Giobbe, E. (1990) 'Confronting the liberal lies about prostitution', in D. Leidholdt and J.G. Raymond (eds) *The Sexual Liberals and the Attack on Feminism*, New York: Pergamon Press, 67–81.

Glick, E. (2000) 'Feminism, queer theory, and the politics of transgression', *Feminist Review*, 64: 19–41.

Gordon, C. (1991) 'Governmental rationality: an introduction', in G. Burchell, C. Gordon and P. Miller (eds) *The Foucault Effect: Studies in Governmentality*, London: Harvester Wheatsheaf, 1–52.

Gore, L.L.P (1999) 'The communist legacy in post-Mao growth', *China Journal*, 41: 25–54.

Gould, A. (2001) 'The criminalisation of buying sex: the politics of prostitution in Sweden', *Journal of Social Policy*, 30: 437–56.

Grosz, E. (1994) *Volatile Bodies: Towards a Corporeal Feminism*, St. Leonards, NSW: Allen & Unwin.

Grosz, E. (1995) *Space, Time and Perversion: Essays on the Politics of Bodies*, New York: Routledge.

'Guangdong court judge sacked for hiring prostitutes' (2000) *Xinhua News Agency Bulletin*, 26 September © Xinhua News Agency.

Guillain, R. (1957) *The Blue Ants: 600 Million Chinese under the Red Flag*, Secker.

Gunning, I.R. (1992) 'Arrogant perception, world-travelling and multicultural feminism: the case of female genital surgeries', *Columbia Human Rights Law Review*, 23: 189–99.

Haraway, D.J. (1991) *Simians, Cyborgs, and Women: The Reinvention of Nature*, London: Free Association.

Harootunian, H.D. (1999) 'Postcoloniality's unconscious/area studies' desire', *Postcolonial Studies*, 2: 127–48.

Hart, L. and Dale, J. (1997) 'Sadomasochism', in A. Medhurst and S.R. Munt (eds) *Lesbian and Gay Studies: A Critical Introduction*, London: Cassell, 341–55.

Heath, M. (1997) 'Catharine MacKinnon: toward a feminist theory of the state', *Australian Feminist Law Journal*, 9: 45–63.

Hershatter, G. (1993) 'The subaltern talks back: reflections on subaltern theory and Chinese history', *positions: East Asia cultures critique*, 1: 103–30.

Hershatter, G. (1996a) 'Chinese sex workers in the reform period', in E.J. Perry (ed.) *Putting Class in Its Place: Worker Identities in East Asia*, Institute of East Asian Studies, University of California, Berkeley: Center for Chinese Studies, 199–224.

Hershatter, G. (1996b) 'Sexing modern China', in G. Hershatter, E. Honig, J.N. Lipman and R. Stross (eds) *Remapping China: Fissures in Historical Terrain*, Stanford, CA: Stanford University Press, 42–93.

Hershatter, G. (1997) *Dangerous Pleasures: Prostitution and Modernity in Twentieth-Century Shanghai*, Berkeley, CA: University of California Press.

Hershatter, G., Honig, E., Lipman, J.N. and Stross, R. (eds) (1996) *Remapping China: Fissures in Historical Terrain*, Stanford, CA: Stanford University Press.

Hindess, B. (1993) 'Liberalism, socialism and democracy: variations on a governmental theme', *Economy and Society*, 22: 300–13.

Howe, A. (1995) 'White western feminism meets international law: challenges/complicity, erasures/encounters', *Australian Feminist Law Journal*, 4: 63–91.

Howell, J. (1999) 'Keeping the political in: a response to William Jankowiak's "Chinese women, gender and sexuality: a critical review of recent studies"', *Bulletin of Concerned Asian Scholars*, 31: 37–9.

Hu Qihua (2000) 'Amendments to oust mistresses', *China Daily*, New York, 24 October: 2.

Huang Jingpin, Li Tianfu and Wang Zhimin (1988) 'Gongan guanli xianzhuang' [The situation with regard to public security management], *Gongan yanjiu*, 4: 42–6.

Human Rights in China (1999), 'Not welcome at the party: behind the "clean-up" of China's cities? A report on administrative detention under "custody and repatriation"', <http://www.hrichina.org/report/cleanup.html> (accessed 8 May 2000).

Human Rights in China, Asia Monitor Resource Centre, China Labour Bulletin, and the Hong Kong Christian Industrial Committee (1998) 'Can dialogue improve China's human rights situation? Report on implementation of CEDAW (Committee on the elimination of all forms of discrimination against women) in the People's Republic of China', <http://www.hrichina.org/reports/cedaw.html> (accessed 8 May 2000).

Hunter, A. (1992) 'The development of theoretical approaches to sex-work in

Australian sex-worker rights groups', in S. Gerrull and B. Halstead (eds) *Sex Industry and Public Policy: Proceedings of a Conference Held 6–8 May 1991*, Canberra, ACT: Australian Institute of Criminology, 109–15.

Information Office of the State Council (1992) 'Criminal reform in China', *Beijing Review*, 17–23 August: 9–24.

Information Office of the State Council (1994) *The Situation of Chinese Women*, Beijing.

International Committee for Prostitutes' Rights, February 1985, Amsterdam (1993) 'World charter for prostitutes' rights', *Social Text*, 37: 183–5.

'International scrutiny in action: CEDAW reviews report from China' (1999) *China Rights Forum*, <http://www.hrichina.org/crf/english/99spring/e10_ scrutiny.html> (accessed 17 August 2000).

Jaivin, L. (1994–5) 'Sex', a special edition of *Chinese Sociology and Anthropology: A Journal of Translations*, 27.

Jankowiak, W. (1999) 'Chinese women, gender, and sexuality: a critical review of recent studies', *Bulletin of Concerned Asian Scholars*, 31: 31–7.

'Jasmin' (1993) 'Prostitution is work', *Social Text*, 37: 33–7.

Jeffreys, E. (1997a) 'Dangerous amusements: prostitution and karaoke halls in contemporary China', *Asian Studies Review*, 20: 43–54.

Jeffreys, E. (1997b) 'Guest editor's introduction', *Chinese Sociology and Anthropology: A Journal of Translations*, 30: 3–27.

Jeffreys, E. (1998) 'The problem of prostitution and sex work in twentieth-century China' (A Review of *Dangerous Pleasures: Prostitution and Modernity in Twentieth-Century Shanghai* by Gail Hershatter), *China Journal*, 39: 215–18.

Jeffreys, E. and Ross, K. (1998) 'Gender trouble in China' (a review of Harriet Evans' *Women and Sexuality in China: Dominant Discourses of Female Sexuality and Gender since 1949*, Cambridge, UK: Polity Press, 1997), *China Journal*, 40: 207–10.

Jeffreys, S. (1997) *The Idea of Prostitution*, Melbourne: Spinifex Press.

Jeffreys, S. (2000) 'Challenging the child/adult distinction in theory and practice on prostitution', *International Feminist Journal of Politics*, 2: 359–79.

Jenness, V. (1990) 'From sex as sin to sex as work: COYOTE and the reorganization of prostitution as a social problem', *Social Problems*, 37: 403–19.

Jiang Bo and Dai Yisheng (1990) 'Mobilize all possible social forces to strengthen public security – a must for crime prevention', *Police Studies*, 13: 1–9.

Jiang Jingen (1998) 'Club boss gets five years in sex case', *China Daily*, 12 October: 3.

Jiang Rongsheng (1992) 'Maiyin piaochang xingwei de rending' [Identifying prostitution], *Renmin gongan*, 6: 34.

Jin Jushin (1997) 'Chinese child sex scandal shocks Beijing experts', *Reuters News Service*, Beijing, 7 November © Reuters.

'Jingcheng qudi yixing anmo' [Beijing bans opposite-sex massage] (1996) *Minzhu fazhi*, 225: 4–7.

'Jinyibu ba jinchang gongzuo tuixiang shenru' [Towards advancing and developing the work of banning prostitution] (1992) *Renmin gongan*, 10: 7–11.

John, M.E. (1996) *Discrepant Dislocations: Feminism, Theory, and Postcolonial Histories*, Delhi: Oxford University Press.

Jolin, A. (1994) 'On the backs of working prostitutes: feminist theory and prostitution policy', *Crime and Delinquency*, 40: 69–83.

'Ju dang sanpei tiaolou zhitan de chuanmeizi hanlei hujiao "saohuang" qianwan buneng shouruan' [A young Sichuanese woman physically disabled after leaping from a building to resist being forced into 'hostessing' makes an emotional call: 'we must never slacken in the struggle to clear away pornography and illegality!'] (1998) *Renmin ribao*, 8 January.

'Ju "sanpei" you you san nü tiaolou' [Three more women leap from buildings to resist being forced into 'hostessing'] (1998) *Nanfang zhoumu*, 15 May: 5.

'Karaoke women to get cards' (1998) *South China Morning Post*, 2 December.

Kong Wen and Meng Qingfeng (2000) 'Yule changsuo guanli tanxi' [Assessing the management of public places of entertainment], *Gongan yanjiu*, 1: 40–2.

Koureskas, H. (1995) 'In a different voice: the prostitute's voice', *Australian Feminist Law Journal*, 5: 99–107.

Kristeva, J. (1977) *About Chinese Women*, trans. A. Barrows, London: M. Boyars.

Kristof, N.D. (1996) 'Fear of AIDS helps bolster child prostitution in Asia', *Plain Dealer*, Cleveland, OH, 14 April.

Kruhse-Mountburton, S. (1996) 'The contemporary client of prostitution in Darwin, Australia', unpublished thesis, Griffith University.

Kuo, D. (1999) 'Taiwan men prosecuted for bogus marriages to mainland women', *Asian Intelligence Wire*, 24 May © Central News Agency (Taiwan), Chamber World Network International.

Kwan, D. (1995a) 'Cadres attacked for backing prostitution', *South China Morning Post*, 11 March.

Kwan, D. (1995b) 'Speaker berates cadres' liberal view of prostitution', *South China Morning Post*, 11 March: 6.

Kwan, D. (2000) 'Minister decries vice levels', *South China Morning Post*, 29 February.

Kwang, M. (1999) 'Women's group slams tax on sex trade', *Straits Times*, 14 March © Reuters.

Kwang, M. (2000) 'Undercover dealings in flesh trade', *Straits Times*, 8 November © Singapore Press Holdings.

Lander, M. (2000) 'Dongguan journal: for Hong Kong men, mistresses on the mainland', *New York Times*, 14 August: A4.

'Law faces sex problems – Sichuan teahouse case' (1999) *SinoFile Chinese News Abstracts and Translations*, 13 May.

'Law on administrative punishments' (1996) Xinhua News Agency, Beijing, 21 March 1996, trans. *Selected World Broadcasts – China*, 13 April 1996, FE/2585 S2/1–7.

Leng, K.W. (1997) 'Sex and sexualities: contemporary feminist debates', in K.P. Hughes (ed.) *Contemporary Australian Feminism* 2, South Melbourne: Longman, 77–103.

Levine, P. (1996) 'Response to Valenze and Berger', in N.R. Keddie (ed.) *Debating Gender, Debating Sexuality*, New York: New York University Press, 208–13.

Leys, S. (1977) *The Chairman's New Clothes: Mao and the Cultural Revolution*, trans. C. Appleyard and P. Goode, New York: St. Martin's Press.

Leys, S. (1981) 'The China experts', *Quadrant*, 25: 17–22.

Leys, S. (1989) 'China and the pundits', *Quadrant*, 33: 8–9.

Li Dun (1996) 'Dui aizibing yu maiyin de zhengce he falü pingjia' [An evaluation of China's policies and laws concerning AIDS and prostitution], in *Aizibing: shehui, lunli he falü wenti zhuanjia yantaohui* [Report of the Expert Workshop on HIV and Prostitution: social, ethical and legal issues], Beijing: Chinese Academy of Social Sciences, 29–31 October, 16–17.

Li Juqing (1993) 'Wuguang-shise de "falangnü" [The many kinds of women who work in hairdressing salons], *Qingnian yu shehui*, September: 40–1.

Li Rongxia (2000) 'Cracking down on the abduction of women and children', *Beijing Review*, 8 May, 43, 19: 13–19.

Li Shi and Gao Ling (1993) 'Chuncheng' [Spring city], *Qingnian yu shehui*, December: 10–13.

Li Yinhe (1997) *Zhongguo nüxing de xing yu ai* [Sex, Love, and Chinese Women], Hong Kong: Oxford University Press.

Li Yinhe and Wang Xiaobo (1992) *Tamen de shijie: Zhongguo nan tongxinglian qunluo toushi* [Their World: A Perspective on China's Male Homosexual Community], Taiyuan: Shanxi renmin chubanshe.

Lim, L.L. (ed.) (1998) *The Sex Sector: The Economic and Social Bases of Prostitution in Southeast Asia*, Geneva: International Labour Office.

Lin, M. and Wu, Y. (1999) 'Government law and policy hinders AIDS prevention effort', *China News Digest* (Global News, No. GL99–148), 3 November.

Liu Dong (1995) 'Jingti renwei de "yangjingbang xuefeng"' ['Watch out for "purposeful pidgin scholarship"'], *Ershiyi shiji*, 32: 4–13.

Liu Fanqui (1993) 'Dangbuzhu de youhou?' [A hidden but unceasing attraction?], *Fayuan*, 152: 24–6.

Liu Yinglang (1997) 'Experts push for amendments to marriage law', *China Daily*, New York, 26 April: 4.

Liu, W. and Wu, Y. (2000) 'Police arrest 37 gays in social vice sweep', *China News Digest* (Global News, No. GL00–085), 10 July.

Ma Weigang (ed.) (1993) *Jinchang jindu* [On Strictly Forbidding Prostitution and Drugs], Beijing: Jingguan jiaoyu chubanshe.

McClintock, A. (1992) 'Screwing the system: sexwork, race, and the law', *Boundary* 2, 2: 70–95.

McClintock, A. (1993) 'Sex workers and sex work: introduction', *Social Text*, 37: 1–10.

McCloskey, J. and Lazarus, M. (1992) 'Community policing and the policing factor of on-street prostitution in the Kings Cross police patrol', in S. Gerrull and B. Halstead (eds) *Sex Industry and Public Policy: Proceedings of a Conference Held 6–8 May 1991*, Canberra, ACT: Australian Institute of Criminology, 233–47.

McElroy, D. (1998) 'Oldest profession thrives in China's economic boom, *Sunday Telegraph*, 6 December © Telegraph Group.

McElroy, D. (1999) 'Beijing regime lowers the red lantern – in Beijing', *Scotsman*, 2 September: 13.

McGivering, J. (1998) 'Two-timers to do time', *Australian*, 17 December: 8.

MacKinnon, C. (1989) *Toward a Feminist Theory of the State*, Cambridge, MA: Harvard University Press.

McMillan, J. (1999) 'Problems for Adam and Eve: Chinese sex shops and the biomedical construction of sexuality', *Bulletin of the British Association for Chinese Studies*, 10–26.

Mahoney, K. and Mahoney, P. (eds) (1993) *Human Rights in the Twenty-First Century: A Global Challenge*, Dordrecht: M. Nijhoff Publishers.

Malhotra, A. (1994) 'Prostitution, triads and corruption – Shanghai's dark side',

Asia, Inc., February: 32–9, electronically reprinted in *China News Digest Books and Journal Reviews*, 20 March.

Mao Lei (1993) 'Zhongguo nüxing xing fanzui toushi' [A perspective on female sex crimes in China], *Minzhu yu fazhi*, 2: 2–6 (trans. S. Rosen (1994), 'A perspective on sexual crimes among women in China', in *Chinese Education and Society*, 27: 77–88).

Marenin, O. (ed.) (1996) *Policing Change, Changing Police: International Perspectives*, New York: Garland Publishing.

Massonnet, P. (1999) *The New China: Money, Sex and Power*, Boston, MA: Tuttle Publishing.

Miller, P. and Rose, N. (1990) 'Governing economic life', *Economy and Society*, 19: 1–31.

Millet, K. (1971, 2nd edn 1975) *The Prostitution Papers*, St. Albans: Paladin Books.

'Million bars closed' (2001) *Advertiser* (Adelaide), 30 January: 22.

Milton, N. (1973) 'A response to "women and revolution"', in M.B. Young (ed.) *Women in China: Studies in Social Change and Feminism*, University of Michigan: Center for Chinese Studies, 179–92.

Minson, J. (1993) *Questions of Conduct: Sexual Harassment, Citizenship, Government*, Basingstoke: Macmillan.

Moraga, C. (1983) *Loving in the War Years*, Boston: Southend Press.

Murray, A. and Robinson, T. (1996) 'Minding your peers and queers: female sex workers in the AIDS discourse in Australia and South-East Asia', *Gender, Place and Culture*, 3: 43–59.

Nagle, J. (ed.) (1997) *Whores and Other Feminists*, New York: Routledge.

Niu Yangzi (1993) '"Yangji" xianxiang saomao' [Exploring the phenomenon of 'foreign prostitutes'], *Fazhi yuekan*, 11: 32–4.

O'Neill, M. (1999) 'Vice-like grip on oldest profession loosened', *South China Morning Post*, 28 September © Reuters.

Ouyang Tao (1994) 'Dangjin woguo maiyin piaochang fanzui de zhuangshi tedian ji duice' [Prostitution offences in contemporary China: characteristics and countermeasures], *Fanzui yu gaizao yanjiu*, 10: 15–18.

Overall, C. (1992) 'What's wrong with prostitution? Evaluating sex work', *Signs: Journal of Women in Culture and Society*, 17: 705–25.

Paloczi-Horvath, G. (1962) *Mao Tse-tung: Emperor of the Blue Ants*, London: Secker & Warburg.

Pan Suiming (1992a) 'Maiyin shenhua de bianzheng' [Decipher the myth of prostitution], *Shehui*, 87: 25–6.

Pan Suiming (1992b) 'Nanren, ye zai bei xing saorao' [Men, too, are sexually harassed], *Funü yanjiu*, 4: 39.

Pan Suiming (1993) 'A sex revolution in current China', *Journal of Psychology and Human Sexuality*, 6: 1–14.

Pan Suiming (1995) *Zhongguo xing xianzhuang* [The State of Sex in China], Beijing: Guangming ribao chubanshe.

Pan Suiming (1996a) 'Jinchang: wei shui fuwu?' [The prohibition of prostitution: whom does it serve?], in *Aizibing: shehui, lunli he falü wenti zhuanjia yantaohui* [Report of the Expert Workshop on HIV and Prostitution: Social, Ethical and Legal Issues], Beijing: Chinese Academy of Social Sciences, 29–31 October, 19–21.

Pan Suiming (1996b) 'San tan "dixia xing chanye"' [The 'underground sex industry': no. 3], *Aizibing: shehui, lunli he falü wenti zhuanjia yantaohui* [Report of the Expert Workshop on HIV and Prostitution: Social, Ethical and Legal Issues], Beijing: Chinese Academy of Social Sciences, 29–31 October, 52–7.

Parker, R.G. and Gagnon, J.H. (eds) (1995) *Conceiving Sexuality: Approaches to Sex Research in a Postmodern World*, New York: Routledge.

'Party official maps out "spiritual civilization" work for 2000' (1999) Xinhua News Agency, Beijing, 28 December 1999, trans. *Selected World Broadcasts – China*, 31 December 1999, FE/3728 G/6–8.

Pateman, C. (1988) 'What's wrong with prostitution?', in C. Pateman *The Sexual Contract*, Cambridge: Polity Press, 189–218.

Peratis, K. and Flores, J.R. (2000) 'Symposium (voluntary prostitution)', *Insight on the News*, 17 July, <http://web4.infotrac.galegroup.com> (accessed 9 August 2000).

Peters, J. and Wolper, A. (eds) (1995) *Women's Rights, Human Rights: International Feminist Perspectives*, New York: Routledge.

Pheterson, G. (ed.) (1989) *A Vindication of the Rights of Whores*, Seattle: Seal Press.

Pheterson, G. (1996) *The Prositution Prism*, Amsterdam: Amsterdam University Press.

'Police "hotmail" hot in Beijing' (2001) *Xinhua News Agency Bulletin*, 20 February.

'Police say one-fifth of inspected massage parlours involved in vice' (1999) *BBC Worldwide Monitoring Service: Asia Pacific*, 11 June © BBC.

'Police strengthen inspection of recreational places' (1999) Xinhua News Agency, 18 October, *BBC Worldwide Monitoring Service: Asia Pacific*, 19 October © BBC.

Poole, T. (1999) 'Carnal pleasures on road to nirvana', *Independent*, 4 August: 11.

Pratt, M.L. (1986) 'Fieldwork in common places', in J. Clifford and G.E. Marcus (eds) *Writing Culture: The Poetics and Politics of Ethnography*, Berkeley, CA: University of California Press, 27–50.

Prestage, G. and Perkins, R. (1994) 'Introduction', in G. Prestage, R. Sharp and F. Lovejoy (eds) *Sex Work, Sex Workers in Australia*, Sydney: UNSW Press, 6–21.

Prostitutes' Education Network (n.d.) 'Prostitution law reform: defining terms', <http://bayswan.org/defining.html> (accessed 17 August 1998).

'Prostitution tax' (1999) *SinoFile Chinese News Abstracts and Translations*, 13 July: 3.

Qian Changfu (1995) 'Juzhong maiyin piaochang xingwei de dingxing ji chuli' [The nature and handling of group participation in prostitution behaviour], *Renmin jiancha*, 1: 51.

Qiu Renzong (1996) 'Ethical and policy issues in the prevention of HIV/AIDS in China', in *Aizibing: shehui, lunli he falü wenti zhuanjia yantaohui* [Report of the Expert Workshop on HIV and Prostitution: Social, Ethical and Legal Issues], Beijing: Chinese Academy of Social Sciences, 29–31 October, 42–4.

Quanguo renda changweihui, xingfashi bianzhu, fazhi gongzuo weiyuanhui [Criminal Law Office and the Legal Council of the Standing Committee of the National People's Congress] (1991) *Guanyu yanjin maiyin piaochang de jueding he guanyu yancheng guaimai bangjiafunü, ertong de fanzui fenzi de jueding shiyi* [An Explanation of the Decision on Strictly Forbidding the Selling and Buying of

Sex and the Decision on the Severe Punishment of Criminals Who Abduct and Traffic in or Kidnap Women and Children], Zhongguo jiancha chubanshe.

Ramazanoglu, C. (ed.) (1993) *Up Against Foucault: Explorations of Some Tensions between Foucault and Feminism*, London: Routledge.

Rao, A. (1995) 'The politics of gender and culture in international human rights discourse', in J. Peters and A. Wolper (eds) *Women's Rights, Human Rights: International Feminist Perspectives*, New York: Routledge.

Raymond, J. (1995) 'Report to the Special Rapporteur on violence against women: the United Nations, Geneva, Switzerland', P.O. Box 9338, N. Amherst, MA 01059 USA.

Raymond, J. (n.d.) 'Legitimating prostitution as work: UN Labor Organization (ILO) calls for recognition of the sex industry', <http://www.uri.edu/artsci/wms/hughes/catw/legit.html> (accessed 1 March 2000).

Resolution on CPC History (1949–81) (1981) Oxford; New York: Pergamon Press.

Rich, A. (1980) 'Compulsory sexuality and lesbian existence', *Signs: Journal of Women in Culture and Society*, 5: 631–60.

Romany, C. (1994) 'State responsibility goes private: a feminist critique of the public/private distinction in international human rights law', in R.J. Cook (ed.) *Human Rights of Women: National and International Perspectives*, Philadelphia, PA: University of Pennsylvania Press.

Rose, N. (1989) *Governing the Soul: The Shaping of the Private Self*, London: Routledge.

Rose, N. and Miller, P. (1992) 'Political power beyond the state: problematics of government', *British Journal of Sociology*, 43: 113–205.

Rosenthal, E. (1998) 'In China, 35+ and female = unemployable', *New York Times*, 13 October.

Rowland, R. and Klein, R. (1996) 'Radical feminism: history, politics, action', in D. Bell and R. Klein (eds), *Radically Speaking: Feminism Reclaimed*, Melbourne: Spinifex, 9–36.

Ruan, F. (1991) *Sex in China: Studies in Sexology in Chinese Culture*, New York: Plenum Press.

Ruan, F. and Bullough, V.L. (1989) 'Sex repression in contemporary China', in P. Kurtz (ed.) *Building a World Community: Humanism in the Twenty-First Century*, Buffalo, New York: Prometheus Books, 198–201.

Rubin, G.S. (1984) 'Thinking sex: notes for a radical theory of the politics of sexuality', in C. Vance (ed.) *Pleasure and Danger: Exploring Female Sexuality*, Boston: Routledge and Kegan Paul.

Russo, A. (1998) 'The probable defeat: preliminary notes on the Chinese cultural revolution', *positions: East Asia cultures critique*, 6: 179–202.

Ryckmans, P. (1984) 'Orientalism and Sinology', *ASAA Review*, 7: 18–20.

Said, E.W. (1978) *Orientalism*, London: Routledge & Kegan Paul.

Sargant, L. (ed.) (1981) *Women and Revolution: A Discussion of the Unhappy Marriage of Marxism and Feminism*, London: Pluto.

Satz, D. (1995) 'Markets in women's sexual labor', *Ethics*, 106: 63–85.

Schwartz, B. (1964) 'The fetish of the "Disciplines" (Symposium on Chinese studies and the Disciplines)', *Journal of Asian Studies*, 23: 537–8.

Selden, M. (1971) *The Yenan Way in Revolutionary China*, Cambridge, MA: Harvard University Press.

Selden, M. (1995) 'Yan'an communism reconsidered', *Modern China*, 21: 8–44.

Seymour, J.D. and Anderson, R. (1998) *New Ghosts, Old Ghosts: Prisons and Labour Reform Camps in China*, Armonk, NY: M.E. Sharpe.

Shan Guangnai (1995) *Zhongguo changji – guoqu he xianzai* [Chinese Prostitution – Past and Present], Beijing: Falü chubanshe.

Sharpe, K. (1998) *Red Light, Blue Light: Prostitutes, Punters and the Police* Aldershot: Ashgate.

Shrage, L. (1994) *Moral Dilemmas of Feminism: Prostitution, Adultery, and Abortion*, New York: Routledge.

Shrage, L. (1996) 'Prostitution and the case for decriminalization', *Dissent*, 43: 41–5.

Sigley, G. (1996a) 'Governing Chinese bodies: population, reproduction, and the civilising process in contemporary China', unpublished thesis, Griffith University.

Shrage, L. (1996b) 'Governing Chinese bodies: the significance of studies in the concept of governmentality for the analysis of government in China', *Economy and Society*, 25: 457–82.

Sigley, G. (ed.) (1998) 'Getting it right: marriage, sex, and pleasure', a special issue of *Chinese Sociology and Anthropology: A Journal of Translations*, 31.

Song Zhenyong (1996) 'Shenyang 90 ming "sanpei" xiaojie beisha' [90 'hostesses' murdered in Shenyang], *Beijing zhichun*, January: 69–70.

Spivak, G.C. (1986–7) 'Strategy, identity, writing: an interview with Gayatri Spivak', *Melbourne Journal of Politics*, 18: 44–59.

Spivak, G.C. (1995) 'Can the subaltern speak?', in B. Ashcroft, G. Griffiths and H. Tiffen (eds) *The Post-Colonial Studies Reader*, London: Routledge, 24–8.

St. James, M. (1989) 'Preface', in G. Pheterson (ed.) *A Vindication of the Rights of Whores*, Seattle: Seal Press, xvii–xx.

Stacey, J. (1975) 'When patriarchy kowtows: the significance of the Chinese family revolution for feminist theory', *Feminist Studies*, 2: 64–112.

Stacey, J. (1976) 'A feminist view of research on Chinese women', *Signs: Journal of Women in Culture and Society*, 2: 485–97.

Stanton, D.C. (ed.) (1992) *Discourses of Sexuality: From Aristotle to AIDS*, Ann Arbor, MI: University of Michigan Press.

'State never collects "Miss taxes"' (1998) *China Youth Daily*, 1 December, © SinoFile Information Services.

Sullivan, B. (1992) 'Feminist approaches to the sex industry', in S. Gerrull and B. Halstead (eds) *Sex Industry and Public Policy: Proceedings of a Conference Held 6–8 May 1991*, Canberra, ACT: Australian Institute of Criminology, 7–15.

Sullivan, B. (1995) 'Rethinking prostitution', in B. Caine and R. Pringle (eds) *Transitions: New Australian Feminisms*, St. Leonards, NSW: Allen & Unwin, 184–97.

Sullivan, B. (1997) *The Politics of Sex: Prostitution and Pornography in Australia since 1945*, Cambridge: Cambridge University Press.

Symanski, R. (1981) *The Immoral Landscape: Female Prostitution in Western Societies*, Toronto: Butterworths.

'Symposium on Chinese Studies and the Disciplines' (1964) *Journal of Asian Studies*, 23: 505–38.

Tanner, H. (1995) 'Policing, punishment, and the individual: criminal justice in China', *Law and Social Inquiry*, 20: 277–303.

Tanner, H. (1999) *Strike Hard! Anti-Crime Campaigns and Chinese Criminal Justice, 1979–1985*, East Asia Series 104, Ithaca, NY: Cornell University Press.

Tanner, M.S. (1999) 'Ideological struggle over police reform, 1988–1993', in E.A. Winkler (ed.) *Transition from Communism in China: Institutional and Comparative Analysis*, Boulder, CO: Lynne Rienner Publishers, 111–28.

Tanner, M.S. (2000) 'State coercion and the "balance of awe": the 1983–1986 stern blows anti-crime campaign', *China Journal*, 44: 93–125.

Teng, J.E. (1996) 'The construction of the "traditional Chinese woman" in the western academy: a critical review', *Signs: Journal of Women in Culture and Society*, 22: 115–51.

Thorbek, S. and Pattanaik, B. (eds) (2002) *Transnational Prostitution: Changing Global Patterns*, London: Zed Books.

'Three escorts' (1994) *China News Analysis*, 1–13 August, 1515–16: 6.

'Tibet anti-pornography, drugs, prostitution campaign' (1996) excerpts from a report by Chinese Regional TV from Tibet, Lhasa, 10 December, trans. *Selected World Broadcasts – China*, 14 December, FE/2795, G/7–8.

Tong, R. (1984) *Women, Sex, and the Law*, Totowa, NJ: Rowman & Allanheld.

'TV programme helps raise awareness of law' (1996) Xinhua News Agency, 24 October, in *Selected World Broadcasts – China*, 4 November, FE/2760, S2/12–13.

United Nations (1949) *Convention for the Suppression of the Traffic in Persons and of the Exploitation of the Prostitution of Others*, approved by General Assembly resolution 317 (IV) of 2 December 1949, entry into force 25 July 1951, <http://www.unhchr.ch/html/menu3/b/33.html> (accessed 1 March 2000).

United Nations (1979) *Convention on the Elimination of All Forms of Discrimination Against Women*, General Assembly Resolution 34/180.

United Nations (1995) 'Harmful traditional practices affecting the health of women and children', Fact Sheet 23.

Valenze, D. (1996) 'Is Marxism still a useful tool of analysis for the history of British women?', in N.R. Keddie (ed.) *Debating Gender, Debating Sexuality*, New York: New York University Press, 181–92.

Valverde, M. (1999) 'Identity politics and the law in the United States', *Feminist Studies*, 25: 345–61.

van der Poel, S. (1995) 'Solidarity as boomerang: the fiasco of the prostitute's rights movement in the Netherlands', *Crime, Law and Social Change*, 23: 41–65.

van der Vleuten, N. (1991) *Survey on "Traffic in Women": Policies and Policy – Research in an International Context*, Leiden: Research and Documentation Centre: Women and Autonomy Centre, Leiden University.

'Voice from women' (1999) *SinoFile Chinese News Abstracts and Translations*, 12 March: 2.

Walkowitz, J. (1980) *Prostitution and Victorian Society: Women, Class, and the State*, Cambridge: Cambridge University Press.

Wan Yanhai (1996) 'Tongxinglian he maiyin' [Homosexuality and prostitution], in *Aizibing: shehui, lunli he falü wenti zhuanjia yantaohui* [Report of the Expert Workshop on HIV and Prostitution: Social, Ethical and Legal Issues], Beijing: Chinese Academy of Social Sciences, 29–31 October, 28–30.

Wang Dazhong (1995) 'Guanyu maiyin piaochang renyuan de laojiao yu qiangzhi jizhong jiaoyu de wenti' [Some problems concerning the sending of prostitution offenders to education through labour and compelling them to undergo joint detention and education], *Fanzui yu gaizao*, 6: 57.

Wang Fengbin (1998) 'Xiang "fuwu xiaojie" zhengshui nan zai nali?' [What's so difficult about taxing 'female service workers'?], *Fazhi ribao*, 17 August: 1.

Wang Huanju (1995) 'Yixing anmo' [Opposite-sex massage], *Renmin jingcha*, 430: 44–9.

Wang Jinling, Gao Xueyu and Jiang Ming (1998) 'Dui shangyexing xingjiaoyizhe de xingbie bijiao fenxi' [A comparative analysis of gender differences amongst participants in commercialised sex], *Zhejiang xuekan*, 3: 53–9.

Wang Shouzhi (1995) '"Lakenan", "peikenü" wei shayao chufa?' [Why should we punish the activities of 'male touts' and 'female hostesses'?], *Renmin jingcha*, 6: 47.

Wang Tie (1993) 'Gongzhi renyuan de fubai duzhi yanjiu' [Research on corruption and neglect of work by public employees], *Shehuixue yanjiu*, 3: 30–41.

Wang Xingjuan (1996) 'Dangqian maiyin piaochang de xianxiang wenti' [Some problems concerning the current phenomenon of selling and buying sex] an abstract in *Aizibing: shehui, lunli he falü wenti zhuanjia yantaohui* [Report of the Expert Workshop on HIV and Prostitution: Social, Ethical and Legal Issues], Beijing: Chinese Academy of Social Sciences, 29–31 October, 27–8.

Wang Zheng (1997) 'Maoism, feminism, and the UN conference on women: women's studies research in contemporary China', *Journal of Women's History*, 8: 126–52.

Wang Zheng (2000) 'Gender, employment and women's resistance', in E.J. Perry and M. Selden (eds) *Chinese Society: Change, Conflict and Resistance*, London: Routledge, 126–52.

Wang Zhimin (1993) *Pingjia shehui zhian zhuangkang gailun* [Towards an Assessment of the Social Order Situation], Beijing: Qunzhong chubanshe.

Wehrfritz, G. (1996) 'Unbuttoning a nation', *Newsweek*, 15 April: 8–11.

Weitzer, R. (1991) 'Prostitutes' rights in the United States: the failure of a movement', *Sociological Quarterly*, 32, 1: 23–41.

Winter, B. (1994) 'Women, the law, and cultural relativism in France: the case of excision', *Signs: Journal of Women in Culture and Society*, 19: 939–74.

Wittig, M. (1981) 'One is not born a woman', *Feminist Issues*, 1: 47–54.

Wolf, M. and Witke, R. (eds) (1975) *Women in Chinese Society*, Stanford, CA: Stanford University Press.

'Women's lobby tackles bar sex' (1999) *South China Morning Post*, 4 March.

'Wu ge nanji de zaoyu' [The experiences of five male prostitutes] (1995) *Fazhi zhuanji*, 65: 37–47.

Wu Yaonong (2000) 'Chengzhi "xinghuilu"' [Penalizing sex-related bribery/corruption], *Zhongguo qingnian bao*, 13 December.

Wu Zhong (1997) 'Tax on hostesses possible move to legalise prostitution', *Hong Kong Standard*, 29 September © East Asian World Sources Online.

Xia Yinlan (1996) 'The protection of women's rights relating to the person', *Australian Feminist Law Journal*, 7: 165–9.

Xian, K. and Wu, Y. (2000) 'Thousands rescued from human trafficking in police crackdown', *China News Digest* (Global News, No. GL00–048), 14 April.

Xin Ran (1996) 'Jingcheng yixing anmoye tan wei' [An inquiry into the opposite-sex massage industry in Beijing], *Renmin jingcha*, 8: 14–20.

Xin Ren (1993) 'China', in N.J. Davis (ed.) *Prostitution: An International Handbook on Trends, Problems, and Policies*, Westport, CT: Greenwood Press.

Xin Ren (1999) 'Prostitution and economic modernization in China', *Violence Against Women*, 5: 1411–36.

Xu, S. (1999) 'China: centre helps prostitutes', *Shanghai Star*, 24 December © Reuters.

Xu Hu (1993) 'Zhongguo maiyin piaochang de xianzhuang yu duice' [Prostitution in China: the current state of affairs and countermeasures], *Shehuixue yanjiu*, 3: 42–51.

Xu Xiaoqun (1996) 'The discourse on love, marriage, and sexuality in post-Mao China: a reading of the journalistic literature on women', *positions: East Asia cultures critique*, 4: 381–414.

Xue Jing (1999) 'Qiyue chajin sanpeinü' [July ban on 'hostesses'], *Beijing qingnian zhoukan*, 18 July.

Yang Xiaobing (1991) 'China launches anti-prostitution campaign', *Beijing Review*, 16–22 December: 23–5.

Young, M. (ed.) (1973) *Women in China: Studies in Social Change and Feminism*, Anne Arbor, MI, Center for Chinese Studies, University of Michigan.

Young, M. (1976) 'Introduction', *Signs: Journal of Women in Culture and Society*, 2: 1–4.

Yu Hongyuan (1999) 'Dangqian guanche qunzhong luxian de sixiang zhangai ji gaijin cuoshi' [Current ideological obstacles to the implementation of the mass line and measures for improvement], *Gongan yanjiu*, 3: 40–2.

Zatz, N.D. (1997) 'Sex work/sex act: law, labor and desire in constructions of prostitution', *Signs: Journal of Women in Culture and Society*, 22: 277–309.

Zha Jianying (1995) *China Pop: How Soap Operas, Tabloids, and Bestsellers are Transforming a Culture*, New York: New Press.

Zhang Beichuan, Chen Guanzhi, Li Kefu and Li Xiufang (1996) 'Zhongguo mou chengshi jinü diaocha' [A survey of female prostitutes in a Chinese city], in *Aizibing: shehui, lunli he falü wenti zhuanjia yantaohui* [Report of the Expert Workshop on HIV and Prostitution: Social, Ethical and Legal Issues], Beijing: Chinese Academy of Social Sciences, 29–31 October.

Zhang Heqing (2002) *Ruoshi qunti de shengyin yu shehui gongzuo jieru* [Subaltern Voices and Activist Social Work], Beijing: Zhongguo caizheng jingji chubanshe.

Zhang Ping (1993) 'Dangjin Zhongguo shehui bing' [Social problems in contemporary China], *Shehui yanjiu*, 3: 25–9.

Zhang Yanshang (1993) 'Piaochangzhe xintai lu' [A series of psychological profiles of prostitute clients], *Jindun*, 12: 12–19.

Zhang Yiwu (1995) 'Chanshi "Zhongguo" de jiaolü' [The anxiety of interpreting 'China'], *Ershiyi shiji*, 28: 128–35.

Zhang Zhiping (2000) 'Does China need a red-light district?', *Beijing Review*, 12 June: 28–33.

Zhao Jianmei (1994) 'Manhua "chi he wan le quan baoxiao"' [An informal discussion: 'eat, drink, play, and ask for complete reimbursement'], *Dashidai*, 6: 35.

Zhao Qinggui (1994) 'Nüxing fanzui de tedian yuanyin ji duice' [The characteristics of female crime: reasons and countermeasures], *Fanzui yu gaizao yanjiu*, 8: 10–14.

Zhao Shukai (2000) 'Criminality and the policing of migrant workers', trans. A. Kipnis, *China Journal*, 43: 101–10.

'Zhifa renyuan baoyang "sanpei" yishen shifa diudiao "wusha"' [Law enforcement officials who keep 'hostesses' to lose their 'posts'] (1999) *Renmin ribao*, 21 January.

Zhong Wei, 'A close look at China's "sex industry"', *Lianhe zaobao* (Singapore), 2 October 2000, <http://www.usembassy-china.org.cn/english/sandt/sex-industry.html> (accessed 24 October 2000).

Zhonghua renmin gongheguo guowuyuan [State Council of the PRC] (1999) *Yule changsuo guanli tiaoli* [Regulations concerning the management of public places of entertainment], Wenhua chubanshe.

Zhonghua renmin gongheguo hunyinfa, Zhonghua renmin gongheguo funü quanyi baozhangfa [The Marriage Law of the People's Republic of China and the Law of the People's Republic of China on the Protection of Women's Rights and Interests] (1994) Zhongguo fazhi chubanshe.

Zhou Wenhui and Wang Dekang (1993) 'Dayawan bian jiu miaonü' [The rescue of four Miao women Near Dayawan], *Fayuan*, 152: 34–7.

Zito, A. and Barlow, T.E. (eds) (1994) *Body, Subject and Power in China*, Chicago: University of Chicago Press.

Index